Hitler: Dictator or Puppet?

Also by Andrew Norman

By Swords Divided: Corfe Castle in the Civil War, Halsgrove, Tiverton, 2003
Thomas Hardy: Behind the Inscrutable Smile, Halsgrove, Tiverton, 2003
Tyneham: The Lost Village of Dorset, Halsgrove, Tiverton, 2003
Sir Francis Drake: Behind the Pirate's Mask, Halsgrove, Tiverton, 2004
Dunshay: Reflections on a Dorset Manor House, Halsgrove, Tiverton, 2004
Robert Mugabe and the Betrayal of Zimbabwe, McFarland & Company Inc., Jefferson, NC, USA, 2004
Enid Blyton and her Enchantment with Dorset, Halsgrove, Tiverton, 2005
Thomas Hardy: Christmas Carollings, Halsgrove, Tiverton, 2005
Adolf Hitler: The Final Analysis, Spellmount, Staplehurst, 2005
Agatha Christie: The Finished Portrait, Tempus Publishing, Stroud, 2007
Mugabe: Teacher, Revolutionary, Tyrant, The History Press, Stroud, 2008
HMS Hood: *Pride of the Royal Navy,* The History Press, Stroud, 2008
T E Lawrence: Unravelling the Enigma, The History Press, Stroud, 2008
The Story of George Loveless and the Tolpuddle Martyrs, Halsgrove, Tiverton, 2008
Agatha Christie: The Pitkin Guide, Pitkin Publishing, 2009
Purbeck Personalities, Halsgrove, Tiverton, 2009
Arthur Conan Doyle: The Man behind Sherlock Holmes, The History Press, Stroud, 2009
Father of the Blind: A Portrait of Sir Arthur Pearson, The History Press, Stroud, 2009
Jane Austen: An Unrequited Love, The History Press, Stroud, 2009
Bournemouth's Founders and Famous Visitors, The History Press, Stroud, 2010
A Brummie Boy Goes to War, Halsgrove, Tiverton, 2011

Hitler

Dictator or Puppet?

Dr Andrew Norman

Pen & Sword
MILITARY

First published in Great Britain in 2011 by
Pen & Sword Military
an imprint of
Pen & Sword Books Ltd
47 Church Street
Barnsley
South Yorkshire
S70 2AS

Copyright © Dr Andrew Norman 2011

ISBN 978-1-84884-523-7

A CIP catalogue record for this book is available from the British Library.

Typeset in 11pt Ehrhardt by
Mac Style, Beverley, E. Yorkshire

Printed and bound in the UK by CPI

Pen & Sword Books Ltd incorporates the imprints of Pen & Sword Aviation,
Pen & Sword Maritime, Pen & Sword Military, Wharncliffe Local History,
Pen & Sword Select, Pen & Sword Military Classics, Leo Cooper, Seaforth
Publishing and Frontline Publishing.

For a complete list of Pen & Sword titles please contact
PEN & SWORD BOOKS LIMITED
47 Church Street, Barnsley, South Yorkshire, S70 2AS, England
E-mail: enquiries@pen-and-sword.co.uk
Website: www.pen-and-sword.co.uk

Contents

Rupprecht von Bayern was Crown Prince of the German State of Bavaria. In the summer of 1934 at a luncheon in London with King George V, Rupprecht told the British king that he 'remained convinced that the Führer was insane'.

(NA, Kew: FO 371/18859. Ambassador Eric
Phipps to Foreign Office, 27 December 1935)

He began to speak, and I immediately disliked him. I didn't know then what he would later become. I found him rather comical with his funny little moustache. He had a scratchy voice and a strange appearance; and he shouted so much. He was shouting in this small room and what he was saying was really quite simplistic. I thought he wasn't quite normal. I found him spooky.

(Observations about Hitler by Herbert Richter, a German soldier of the
Great War in 'The Nazis: A Warning from History', Part 1)

Acknowledgements

The British Library, London; the National Archives, Kew, Richmond, Surrey; King's College (Liddell Hart Centre for Military Archives), University of London; the manager and staff of Poole Library; Isle of Wight Record Office, Newport, Isle of Wight; Ventnor and District Local History Society, Ventnor, Isle of Wight.

The Daily Telegraph; *The Times.*

Martin A. Clay; Peter Devlin; Nicholas Dragffy; Tom Gillibrand; Howard Waldin; George Willey.

Oberösterreichisches Landesarchiv, Linz; The Kunsthistorisches Museum, Vienna.

I am especially grateful to my beloved wife Rachel for all her help, expertise and encouragement.

Preface

Hitler's crimes against humanity cast a shadow over the world, and continue to do so even to this day. They were so heinous and revolting, and on such an unimaginably horrifying scale, that people are either rendered speechless or they are obliged to fall back on inadequate words in their attempt to describe both him and them.

In the intervening decades, more than six of which have passed since his death, the Führer has been caricatured on the one hand as a comical figure with a tiny moustache and ridiculous mannerisms and on the other as 'evil', 'a devil', or 'a monster', a two-dimensional figure somehow set apart from the rest of the human race. But are his beliefs and actions to be dismissed simply as those of an inherently wicked person? Or is there more to the story of the man who was responsible for the deaths of millions of people worldwide?

Hitherto, it has been assumed that Hitler's ideas were self-generated. But this is not the case for, instead, they were lifted, lock, stock and barrel, from a series of long-since-forgotten, pseudo-scientific pamphlets called *Ostara* (the product of the febrile brain of a deluded ex-monk called Liebenfels). What kind of person was it that could give credence to such 'mad' ideas? Only someone who was equally as deluded as the monk, of course.

Had the Führer simply been a person who suffered from delusions, then his life might well have passed relatively unnoticed. But what made him so dangerous was that he attempted – by force of oratory and willpower – to convince others of these delusional beliefs. Why?

What has not hitherto been appreciated is that Hitler himself, the great dictator, who was able to manipulate the masses at will, was himself being manipulated, like a puppet on a string, by forces beyond even his control. The evidence for this, which has lain unnoticed in the literature for over half a century, comes not only from two highly reputable, yet independent, sources, both of which were close to the Führer, but also from Hitler himself.

Who or what the puppeteer who controlled the Führer was will be explained for the very first time in this volume. Then, and only then, is it possible to enter into and understand the workings of the mind of Adolf Hitler.

Chapter 1

Hitler and his Family Background

Adolf Hitler was born on 20 April 1889 at Braunau am Inn in Austria. Of his five siblings, only one, Paula, survived into adulthood.

Hitler's father, Alois

Alois senior, born in Strones, Austria in 1837, was an employee of the Imperial Customs Service. Born out of wedlock, he took his mother's maiden name of Schicklgruber. He later named [Johann] Georg Heidler as his father, and in 1876, almost two decades after Georg's death, Alois assumed the surname of 'Hitler'.

In 1873, Alois married Anna Glassl-Hörer, but the marriage was annulled.[1] A decade later, in 1883, he married Franzisca Matzelsberger. The couple already had one child, Alois junior (born 1882), and in the year of their marriage their second child, Angela, was born. However, in 1884, Franzisca died of tuberculosis. In January 1885, Alois was married a third time, to Klara Pölzl, who bore him 6 children – only two of whom were to survive into adulthood: Adolf, and his younger sister, Paula (born in 1896). Alois senior died in 1903.

Hitler's mother, Klara

Klara, born in Spital, Austria in 1860, was of Czech descent. She was devoted to Adolf and tried to protect him from his father, who was violent to both him and Alois junior. According to Erna Patra Hitler[2] (wife of Hans, the illegitimate son of Hitler's brother Alois), when Adolf was beaten, his

> bawling was accompanied by the father's swearing, and the mother [Klara] cringed at each smack. [In tears, Klara] went up to the attic and shielded Adolf, who was lying on the floor, with her own body, but she was unable to ward off the father's final blow.[3]

It was later revealed that Alois (II) was the possessor of a hippopotamus-hide riding whip.[4]

Hitler's sister, Paula

Paula was born in 1896 in Hafeld, Austria. Prior to the Great War, she worked as a secretary in Vienna. According to her,

Adolf was never a healthy child. His lungs were weak. Twice he was stricken with pneumonia and recovered only through some miracle. [He was a] weakling, and behind at school. He was a difficult child, indifferent to everything around him.[5]

Her brother, Adolf, said Paula, inherited from his father a

love of uniforms. If his father was out, Adolf would sneak into his room, put on his uniform jacket and with a wooden sword, march through the garden. In a loud voice he'd shout military commands, salute and demand a salute from an imaginary passing subordinate. His favourite games were Court-Martial and Execution afterwards.[6]

Paula also revealed that Adolf liked to be in control.

When we children played Red Indians, my brother Adolf was always the leader. All the others did what he told them. They must have had an instinct that his will was stronger than theirs.[7]

Paula also confirms that, as a child, Adolf was subjected to violent physical abuse from his father. She also states:

Adolf, who so often played hookey from school, had built a little boat of odds-and-ends and took it down to the river. When our father heard of it he followed Adolf, snatched up the boat and smashed it to pieces, then he grabbed Adolf by the throat and held him against a tree, until he half-choked. Adolf dropped in a faint. Only then did the old man wake up to what he was doing; he picked Adolf up and carried him home. For a week Adolf was more dead than alive.[8]

However, according to Paula, Adolf was also capable of violence, which he displayed towards both herself and his half-sister Angela. He behaved 'abominably', said Paula to her half-brother Alois's wife, Bridget, and was 'always threatening them with blows and pulling their hair'.[9]

Hitler's half-brother, Alois
Alois junior was born in Vienna in 1882. He was also beaten by his father. And matters worsened when his mother, Franzisca, died, and his father was remarried to Klara. When Hitler (Adolf) was born, said Alois junior, his step-mother Klara

needed all the available money for her favourite, Adolf, whom she kept at home. He hid behind her skirts, never doing a day's work or earning a *Heller* [German monetary coin][10]

Alois left home at fourteen and commenced work as an apprentice waiter. Having been convicted and imprisoned twice for theft, he relocated to Ireland, becoming a waiter at Dublin's prestigious Shelbourne Hotel. It was in 1909 at the Dublin Horse Show, that he met an Irish girl called Bridget Elizabeth Dowling. Having failed to obtain the consent of Bridget's parents to marry, the couple ran away and were married in London in June 1910. They then moved to Liverpool where, the following March, their only child, William Patrick, was born in a flat in Upper Stanhope Street in the Toxteth district of the city.

Alois junior told his wife Bridget that when his father, Alois senior, died in 1903

he left a house and a small piece of land. One fourth was to be mine. Do you know what Adolf did? After my stepmother [Klara] died [in December 1908] he sold the house and the land – my share too.[11] [Hitler now] went to Vienna and lived on our inheritance: mine as well as his. He had never learned a trade, so when the money ran out, instead of getting a job he just moved in on my sister Angela. He lived in her house and ate her food until even she got tired of it and made him leave. In the end, he sank so low that he had to seek shelter in the Vienna Municipal Lodgings. Imagine how I felt when I heard that. What a disgrace! There's some excuse for old men who have nowhere to go and can't work, but Adolf was only 20 when he went there and he has stayed ever since. A man in his early 20s so shiftless that he lives in a lodging for old men at the city's expense! Isn't that shameful! And he's my brother.

'But you told me he was an artist,' said Bridget. To which Alois replied, 'Don't be ridiculous. Artist! He's nothing but a cheap dauber. They wouldn't even accept him as a student in the *Kunstakademie*. (Academy of Fine Art).[12]

In May 1914, as their fourth wedding anniversary approached, Alois abandoned his wife and son and returned to Germany where he hoped to establish a business, whereby he would 'launch an English [safety] razor on the Continent'.[13] He subsequently became a restaurateur. Two years later, in 1916, despite the fact that he was already married to Bridget, he married Hedwig Heidemann. In 1923, he was charged with bigamy.

Hitler's half-sister, Angela
Angela was born in Braunau am Inn in 1883. In 1903 she married Leo Raubal, an assistant tax collector, and bore him three children, including her namesake Angelika ('Geli') – about whom more will be said later.

Hitler's half-brother Alois's wife, Bridget (née Dowling)
Bridget was born in Dublin, Ireland in 1891. In her memoirs,[14] Bridget makes an extraordinary claim: that from November 1912 to April 1913, Hitler was a guest in her Liverpool flat. And it has to be said that, because of the detail which she provides, and because a great deal of what she says is verifiable from other sources, there can be little doubt as to its authenticity. And during this period, says Bridget, her husband, Alois, in his spare time, took Adolf to see the sights of London, including Tower Bridge. 'They both had an intense interest in anything English and

were always going sight-seeing.' (Here there is a slight discrepancy since with the records of the Vienna police, which state that Hitler was resident in Vienna from 1907 to the beginning of 1913.[15]) Further corroboration of Bridget's account comes from Hitler himself in Volume I, Chapter 3 of his book, *Mein Kampf (My Struggle,* written in 1923), where he mentions the statues and paintings contained in both British Houses of Parliament, which he describes as a 'magnificent edifice'. And journalist and author, David Gardner, quotes a 'key family source' who confirmed that not only did Hitler visit Liverpool, he also visited Ireland.[16]

When Alois told Bridget that the Austrian authorities desired to put Adolf in jail, and she asked why, he replied,

> He's a deserter from the army ... Every man has to serve three years in the army in Austria. Adolf has been hiding from the military authorities, consequently from the police for the last eighteen months. That's why he came here to me. He had no choice ... [And this was why] In order to evade capture he [had] registered at the Vienna Municipal Lodging House under the name of his younger brother Edmund – Edmund was born five years after Adolf and died at the age of 2. By using Edmund's birth certificate he managed to identify himself as his younger and dead brother. That was how he dodged military service, living under the name of Edmund Hitler, while the Viennese police searched high and low for Adolf Hitler. When he was nearly cornered, Adolf threw himself on [his half-sister] Angela's mercy and she, poor soft-hearted woman, gave him the money I had sent for her and her husband to come and visit us. That was how Adolf got out of the country and saved his skin.[17]

When Adolf's time at Liverpool came to an end, 'he could not return to his own country, for he would have been arrested,' said Alois, who advised him to go to the German city of Munich in Bavaria. This was a place with which he himself (Alois) was familiar

> because it was in every way – scenery, food, manner of dressing, customs and particularly language – the most like their own Austria.[18]

The Hitler family's doctor, Eduard Bloch

Another person with first-hand knowledge of the young Hitler was Dr Eduard Bloch, a Jew, who was affectionately known as the 'poor people's doctor', who has also left a record of his acquaintance with the young Hitler.

According to Bloch, when in 1903 the Hitler family moved from their home-town of Braunau am Inn to the vicinity of the city of Linz, it was because there were some 'good schools there', where Alois believed that 'his son would have the education which had been denied him; an education which would secure him a good government job'.[19] To this end, Alois (who by this time had retired from his post as customs inspector) purchased a small farm in Leonding, a suburb of Linz.

However, 'the family had barely settled in[to] their new home outside of Linz when Alois, the father, died suddenly from an apoplectic stroke'.[20]

It now became apparent that Adolf was 'too young and altogether too frail to become a farmer' – which was evidently the occupation intended for him – so his mother Klara, decided to sell the farm and rent a small apartment in a two-storey house, Number 9 Bluetenstrasse, situated 'across the Danube from the main portion of Linz'.

At this time, said Bloch, Hitler

read extensively and was particularly fascinated by stories about American Indians. He devoured the books of James Fenimore Cooper, and the German writer Karl May [who wrote about the native Indians of America, even though he himself had never visited that country, let alone seen an Indian!]

This accords with the account of Hitler's sister, Paula, who stated that, as a teenager, Hitler's reading matter had

consisted exclusively of adventure stories set in America or Asia. Thrillers, written for children of 10 or 12. He read them over and over again until he literally knew them by heart.[21]

Bloch describes the young Hitler as 'a quiet, well-mannered and neatly dressed' youth who 'like any well-bred boy of 14 or 15 … would bow and thank me courteously' whenever he was treated for a minor illness. 'While he was not a "mother's boy" in the usual sense,' said the doctor, 'I have never witnessed a closer attachment' [than that between Hitler and his mother, Klara].

It was in 1908 that Dr Bloch was obliged to summon the Hitler children to his office to tell them the sad news that their mother had an extensive tumour of the breast. Said he,

Adolf Hitler's reaction to this news was touching. His long, sallow face was contorted. Tears flowed from his eyes. Did his mother, he asked, have no chance? Only then I realized the magnitude of the attachment that existed between mother and son.[22]

Early in the summer of 1908, Klara entered the Hospital of the Sisters of Mercy in Linz to be operated on by Dr Karl Urban, Chief of the Surgical Staff in the presence of Dr Bloch, who stated that

As weeks and months passed after the operation, Frau Hitler's strength began visibly to fail. At most she could be out of bed for an hour or two a day. During this period Adolf spent most of his time around the house, to which his mother had returned. He slept in the tiny bedroom adjoining that of his mother so that he could be summoned at any time during the night. During the day he hovered about the large bed in which she lay.

Klara, having received numerous home visits from Dr Bloch, died during the night of 20/21 December 1908 at the age of forty-seven. Wrote the doctor,

Adolf, his face showing the weariness of a sleepless night, sat beside his mother. In order to preserve a last impression, he had sketched her as she lay on her death-bed. In all my career I had never seen anyone so prostrate with grief as Adolf Hitler.

Klara's funeral took place on Christmas Eve. She was buried beside her husband in the Catholic cemetery at Leonding. Continued Bloch,

After the others … had left, Adolf remained behind; unable to tear himself away from the freshly filled grave. A few days after the funeral the family came to my office. [When his turn came around, Adolf, who] wore a dark suit and a loosely knotted cravat … stepped forward and took my hand. Looking into my eyes he said: 'I shall be grateful to you forever.' That was all. Then he bowed.[23]

Adolf Hitler
Family Tree

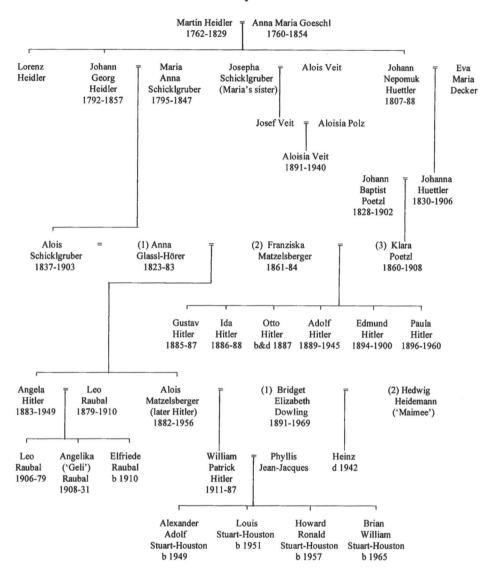

NB Alois Hitler also had an illegitimate son, Hans Hitler, who married (2) Erna Patra.

Notes

1. Olden, *Hitler the Pawn*, p. 15.
2. (Gilera) Erna Patra Hitler was the wife of Hans Hitler, the illegitimate son of Hitler's half-brother Alois. Erna and Hans are buried in Hamburg Cemetery, in the same tomb as Alois and his second wife, Hedwig.
3. *The Hitler Family: in the Shadow of the Dictator*. Quotation from the Chronicle of Erna Patra Hitler.
4. Walter Langer: Interview with Walter Patrick Hitler, in Gardner, *The Last of the Hitlers*, p. 70.
5. Unger, Michael (editor), *The Memoirs of Bridget Hitler*, pp. 171–2.
6. Ibid, p. 172.
7. *Tyranny: the Years of Adolf Hitler*. 1958. Television documentary in which Paula Hitler is interviewed by British film-maker Peter Morley.
8. Unger, op. cit., p. 170.
9. Ibid, pp. 171–72.
10. Ibid, p. 25.
11. Ibid, p. 26.
12. Unger, op.cit., pp. 26–7.
13. Ibid, p. 37.
14. Bridget Hitler's (née Dowling) memoirs were discovered in the Manuscript Division of the New York Public Library in the early 1970s by historian Robert Payne. They were written in the USA, where Bridget spent her latter years, and published in full in 1979. The manuscript ends abruptly in mid-sentence, the last dates mentioned being '1938', followed by 'months later.' In Unger, op. cit., pp. 186, 190.
15. Olden, op. cit., p. 30.
16. Gardner, op. cit., p. 188.
17. Unger, op.cit., pp. 27–8.
18. Ibid, p. 36.
19. Bloch, *My Patient Hitler*, in Colliers, Vol. 1, 15 March, pp.11, 35–9; and 22 March, pp. 69–73.
20. Ibid, p. 35.
21. Unger, op. cit., p. 172.
22. Bloch, op.cit, p. 36.
23. Ibid, p. 39.

* Film Documentary.

Chapter 2

Vienna

Almost immediately after his mother's funeral in December 1908, Hitler left for Vienna to attempt, once more, a career as an artist. Here, said Dr Bloch,

> he worked as a hod carrier on building-construction jobs until workmen threatened to push him off a scaffold [the reason for this is not recorded] and we know that he shovelled snow and took any other job that he could find.
> It was during the following three years, during which time Hitler lived in a men's hostel, that the vitriol of hate began to creep through his body. The grim realities of the life he lived encouraged him to hate the government, labour unions, the very men he lived with. But he had not yet begun to hate the Jews.[1]

This is borne out by the fact that, during this period he took time out to send me a penny postcard. On the back was a message: 'from Vienna I send you my greetings. Yours, always faithfully Adolf Hitler.' [This was despite the fact that Dr Bloch was a Jew].

The doctor also described how he received a card from Hitler depicting 'a hooded Capuchin monk, hoisting a glass of bubbling champagne', which he had painted himself.

Under the picture was a caption: *Prosit Neu Jahr* – 'A Toast to the New Year'. On the reverse side he had written a message: 'The Hitler family sends you the best wishes for a happy New Year. In everlasting thankfulness, Adolf Hitler.'

(Was it the mad monk, Liebenfels, whom Hitler had in mind when he painted this portrait, even though the former was a Cistercian and not a Capuchin?)

Reinhold Hanisch, an etcher from Bohemia, also wrote an account of his acquaintance with Hitler with whom, in the autumn of 1909, he lived in the asylum for the homeless, situated at the rear of Vienna's South Railway Station. This shelter was a Jewish (charitable) foundation, as was another at Erdberg (also visited by Hitler) which 'had been endowed by the Jewish Baron Königswarter'.[2] Hanisch stated that Hitler 'also received benefits [presumably financial support] from (Catholic) convents'.[3]

Soon after Christmas 1909, Hitler moved from the asylum to the *Mannerheim* (men's hostel) in the Meldemannstrasse in the Twentieth District of Vienna, and it was here [according to Hanisch] that he 'had helpful advisers who were Jews'.[4] For example, Hanisch cites 'a one-eyed locksmith called Robinsohn who often assisted him, since he [Robinsohn] was a beneficiary of an accident insurance annuity, and was able to spare a few pennies'. There were other Jews in the *Mannerheim* who often 'listened to his [Hitler's] political debates'.

Hanisch stated that a certain salesman called Neumann, who sold signboards produced by the inmates of the hostel 'became a real friend [to Hitler]'. And when Neumann found himself working 'with another Jew who was buying old clothes and pedalling them in the streets', he often gave Hitler old clothes including 'a long coat'. 'Hitler told me once,' said Hanisch,

> that Neumann was a very decent man, because if any of us had small debts, Neumann paid them [even] though he himself was very much in want.

Hanisch proceeded to describe Hitler's personality and habits. As he, Hitler 'was much too weak for hard physical work', Hanisch suggested to him that he should paint postcards, which he did. Soon after Christmas 1909, Hanisch began to peddle [sell] Hitler's postcards; the latter having told Hanisch that 'he [himself] wouldn't be able to sell them because he wasn't well enough dressed ...'.[5] Hanisch sold these postcards (which were not originals but copies, mainly views of Vienna) on Hitler's behalf in taverns and furniture stores, and to art dealers and upholsterers, 'for in those days divans [long, cushioned seats] were made with pictures inserted in their backs'. Said Hanisch,

> In those days, Hitler was by no means a Jew-hater. He became one afterward[s]. Hitler often said that it was only with the Jews that one could do business, because only they were willing to take chances. They are really the most efficient businessmen. He [Hitler] also appreciated the charitable spirit of the Jews ... [but he] admired the Jews most for their resistance to all persecutions.[6]

In fact, according to Hanisch, it was 'almost solely... Jewish dealers' who purchased Hitler's watercolours. They included Jacob Altenberg; a person called Landsberger who had a shop in the Favoritenstrasse, and another called Morgenstern, whose shop was in the Liechtensteinstrasse. The latter often bought from Hitler and sometimes recommended him to private customers. Tragically, Hitler's attitude to the Jewish community, which had shown him nothing but kindness, was to change dramatically.

Time and again, said Hanisch, he was driven to despair by

bringing in orders [for watercolour postcards] that he [Hitler] simply would not carry out.[7] In the morning he wouldn't even work until he had read several newspapers, and if anyone should come in with another newspaper he would read that too. Meanwhile the orders I brought in weren't carried out.[8] At such laziness I was very angry and resentful.

Hanisch could finally bear it no longer. He moved out of the asylum into private lodgings and 'decided to work independently'.

Despite having befriended and supported Hitler, Hanisch was to discover the duplicity of his so-called friend's character, when, to his astonishment, he [Hanisch] was taken to the Brigittenau Police Commissariat and confronted with Hitler who accused him of misappropriating a watercolour of his, worth 50 Kronen. The outcome was that Hanisch was sentenced to a term of seven days' imprisonment.

* * *

Did Hitler, as a young man, have any girlfriends? Yes, but not in the conventional sense of the word for, in the autumn of 1905 when he was aged 15 and living with his mother in Linz, he became infatuated with a young lady called Stefanie, whom he admired from afar. However, he never plucked up the courage to speak to her.

Historian, Anton Joachimsthaler, has discovered, in the Linz City Archive, that Stefanie's surname was Isak, which indicates that she was Jewish. Hitler may or may not have been aware of this, and if he was, he may have regarded it as of no importance, his anti-Semitic feelings being as yet unborn.[9]

* * *

On 4 August 1914, Britain declared war on Germany, following that country's invasion of Belgium. On this occasion Hitler was only too willing to enlist, and on 21 October he entered the front line as a volunteer corporal in the Sixteenth Bavarian Reserve Infantry Regiment, where he fulfilled the function of *Meldeganger* (despatch runner) – one who relays messages between his company and the regimental headquarters.

On 7 October 1916, having been wounded in the leg, Hitler was invalided back to Germany. He returned from hospital to the Front in March 1917 and was promoted to the rank of lance corporal. On the night of 13/14 October 1918 he was gassed during a British attack near Werwick, south of Ypres. This time he was invalided out to the military hospital at Basewalk in Pomerania in the Baltic region, where he remained until the war ended on 11 November 1918.

During the war, Hitler received the Iron Cross Second Class, in December 1914, and the Iron Cross First Class, on 4 August 1918.

Notes

1. Bloch, op. cit., Vol. 1, 15 March, pp. 11, 35–9; and 22 March, pp. 69–73.
2. Hanisch, Reinhold, *I was Hitler's Buddy*, 5 April, 1939, pp. 239–42 (I); 12 April, pp. 270–72 (II); 19 April, 1939, pp. 297–300 (III).
3. Ibid, II.
4. Ibid.
5. Ibid, I.
6. Ibid, II.
7. Ibid, I.
8. Ibid, III.
9. *Sex and the Swastika: The Making of Adolf Hitler.*

Chapter 3

Germany in Crisis

The First World War came to an end with the signing of the Armistice by Germany and the Allies on 11 November 1918. This was despite the fact that, just prior to the cessation of hostilities, a large area of Belgium, and parts of France and Luxemburg were still in German hands. Nonetheless, the armies of Germany were being progressively driven back at this time. The war's aftermath aroused in Hitler a fury and an intense indignation. Germany had been defeated – in his view because the country had been betrayed by its own leaders. It had also been humiliated. Others, in particular those serving in the armed forces, shared these sentiments. Commented German soldier, Herbert Richter,

> Of course we were angry. The Front Line troops did not feel defeated, and we wondered why the Armistice occurred so quickly, and why we had to vacate all our positions in such a hurry, because everywhere we were still on enemy territory.[1]

German soldier and statesman, Paul von Hindenburg, later declared: 'As an English general has very truly said, the German Army was "stabbed in the back".'[2]

Some were more sanguine; for the truth of the matter was that the offensive at Amiens, launched by the British and the French on 8 August 1918, had been catastrophic for Germany, having resulted in the capture of 30,000 German prisoners. German General, Erich von Ludendorff, wrote:

> The 8th August demonstrated the collapse of our fighting strength, and in the light of our recruiting situation it took from me any hope of discovering some strategic measure which would re-establish the position in our favour ... An end must be put to the war.[3]

Kaiser Wilhelm II reached the same conclusion, stating when the battle was still in progress: 'I see that we must strike the balance. We are at the limits of our endurance. The war must be brought to an end.'[4] Senior Staff Officer, General Hermann von Kuhl, in evidence to the Reichstag Committee of Inquiry said: 'The heavy losses could no longer be replaced. Our reinforcements were exhausted.'[5] In Hitler's opinion, however, there was no doubt as to where the true blame lay.

I intensely loathe the whole gang of miserable party politicians who had betrayed the people. I had long ago realized that the interests of the nation played only a very small part with this disreputable crew, and that what counted with them was the possibility of filling their own empty pockets. My opinion was that those people thoroughly deserve to be hanged, because they were ready to sacrifice the peace and if necessary, allow Germany to be defeated, just to serve their own ends. To consider their wishes would mean to sacrifice the interests of the working classes for the benefit of a gang of thieves. To meet their wishes meant that one should agree to sacrifice Germany.[6]

Hitler never forgot what he perceived as this humiliation, which would rankle with him for the rest of his life. 'The fighting Siegfried' [i.e., the German nation], he said, had 'succumbed to the dagger plunged in his back.'[7] And he subsequently remarked, 'Germany once laid down its arms at a quarter to twelve. On principle, I've never stopped [work] until five past twelve,'[8] as if to imply that the task of defeating the Allies ought to have been completed.

Germany's situation was now made worse by the Allies who continued to blockade the country, causing hunger and debilitation amongst the population, with resulting outbreaks of tuberculosis and influenza.

* * *

Prior to the Armistice being signed, political unrest in Germany had been considerable – opinions tending to become polarized, with people lending their support either to the fascists, or to the socialists, or to the communists. Gangs marched through the streets fighting for control of Germany's cities and towns.

On 3 November 1918 the seriousness of the situation manifested itself, when at Germany's Baltic port of Kiel, some 20,000 or so sailors from her Baltic fleet mutinied, demanding the abdication of the Kaiser and the setting up of Workers and Soldiers Councils. On 7 November 1918 in Munich, capital of Germany's south-eastern region of Bavaria, a Workers and Soldiers Council, led by journalist and politician Kurt Eisner (who, the previous year, had founded the Bavarian branch of the Independent Socialist Party), proclaimed, in a bloodless revolt, a Bavarian Socialist Republic. There would now be a proliferation of such Workers and Soldiers Councils throughout Germany.

On 9 November 1918 a general strike commenced in many German cities including the capital, Berlin, where hostile crowds converged on the chancellery building, forcing Prince Max of Baden (Germany's last Imperial Chancellor, who had been appointed on 3 October by Wilhelm II) to announce the abdication of the Kaiser, before he himself resigned. That same day, the so-called Majority Socialists, under the leadership of Friedrich Ebert and Philipp Scheidemann, proclaimed the new German Republic, and a deal was struck between Ebert and General Paul von Hindenburg (commander of the entire army on the Western Front) when it was agreed that if Ebert acted against the Communists, then the Army would, in return, support his new government and him personally, as the legitimate Chancellor of Germany. On 10 November 1918 a Council of People's Representatives was elected to govern the country with Ebert at its head. Meanwhile, Prince Max was seeking an armistice with the Allies and had despatched a commission to meet with Allied representatives in France's Compiègne Forest.

For Ebert, there arose a major problem in that armed Spartacists, under the command of Communist revolutionary Karl Liebknecht, a German barrister and politician, had established themselves in the former Kaiser's Imperial Palace, from the roof of which now flew a red flag. The Spartacus League had been founded in Berlin by Liebknecht, together with Rosa Luxemburg, a left-wing revolutionary, who had been born in Russian Poland in 1871, at the outbreak of the Great War. Together with fellow revolutionary Liebknecht, she had created the International Group which, in 1915, became the Spartacus League; this in turn became firstly, part of the Social Democratic Party (SDP – later the Independent SDP) and finally, the Communist Party of Germany. Luxemburg now joined Liebknecht in Berlin.

*   *   *

Hitler returned to Munich in November 1918 shortly after the signing of the Armistice to find the streets littered with crippled people and amputees; these were ex-servicemen with no pensions and no possessions. There were demonstrations in which the cry was 'Give us bread!' 'Give us work!' By this time, Hitler had already developed a deep-seated, not to say pathological, hatred of Bolshevism as epitomized by the Bolshevik Revolutionaries who, in November 1917, had overthrown Russia's tsarist regime. 'The menace to which Russia once succumbed,' he said in his book, *Mein Kampf*, 'is hanging steadily over Germany.'[9] As events unfolded in Germany, so this hatred grew.

*   *   *

On 5 January 1919 the Spartacists and Independent Socialists staged a huge demonstration in Berlin and, the following morning, called a general strike with in excess of 200,000 workers, many of them armed, parading through the city.

The Free Corps was a body of right-wing mercenaries, largely composed of veteran soldiers from Germany's defeated army, whose officers were trained professional soldiers and whose weapons and ammunition were supplied covertly by the army. Free Corps troops now moved against the Spartacists. They marched into Berlin, and between 10 and 17 January – so-called Bloody Week – put down the Communist uprising with much brutality. Five hundred or so lives were lost, including those of Luxemburg and Liebknecht who were both hunted down and executed.

On 19 January 1919 when elections were held for the new National Assembly, the Social Democrats (Majority and Independent Socialists) won 185 of the 421 seats, insufficient to form a majority. On 6 February 1919 the National Assembly met at

Weimar, 130 miles south of Berlin on the Elbe river, instead of Berlin, because of continuing violence in that city. A coalition was formed between the Social Democratic Party (SDP), the Democratic Party, and the centre parties, with Philipp Scheidemann of the SDP as Chancellor. Five days later, Friedrich Ebert was elected First President of the so-called Weimar Republic. Germany now had a national assembly with a democratic constitution as opposed to the previous semi-autocratic monarchy of Kaiser Wilhelm II.

The fact that so many communist revolutionaries, not only in Germany but elsewhere, were Jews, gave rise to the impression, in that country, that Bolshevism and Judaism were virtually one and the same thing. On 21 February, Munich socialist revolutionary Eisner was murdered by a disgruntled Austrian army officer. In late March 1919, Béla Kun, a thirty-three-year-old Hungarian Jew and founder of the Hungarian Communist Party, staged a coup in that country and proclaimed the Hungarian Soviet Republic.

Many Germans now came to despise the Weimar Republic for being a talking shop, and for kow-towing to Germany's enemies. They believed that parliamentary democracy had failed them. Many soldiers refused to shed their uniforms and instead formed the right-wing Free Corps militias which indulged in fighting battles with communists.

On 4 April 1919 there was a second revolt in Bavaria, when, encouraged by the success of the communists in Hungary, a coalition of German, radical, left-wing parties, led by Eugen Levine, proclaimed the Bavarian Soviet Republic. With its own Red Army and control of the press, the Republic's aim was to form an alliance with Soviet Russia and with the Hungarian Soviet Republic. Its reign, however, was to be short lived: on 1 May regular army troops and Free Corps troops entered Munich and, in a bloody massacre, overturned the communist régime. Now, a moderate socialist government was established under Johannes Hoffmann. In June that year Levine was executed; according to his son Eugene, he (Levine) met his death bravely, crying out 'Long live the World Revolution!'

*   *   *

The Treaty of Versailles was signed on 28 June 1919. Under its terms, which provided yet further humiliation for Germany, the country was forced to surrender territory to France (Alsace-Lorraine); to Poland (the Polish corridor – between Germany and East Prussia – and Silesia); to Czechoslovakia; to Denmark; and to Belgium. This amounted to one eighth of Germany's territory. Moreover, Germany had already lost her African colonies of South West Africa (Namibia) – which was invaded and seized by South Africa in 1915 – and German East Africa (Tanzania) – which was conquered by British and South African forces in 1916.

Germany was also forbidden to keep troops in her western provinces, namely the Rhineland – a thirty-mile-wide strip of land to the west side of the Rhine river; this region would now be demilitarized and occupied by the Allies for a minimum period of fifteen years. She was also required to limit her army to 100,000 men, and to pay heavy reparations for damage caused during the war. In this year, 1919, the League of Nations was created, although it was not until 1926 that Germany became a member.

* * *

Questions now arose: how would Germany manage to pay the punitive war reparations demanded of her by the Allies and at the same time revitalize her shattered economy; and in political terms, in the forthcoming years of privation and misery, would she drift to the left, or to the right?

Notes

1. *The Nazis: A Warning from History, Part 1.*
2. Shirer, *The Rise and Fall of the Third Reich*, p. 31.
3. Lloyd George, *War Memoirs of David Lloyd George*, Vol.2, p. 1870.
4. Ibid, p. 1871.
5. Ibid, p. 1872.
6. Hitler, *Mein Kampf*, p. 118.
7. Ibid, p. 344.
8. *Hitler: a Profile, The Seducer.*
9. Hitler, op. cit., p. 364.

Chapter 4

Politics: Further Humiliation for Germany

In his youth, Hitler had intended to become a painter, and when thwarted in his ambition, had drifted aimlessly for a number of years. The war had given him a new purpose: to fight for Germany, his country of adoption, but with the Allied victory in 1918, he saw his endeavour, once again, as ending in failure. Nonetheless, a desire to right the wrongs of the past burned within him, and soon an opportunity to take the first steps presented itself.

With the ending of hostilities, Hitler, who was still a serving soldier, was employed by the army to infiltrate left-wing organizations which were seen by it as a threat. To this end he was

> ordered to appear before the Inquiry Commission which had been set up in the 2nd Infantry Regiment for the purpose of watching revolutionary activities.

This, he said, was his 'first incursion into the more or less political field'.[2] A few weeks later, he was ordered to 'attend a course of lectures which were being given for members of the army'. Their purpose was 'to inculcate certain fundamental principles on which the soldier could base his political ideas'[3] He and others, were convinced at that time that Germany

> could not be saved from imminent disaster by those who had participated in the November treachery [i.e., the signing by Germany of the Armistice] – that is to say, the Centre ..., the Social-Democrats ..., and the so-called Bourgeois-National group [the bourgeoisie being the capitalist class].[4]

Hitler and his small circle now 'discussed the project of forming a new party': it would be called the Social Revolutionary Party.[5] In this desire, however, he would be overtaken by events. One day, as a result of attending his lectures, Hitler volunteered to take part in a discussion group. Having found that 'an overwhelming number of those who attended the lecture course supported my views', he was a few days later 'assigned to a regiment then stationed in Munich and given a position there as "instruction officer"'.[6] This gave him 'an opportunity of speaking before quite a large audience', and he was now 'able to confirm what I had hitherto merely felt, namely that I had a talent for public speaking'.[7] Not only that, but becoming a 'platform orator at mass meetings' gave Hitler, by his own admission, 'practice in the pathos and gesture required in large halls that held thousands of people'. In other words, he appreciated the importance of 'body language' as a way of captivating his audience.[8]

In September 1919, Hitler received an order from the army's Political Department to investigate a small political group in Munich, known as the German Labour Party (GLP).[9] This he duly did on the 12th of that month. At the meeting, the National President of the Party, Anton Drexler, a locksmith by trade, gave him a small booklet entitled *My Political Awakening,* the theme of which was 'A Greater Germany and German Unity'. Hitler read it and, to his surprise, found himself much in sympathy with Drexler's aim of creating a political party which would appeal to the working classes, but which, unlike the Social Democrats, would be strongly nationalistic.[10] He was even more surprised the following morning to receive a postcard telling him that he had been accepted as a member of the party.

'When I entered the German Labour Party,' said Hitler, 'I at once took charge of the propaganda, believing this branch to be far the most important for the time being.'[11] 'The receptive powers of the masses are very restricted,' he affirmed

> and their understanding is feeble. On the other hand, they quickly forget. Such being the case, all effective propaganda must be confined to a few bare essentials and those must be expressed, as far as possible, in stereotyped formulae. These slogans should be persistently repeated until the very last individual has come to grasp the idea that has been put forward.[12]

Captain Ernst Röhm of District Command was already a member of the GLP, and had brought with him, covertly and illegally, volunteers and funding from the army, which was sympathetic to the organization. An influential member of the GLP was Dietrich Eckart, poet, playwright, drunkard and one-time drug addict, who regarded Hitler as his protégé.

In October 1919, Hitler addressed the German Workers Party on the subject of the Treaty of Versailles and the Treaty of Brest-Litovsk, which he described as 'one of the most scandalous acts of violence [i.e., against Germany] in the history of the world'.[13]

*   *   *

On 24 February 1920 'the first great mass meeting under the auspices of the new movement took place' in the Banquet Hall of the Munich *Hofbrauhaus* (beer hall for drinking and singing) owned by the brewery Hofbrau.[14] The committees were meeting to elect members and 'to revise the old programme and draw up a new one', said Hitler, who was not impressed by what he saw. Here, he said the swindle begins anew. Once we understand the impenetrable stupidity of our public we cannot be surprised that such tactics turn out [to be] successful. Led by the press and blinded once again by the alluring appearance of the new programme, the bourgeois [capitalist] as well as the proletarian [working class] herds of voters, faithfully return to the common stall and re-elect their old deceivers. Scarcely anything else can be so depressing as to watch this process in sober reality, and to be the eyewitness of this repeatedly recurring fraud.[15]

At this meeting, the Party was renamed the *Nationalsozialistische Deutsche Arbeiterpartei* (National Socialist German Workers Party [NSDAP] or Nazi Party). Hitler wrote that,

> during the first stages of founding our movement, we had to take special care that our militant group which fought for the establishment of a new and exalted political faith should not degenerate into a society for the promotion of parliamentarian interests.[16]

On 13 March 1920 sections of the *Reichswehr* rose up in revolt against the (Weimar) republican government of President Friedrich Ebert, marching into Berlin and installing the sixty-two-year-old civilian Wolfgang Kapp as Chancellor of the Reich. However, *Reichswehr* units in other parts of the country having failed to lend their support to their colleagues, the Reich government was able to suppress the so-called *Kapp Putsch*.

On 14 March 1920 the Munich government of Johannes Hoffman was overthrown by the *Reichswehr* and replaced by a right-wing one under Gustav von Kahr. Munich now became the focus for extremist groups anxious to overthrow the German Republic and repudiate the Treaty of Versailles, the terms of which they considered to be excessively harsh. Included amongst them was German General Erich Ludendorff and many former army officers. Meanwhile, the *Reichswehr* had overthrown the Social Democratic government of Munich and from then on Bavaria was ruled by a state government which had right-wing leanings – in contrast to the central government in Berlin.

The communists remained a potent threat. By 20 March 1920 a Red Army of 50,000 workers had occupied most of the Ruhr, and on this day their newspaper *Das Ruhr Echo* [*The Ruhr Echo*], declared that

> Germany must become a republic of soviets and, in union with Russia, the springboard for the coming victory of the World Revolution and World Socialism.[17]

On 31 March 1920, Hitler was demobilized from the army and became a private citizen. As for the Party, 'It was imperative from the start to introduce rigid discipline into our meetings,' said Hitler 'and establish the authority of the chairman absolutely.' To this end, 'as early as the summer of 1920, the organization of squads of men as hall guards for maintaining order at our meetings was gradually assuming definite shape.'[18]

* * *

On 22 June 1921 an attempt was made by right-wing extremists to assassinate Philipp Scheidemann, the socialist who had proclaimed the Republic. On 21 July 1921, Hitler was confirmed as chairman of the NSDAP, having won the election for the post by the margin of 543 votes to one.

On 26 August 1921, Matthias Erzberger, a Catholic politician who had signed the Armistice Agreement, when the generals had demurred, and who was therefore seen as a traitor, was murdered by right-wing extremists. On the evening of 14 September 1921 at the Munich *Löwenbraukeller* (beer hall owned by the brewery Löwenbrau), Hitler and his SA disrupted a left-wing meeting of the Bavarian League, dragging its leader away and assaulting him. This resulted in Hitler's appearing in court and being given the minimum sentence possible, three months imprisonment. However, for the time being he would remain a free man.

The NSDAP's paramilitary unit led by Röhm, which had now effectively become a uniformed, private army, was largely composed of First World War veteran volunteers, or Free Corps (Freikorps). From November 1921 it was known as the *Sturmabteilung* (Storm Detachment, abbreviated to SA. SA men were often called 'brownshirts', the brown shirt being part of their uniform.) Within the SA was a small, elite unit, established in 1928 as Hitler's personal bodyguard, known as the SS (*Schutztaffel* – Guard Detachment).

The SA was put to the test on 4 November 1921 on the occasion of Hitler's addressing an evening meeting of the Party at the Munich *Hofbrauhaus* when, 'like wolves', they 'threw themselves on the enemy [the communists – or Reds] again and again in parties of eight or ten, and began steadily to thrash them out of the hall'. [19]

* * *

On 16 April 1922, Germany's Foreign Minister, Walther Rathenau, a Jew, signed the Treaty of Rapallo with the Soviet Union: in essence, a trade agreement, this treaty also included secret agreements for military co-operation between the two countries, both of which regarded themselves as outcasts from the international community. The result was that the anti-Bolsheviks were incensed, and on 4 June, Rathenau was assassinated by two former members of the Free Corps.

The Bavarian Government now insisted that Hitler serve the prison sentence which he had been given the previous year. However, following representations in support of Hitler by the presiding judge at the trial to the Appeal Court, the sentence was reduced from three months to just over one month (i.e., 24 June to 27 July).

* * *

On 11 January 1923, French and Belgian troops occupied the Ruhr – the heartland of Germany's heavy industry – in an attempt to enforce reparation payments owed to them. Passive resistance by the local population involved the government in extra expense, which contributed to the already high level of inflation in the country.

Hitler took the opportunity to vent his anger at yet another 'most humiliating kind of capitulation', and described the French 'invasion' as 'insolent'.

> indignation against such a betrayal of our unhappy country broke out into a blaze. Millions of [Deutschmarks] German money had been spent in vain and thousands of young Germans had been sacrificed, who were foolish enough to trust in the promises made by the rulers of the Reich. [By this, Hitler was presumably referring to German losses in the First World War.] Millions of people now became clearly convinced that Germany could be saved only if the whole prevailing system were destroyed, root and branch.

> There never had been a more propitious moment for such a solution. On the one side, an act of high treason had been committed against the country, openly and shamelessly; on the other side, a nation found itself delivered over to die slowly of hunger. Since the State itself had trodden down all the prospects of faith and loyalty, made a mockery of the rights of its citizens, rendered the sacrifices of millions of its most loyal sons fruitless, and robbed other millions of their last penny, such a state could no longer expect anything but hatred from its subjects. This hatred against those who had ruined the people and the country was bound to find an outlet in one form or another.[20]

By September 1923 the communists remained highly influential in Saxony and in industrial centres like Hamburg and the Ruhr, where they threatened to revolt. By the end of October, however, a communist rising in Hamburg had been suppressed by the police; a socialist-communist government in Saxony was arrested by the local *Reichswehr*, and a Reichs Commissioner appointed to rule in its place; a communist government in Thuringia had similarly been removed.

In Munich, on the evening of 8 November 1923, Hitler and 600 *Storm Troopers* (whose job it was to protect Nazi political meetings) launched a surprise attack on the Munich *Bürgerbräukeller* (beer hall owned by Bürgerbräu), where high ranking members of the Bavarian administration (including State Commissioner Gustav Ritter von Kahr, local army commander General Otto von Lossow, and police chief Colonel Hans Ritter von Seisser) were holding a political meeting. Hitler himself mounted the stage and shouted, 'The National Revolution has begun!'[21] and demanded the overthrow of the left-wing government in Berlin.

This *Putsch* (during the course of which the Nazis seized a local bank, hoping to use its premises for their central offices) was swiftly put down by the Munich police who, in the ensuing fracas, shot dead sixteen of Hitler's men. One of those who lost his life was Theodor von der Pfordten, councillor to the Superior Provincial Court, who was part Jewish – though this was never acknowledged by Hitler. Hitler fled the scene, but was soon captured and imprisoned in Bavaria's Landsberg Fortress. Revolutionaries Rudolf Hess (who had been seriously wounded in the action), Hermann Göring, Julius Streicher, Ernst ('Putzi') Hanfstaengl, and others fled to Austria. The Nazi Party was now proscribed and its newspaper, *Der Volkischer Beobachter*, suppressed.

*   *   *

In February 1924, Hitler and nine of his collaborators, including the distinguished military leader of the First World War, General Erich von Ludendorff, together with Captain Ernst Röhm, found themselves appearing before the same judge who had presided over his previous trial, the Bavarian authorities having deliberately chosen this particular person whom they knew would be lenient towards Hitler. At the conclusion of the trial, Hitler states in *Mein Kampf* that he made the following speech.

> The judges of this State may tranquilly condemn us [i.e., himself and his fellow conspirators] for our conduct at that time, but history, the goddess of a higher truth and a better legal code, will smile as she tears up this verdict and will acquit us all of the crime for which this verdict demands punishment.[22]

Nevertheless, he was sentenced to a period of five years' imprisonment. In the event, he would only serve thirteen months. General Ludendorff escaped prison.

Notes

1. Prange, *Hitler's Words*, p. 94.
2. Hitler, op. cit., p. 121.
3. Ibid.
4. Ibid.
5. Ibid, p. 122.
6. Ibid, p. 125.
7. Ibid.
8. Ibid, p. 262.
9. Ibid, p. 126.
10. Shirer, op. cit., p. 37.
11. Hitler, op. cit., p. 318.
12. Ibid, p. 108.
13. Ibid, p. 261.
14. Ibid, p. 210.
15. Ibid, p. 211.
16. Ibid, p. 213.
17. Toland, *Adolf Hitler*, pp. 100–1.
18. Hitler, op. cit., p. 274.
19. Ibid, p. 281.
20. Ibid, p. 377.
21. Bullock, *Hitler: A Study in Tyranny*, p. 106.
22. Hitler, op. cit., p. 377.

Chapter 5

Mein Kampf – Hitler's Manifesto

Mein Kampf was written by Hitler between November 1923 and December 1924, during the time of his imprisonment in Landsberg. In it, his exposition of his philosophy leaves the reader in no doubt as to his intentions, were he ever to come to power.

The Poor

According to Hitler,

> Abject poverty confronted the wealth of the aristocracy and the merchant class face to face. Thousands of unemployed loitered in front of the palaces on the Ring Strasse; and below that Via Triumphalis of the old Austria, the homeless huddled together in the murk and filth of the canals.[1]

In a typical household, he declared,

> the week's earnings are spent in common at home within two or three days. The family eat and drink together as long as the money lasts, and at the end of the week they hunger together. Then the wife wanders about furtively in the neighbourhood, borrows a little, and runs up small debts with the shopkeepers in an effort to pull through the lean days towards the end of the week. They sit down together to the midday meal with only meagre fare on the table, and often even nothing to eat. They wait for the coming pay-day, talking of it and making plans; and while they are thus hungry they dream of the plenty that is to come. And so the little children become acquainted with misery in their early years.[2]

As for the manual labourers of Vienna, they

> lived in surroundings of appalling misery. I shudder even today when I think of the woeful dens in which people dwelt, the night shelters and the slums, and all tenebrous spectacles of ordure, loathsome filth and wickedness. [Then, ominously] What will happen one day when hordes of emancipated slaves [i.e., the poor and the oppressed] come forth from these dens of misery to swoop

down on their unsuspecting fellow men ...? Sooner or later destiny will take its vengeance unless it will have been appeased in time.

For these problems, Hitler proposed the following solution.

> There was a two-fold method by which alone it would be possible to bring about an amelioration of these conditions ... First, to create better fundamental conditions of social development by establishing a profound feeling for social responsibility among the public; second to combine this feeling for social responsibilities with a ruthless determination to prune away all excrescences which are incapable of being improved.[3]

Prostitution and Syphilis

Hitler, who regarded the Weimar Republic as decadent, even though it was generally considered that Berlin had outstripped even Paris as a city of culture, took a lively interest in what he perceived as other social problems. For example, he had much to say about prostitution and the venereal disease, syphilis, which may result from it.

> Those who want seriously to combat prostitution must first of all assist in removing the spiritual conditions on which it thrives. They will have to clean up the moral pollution of our city 'culture' fearlessly and without regard for the outcry that will follow. If we do not drag our youth out of the morass of their present environment, they will be engulfed by it. The fight against syphilis and its pace–maker, prostitution, is one of the gigantic tasks of mankind ...[4]

> The primary cause [of syphilis] is to be found in the manner in which love has been prostituted. Even though this did not directly bring about the fearful disease itself, the nation must still suffer serious damage thereby, for the moral havoc resulting from this prostitution would be sufficient to bring about the destruction of the nation, slowly but surely. This Judaising of our spiritual life and mammonising of our natural instinct for procreation will sooner or later work havoc with our whole posterity. For instead of strong, healthy children, blessed with natural feelings, we shall see miserable specimens of humanity resulting from economic calculation. For economic considerations are becoming more and more the foundations of marriage ...[5]

The Institution of Marriage

Hitler regarded marriage not as

> an end in itself, but [something which] must serve the greater end, which is that of increasing and maintaining the human species and the race [by which Hitler meant his own so-called 'Aryan' race] This is its only meaning and purpose.[6]

Bourgeois (Capitalist) Parties and Trade Unions

Hitler directed his wrath towards the bourgeois parties,

> who had opposed every social demand put forward by the working class. The short-sighted refusal to make an effort towards improving labour conditions; the refusal to adopt measures to insure the workman in case of accidents in the factories; the refusal to forbid child labour; the refusal to consider protective measures for female workers, especially expectant mothers.

As a result of this failure of the bourgeois parties, the masses had no alternative but to join the Social Democratic Party which could claim 'that they alone stand up for the interests of the working class'.

This became the principal ground for the moral justification of the actual existence of the trades unions, so that the labour organization became, from that time onwards, the chief political recruiting ground to swell the ranks of the Social Democratic Party.[7]

However, by the time he had reached the age of twenty, Hitler had

> learned to distinguish between the trade union as a means of defending the social rights of the employees and fighting for better living conditions for them and, on the other hand, the trade union as a political instrument used by the Party in the class struggle.

On balance, therefore, Hitler decided that as far as the trade unions were concerned, he would recommend members of his Party either to leave those unions 'in which they were enrolled, or to remain in them with the idea of causing as much destruction in them as possible'.[8] Employers and employees would 'no longer find themselves drawn into mutual conflict over wages and hours of work ...' but

> questions that are now fought over through a quarrel which involves millions of people will then be settled in the representative chambers of trades and professions, and in the Central Economic Parliament.[9]

Here, Hitler was already indicating to the German people what they might expect were he to come to power, in other words, a centralized, authoritarian state.

The Press

Hitler, in *Mein Kampf*, made his intentions perfectly clear. With regard to the so-called 'freedom of the Press', he stated that

> with ruthless determination, the State must keep control of this instrument of popular education and place it at the service of the State and the Nation.[10]

The Arts
Hitler was also concerned about what he described as 'the Bolshevization of art …'. A person

> need only take a glance at those lucky [sarcasm] states which had become Bolshevized and, to his horror, he will there recognize those morbid monstrosities which have been produced by insane and degenerate people. All those artistic aberrations which are classified under the names of cubism and dadism … [which] showed signs not only of political, but also of cultural decadence.[11]

Race
Mein Kampf is riddled with racist overtones: 'The worth of the State can be determined only by asking how far it actually succeeds in promoting the well-being of a definite race, and not by the role which it plays in the world at large.'[12] 'Those states which do not serve this purpose have no justification for their existence. They are monstrosities.'[13] Referring to his home country of Austria, Hitler describes 'forces … that had their origin in the nationalist yearnings of the various ethnic groups'.[14] In Hitler's opinion, Archduke Franz Ferdinand 'was the chief patron of the movement to make Austria a Slav state',[15] to which Hitler was bitterly opposed.

In respect of racial matters, France was not to escape the wrath of Hitler who was already angered by that country's occupation of Germany's Ruhr in 1923. The fact that the French had included native, colonial soldiers in their army of occupation angered him still further. Said he, 'France is and will remain by far the most dangerous enemy'. And he went on to say,

> The French people, who are becoming more and more obsessed by negroid ideas, represent a threatening menace to the existence of the white race in Europe. For the contamination caused by the influx of negroid blood on the Rhine, in the very heart of Europe, is in accord with the sadist[ic] and perverse lust for vengeance on the part of the hereditary enemy of our people, just as it suits the purpose of the cool, calculating Jew, who would use this means of introducing a process of bastardisation in the very centre of the European continent and, by infecting the white race with the blood of an inferior stock, would destroy the foundations of its independent existence.[16]

Eugenics
Not only would Hitler's State be organized on racial lines, but he would ensure that, within its boundaries, only the fittest would survive.

> In this present State of ours … our national bourgeoisie look upon it as a crime to make procreation impossible for syphilitics and those who suffer from tuberculosis or other hereditary diseases, also cripples and imbeciles.[17]

This was in line with his professed view of the 'struggle between the various species', where

> nature looks on calmly, and is even pleased with what happens ... The struggle for the daily livelihood leaves behind in the ruck everything that is weak or diseased or wavering ... and this struggle is a means of furthering the health and powers of resistance in the species. Thus, it is one of the causes underlying the process of development towards a higher quality of being.[18]

> If for a period of only 600 years those individuals would be sterilized, who are physically degenerate or mentally diseased, humanity would not only be delivered from an immense misfortune, but also restored to a state of general health such as we at present can hardly imagine.

Religion

It, perhaps, comes as a surprise to know that at the time of writing *Mein Kampf*, Hitler regarded himself as a Christian and a 'champion of truth and right'.[19] He was equally in no doubt, that '[Jesus] Christ was an Aryan ...'[20] and that 'Jesus was certainly not a Jew'.[21]

Hitler admired the Catholic Church which he said had 'a lesson to teach us'. Even though

> its dogmatic system is in conflict with the exact sciences and with scientific discoveries, it [the Church] is not disposed to sacrifice a syllable of its teachings. It has rightly recognized that its powers of resistance would be weakened by introducing greater or less trial adaptations to meet the temporary conclusions of science, which in reality are always vacillating.[22]

However, he was soon to make it clear that his objective was change. 'Without a religion of its own the German people has no permanence,' said Hitler. 'What this religion will be, we do not yet know. We feel it, but that is not enough.'[23] This new religion would be based on 'the old beliefs' which 'will be brought back to honour again ... We shall wash off the Christian veneer and bring out a religion peculiar to our race'.[24]

The State

Democracy, 'as practised in Western Europe today,' said Hitler, was 'the forerunner of Marxism ... Democracy is the breeding ground in which the bacilli of the Marxist world pest can grow and spread'.[25] Therefore, in the 'People's State' which he envisaged, 'no vote would be taken in the chambers or senate' which were to be

> organizations for work, and not voting machines ... The right of decision belongs exclusively to the president, who must be entirely responsible for the matter under discussion ... this principle of combining absolute authority with absolute

responsibility will gradually cause a select group of leaders to emerge; which is not even thinkable in our present epoch of irresponsible parliamentarianism.[26]

'The act of inauguration in citizenship [of this new State], shall be a solemn ceremony,' Hitler declared. 'It entitles him [the new citizen] to exercise all the rights of a citizen and to enjoy all the privileges attached thereto'.[27] Quite what these 'privileges' were, was not spelt out.

Education
Hitler was in favour of education, but for him this appears to be with the purpose of fostering nationalistic feelings in the German people, rather than encouraging them to acquire a broader knowledge and wisdom.

> only when family upbringing and school education have inculcated in the individual a knowledge of the cultural and economic and, above all, the political greatness of his own country – then, and then only, will it be possible for him to feel proud of being a citizen of such a country. I can fight only for something that I love. I can love only what I respect. And in order to respect a thing, I must at least have some knowledge of it.[28]

* * *

Volume 1 of *Mein Kampf* ends with the stirring words,

> A fire was enkindled from whose glowing heat the sword would be fashioned which would restore freedom to the German Siegfried [a Wagnerian reference] and bring back life to the German nation. Beside the revival which I then foresaw, I also felt that the Goddess of Vengeance was now getting ready to redress the treason of the 9th November, 1918 … The movement was on the march.[29]

* * *

Alois Hitler's wife, Bridget, has criticized *Mein Kampf* on several counts. For example, in it, Hitler makes no mention of the fact that he had a sister and half-siblings. And he begins Chapter IV with the words, 'At last I came to Munich in the Spring of 1912,' which was patently untrue, for he had in fact arrived in Munich 'a year later than he claimed'[30] – i.e., when he returned to Germany from England.

Notes
1. Hitler, Adolf, *Mein Kampf*, p. 24.
2. Ibid, p. 26.
3. Ibid, p. 27.
4. Ibid, p. 146.

5. Ibid, pp. 141–2.
6. Ibid, p. 144.
7. Ibid, p. 36.
8. Ibid, p. 333.
9. Ibid, p. 331.
10. Ibid, p. 139.
11. Ibid, p. 147.
12. Ibid, p. 222.
13. Ibid, p. 221.
14. Ibid, p. 51.
15. Ibid, p. 19.
16. Ibid, p. 343.
17. Ibid, p. 226.
18. Ibid, p. 161.
19. Prange, op. cit., p. 71.
20. *Hitler's Secret Conversations*, 1941–1944, The New American Library of World Literature Inc., p. 75.
21. Ibid, p. 328.
22. Hitler, op. cit., p. 257.
23. Rauschning, *Hitler Speaks*, p. 59.
24. Ibid, p. 63.
25. Hitler, op. cit., p. 53.
26. Ibid, p. 252.
27. Ibid, p. 247.
28. Ibid, p. 29.
29. Ibid, p. 209.
30. Unger, op. cit., p. 28.

Chapter 6

Hitler: Racist and Liar

In *Mein Kampf*, Hitler reserved some of his most caustic and vituperative comments for the Jews.

First World War
When Hitler was wounded in October 1916 during the Battle of the Somme, he was sent back to hospital in Germany to recuperate and, having done so, he obtained leave to visit Berlin. Here, as he recorded in *Mein Kampf*, he alleged that

> The art of shirking was looked upon almost as proof of higher intelligence, and devotion to duty was considered a sign of weakness or bigotry. Government offices were staffed by Jews. Almost every clerk was a Jew and every Jew was a clerk. I was amazed at this multitude of combatants who belonged to the chosen people and could not help comparing it with their slender numbers in the fighting lines. In the business world the situation was even worse. Here the Jews had actually become 'indispensable'. Like leeches, they were slowly sucking the blood from the pores of the national body. By means of newly-floated War Companies, an instrument had been discovered whereby all national trade was throttled so that no business could be carried on freely. Special emphasis was laid on the necessity for unhampered centralization. Hence, as early as 1916/17, practically all production was under the control of Jewish finance.[1]

What Hitler failed to mention was that, during the course of the Great War, approximately 100,000 German Jews fought for the German Kaiser, of whom about 12,000 lost their lives and 30,000 were decorated for bravery. Some of them, he would undoubtedly have encountered, for they would have fought alongside him. In addition, when he was awarded the Iron Cross First Class, on 4 August 1918, it was a Jewish officer, Lieutenant Hugo Gutmann, whom he had to thank for his nomination.[2] But despite evidence to the contrary, Hitler preferred to believe that all Jews, without exception, were trying to undermine the German war effort.

Jewish Finance and Prosperity
In *Mein Kampf*, Hitler declared that 'practically all [German economic] production was under the control of Jewish finance ... Jewry was busy despoiling the nation

and tightening the screws of its despoliation'.[3] However, as usual, Hitler was selective in his analysis and omitted to mention, for example, that the largest producer of armaments in Germany, at that time, was Krupps, a German and not a Jewish firm. He described a visit to Berlin where

> the luxury, the perversion, the iniquity, the wanton display, and the Jewish materialism disgusted me so thoroughly, that I was almost beside myself.[4]

The Arts and the Press
Referring again to his time spent in Vienna, Hitler declared,

> in my eyes the charge against Judaism became a grave one the moment I discovered the Jewish activities in the press, in art, in literature and the theatre … One needed only to look at the posters announcing the hideous productions of the cinema and theatre, and study the names of the authors who were highly lauded there, in order to become permanently adamant on Jewish questions. Here was a pestilence, a moral pestilence, with which the public was being infected. It was worse than the Black Plague of long ago … The fact that nine-tenths of all the smutty literature, artistic tripe and theatrical banalities, had to be charged to the account of people who formed scarcely one percent of the nation – that fact could not be gain said [i.e., contradicted].[5]

In contrast, said he, 'It was through the Aryan that art and science flourished.'[6]

Creators of Civilizations and States
In Hitler's words, 'It was he [the Aryan] alone, in the final analysis, who knew how to establish states. The Jew is incapable of all this.'[7]

> The Jew has never yet founded a civilization, but he has destroyed hundreds. He can show nothing of his own creation. Everything that he has is stolen. He has foreign people, foreign workers to build his temples; foreigners create and work for him; foreigners shed their blood for him. He has no art of his own; everything has either been stolen from other peoples, or imitated. He does not even know how to preserve these costly possessions. In his hands they turn immediately to filth and dung.[8]

Anyone who took the trouble to peruse the list of Nobel Prize winners for the twentieth century would come to a different conclusion. The first Nobel Prizes had been awarded in the year 1901, under the terms of the will of Swedish chemist, Alfred B. Nobel, to those who had made the greatest contributions in five different fields of endeavour. The results, for Jews, from 1901 until the outbreak of the Second World War in 1939, are as follows: literature 2; world peace 2; chemistry 5; medicine 7; physics – where the recipients included Albert Einstein and Niels Bohr – 6.

It should also be remembered that the Jews had no country which they could call their own. This would be the case until the state of Israel was created in 1948.

Prostitution

In Vienna, Hitler said that

> the part which the Jews played in the social phenomenon of prostitution, and more especially in the white slave traffic, could be studied here better than in any other western European city, with the possible exception of certain ports in southern France ... A cold shiver ran down my spine when I first ascertained that it was the same kind of cold blooded, thick-skinned and shameless Jew who showed his consummate skill in conducting that revolting exploitation of the dregs of the big city. Then I became fired with wrath.

And having

> learned to track down the Jew in all the different spheres of cultural, artistic life, I suddenly came upon him in a position where I had least expected to find him. I now realized that the Jews were the leaders of social democracy. In the face of that revelation the scales fell from my eyes. My long inner struggle was at an end.[9]

The Jews as Robbers

Hitler said, 'The Jews are a people of robbers ... Everything that he [the Jew] has is stolen.'[10] But were the Jews, in reality, any more likely to commit crime than other ethnic groups? The evidence indicates not. According to statistics compiled by Dr Leo Goldhammer, whereas Jews in Vienna in 1910, when Hitler was resident in that city, accounted for 8.63 per cent of the population, in the following two years only 6.38 per cent of committed crimes were attributable to them. This indicates that they were, in fact, less likely to commit crime than other ethnic groups.[11]

Vienna as a 'Mongrelized' City

In Vienna, said Hitler,

> my inner aversion to the Habsburg State was increasing daily ... The conglomerate spectacle of heterogeneous races which the capital of the dual monarchy [i.e., Austro-Hungarian] presented, this motley of Czechs, Poles, Hungarians, Ruthenians, Serbs and Croats etc – and always that bacillus which is the solvent of human society, the Jew, here and there and everywhere – the whole spectacle was repugnant to me. The gigantic city seemed to be the incarnation of mongrel depravity.[12]

This, of course, reveals that Hitler regarded the Jews as having contaminated the pure Aryan race by interbreeding with it.

The Jews as Aliens

In Vienna, said Hitler, referring to the Jews, 'the more I saw of them, the more strikingly they stood out as a different people from other citizens … in outer appearance [they] bore no similarity to the Germans'.[13] Simply being in the presence of a Jew induced in him a feeling of physical revulsion. 'That they were water-shy was obvious … The odour of those people in caftans often used to make me feel ill. Beyond that there were the unkempt clothes and the ignoble exterior.' He enquired,

> was there any shady undertaking, any form of foulness, especially in cultural life, in which at least one Jew did not participate? On putting the probing knife carefully to that kind of abscess one immediately discovered, like a maggot in a putrescent body, a little Jew who was often blinded by the sudden light.[14]

> In the Jew I still saw only a man who was of a different religion, and therefore, on grounds of human tolerance, I was against the idea that he should be attacked because he had a different faith. And so I considered that the tone adopted by the anti-Semitic press was unworthy of the cultural traditions of a great people.[15]

Gradually however, Hitler's attitude towards the Jews hardened.

> Once, when passing through the inner city [of Vienna] I suddenly encountered a phenomenon in a long caftan and growing black side-locks. My first thought was: is this a Jew? They certainly did not have this appearance in Linz. I watched the man stealthily and cautiously, but the longer I gazed at the strange countenance and examined it feature by feature, the more the question shaped itself in my brain: is this a German? Wherever I now went I saw Jews, and the more I saw of them the more strikingly and clearly they stood out as a different people from the other citizens. Especially the inner city and the district northwards from the Danube Canal swarmed with people who, even in outward appearance, bore no similarity to the Germans.[16]

Religion

In a speech delivered on 12 April 1922, Hitler even went so far as to enlist the support of Jesus Christ in his diatribe against the Jews.

> With boundless love, as a Christian and as a man, I read the passage [in the *Bible*] which relates how the Lord finally gathered His strength, and made use of the whip, in order to drive the usurpers, the vipers, and cheats, from the temple. Today, 2,000 years later, I recognize with deep emotion Christ's tremendous fight for the world against the Jewish poison.[17]

And then he performs a volte-face by declaring that 'The heaviest blow that ever struck humanity was the coming of Christianity. Bolshevism is Christianity's illegitimate child. Both are inventions of the Jew'.[18]

Hitler's Threat

To Josef Hell, a resident of Munich and an editor of the weekly magazine, *Der Gerade Weg – The Straight Way*, Hitler said ominously, in January 1922,

> there are few Germans who are not angered here and there about the behaviour of the Jews, or who have not been injured by Jews. In their relatively small number they control an enormous part of the German National Wealth. That is money you can confiscate and use for the state and the general public, just as was done with the property of the monasteries, the bishops, and the nobility ... Once the hate and the battle against the Jews is really fanned and stirred up, their resistance will collapse in the shortest possible time. They cannot even protect themselves, and no-one else will provide protection for them.[19]

* * *

Hitler had once acknowledged the help given to him by the Jews during his time in Vienna. Now, he had nothing but hatred for them. Furthermore, his opinion of Jews had virtually no basis in fact, and more often than not was based on utter falsehood. As far as he was concerned, the opinion of an individual Jew about politics, religion, or anything else, was irrelevant and he hated all Jews, purely by virtue of their ethnicity.

Hitler was undoubtedly deluded about the Jews. The question is, what was the source of his anti-Semitic ideas?

Notes

1. Hitler, op. cit., p. 114.
2. Wiedemann, *Der Mann, der Feldherr werden wollte*, pp. 25–6.
3. Hitler, op. cit., p. 114.
4. Langer, Information obtained from Ernst Hanfstaengl (901), p. 35.
5. Hitler, op. cit., p. 42.
7. *Der Volkischer Beobachter*, Munich, 28 July 1922; 16 Aug. 1922, in Prange, op. cit., p. 75.
8. Hitler, op. cit., p. 171.
9. Ibid, p. 43.
10. *Der Volkischer Beobachter*, 16 August 1922, in Prange, op. cit., p. 75.
11. Goldhammer, *Die Juden Weins*, Vienna and Leipzig.
12. Hitler, op. cit., p. 79.
13. Ibid, p. 41
14. Ibid, p. 42.
15. Ibid, p. 39.
16. Ibid, p. 41.
17. *Der Volkischer Beobachter*, Munich, 12 April 1922; 22 April 1922; in Prange, op. cit., p. 71.
18. Trevor-Roper, *Hitler's Table Talk, 1941–1944*, p. 7.
19. Josef Hell manuscript in Charles Bracelen Flood. 1922. p.245 and p. 649.

Chapter 7

The Origin of Hitler's Ideas

Bearing in mind the strength of Hitler's feelings on certain matters, it is pertinent to enquire as to where his ideas came from. Did they arise spontaneously, or were other factors involved?

School

Hitler's performance at school, and in particular at *Realschule* (secondary school) was undistinguished, and he left having failed to obtain his vital *Abitur* (school leaving examination diploma at 16). Highly critical of his schoolteachers, he complained that 'they had no sympathy with youth ...'. 'If any pupil showed the slightest trace of originality they persecuted him relentlessly, and the only model pupils whom I have ever known have all been failures in later life.'[1] There was one teacher, however, whom he did admire, namely Dr Leopold Potsch, a fervent German Nationalist. He describes the two of them sitting together 'often aflame with enthusiasm, sometimes even moved to tears ...', and it was because of his teacher's influence that history became Hitler's favourite subject.[2]

Georg Ritter von Schönerer

It was in early 1908, when he was living as a nineteen-year-old in the Austrian town of Linz, that Hitler became acquainted with the teachings of Georg Ritter von Schönerer, a Viennese born in 1842.

Schönerer, founder of Austria's Pan-German Nationalist Party, had been elected to the Austrian *Reichsrat* (Upper House of Parliament) in 1873, where he made anti-Semitic speeches. He was vigorously opposed to liberals, socialists, Catholics, Jews, and the Habsburgs, and demanded the separation of the German-speaking provinces of Austria from the multi-national Habsburg Empire, in favour of their economic and political union with the German Reich.

The Schönerer 'code' advocated celibacy until the age of twenty-five, the avoidance of eating meat and drinking alcohol (which were seen as aphrodisiacs), and the avoidance of consorting with prostitutes due to the danger of infection. (Hitler himself was a teetotaller and a vegetarian.) Schönerer also gave himself the title of *Führer*, and instituted the *Heil* greeting.

As Hitler said in *Mein Kampf*, 'When I came to Vienna, all my sympathies were exclusively with the Pan-German movement.'[3] However, in his view, the way

Schönerer's party supported the parliamentary system of democracy and its failure to win over the support of the establishment and, in particular, the army, was a weakness. Instead, he found himself to be more in sympathy with Doctor Karl Lueger, head of Austria's Christian Socialists, whom he admired for his ability to

> adopt all available means for winning the support of long established institutions, so as to be able to derive the greatest possible advantage for his movement from those old sources of power.[4]

However, in Hitler's opinion, both these parties had weaknesses: the Pan-German Party in its failure to arouse the broad masses of the people; the Christian Socialists for their failure to embrace Pan-Germanism.

Literature which Hitler professed to have read

Referring to his time spent in Vienna, Hitler said, 'I now often turn to the *Volksblat*' – a reference to the anti-Semitic Viennese newspaper. Subsequently, during his period of incarceration at Landsberg, which he described as his 'university paid for by the state', he declared that he 'devoured book after book, pamphlet after pamphlet'.[5] In *Mein Kampf* he mentions, by name, the works of Leopold von Ranke, Professor of History in Berlin; Heinrich von Treitschke; Friedrich Nietzsche, German philosopher, scholar and writer; Karl Marx, German social, political and economic theorist; Prince Otto von Bismarck, Prusso-German statesman and the first Chancellor of the German Empire; together with the war memoirs of soldiers and statesmen, both German and Allied.[6]

He also mentions Houston Stewart Chamberlain, writer and propagandist; Arthur Schopenhauer, German philosopher; and Leopold Poetsch, his former schoolteacher. It is interesting, therefore, to find out what these authors actually had to say, and to what extent their ideas coincided with those of Hitler.

Arthur Schopenhauer

Arthur Schopenhauer (1788–1860), German philosopher of metaphysics, postulated a world of suffering and disappointment and took an atheistic and pessimistic view of the world: pessimistic, because of what he perceived as an irrational force in human beings which produces an ever frustrating cycle of desire, from which the only escape is aesthetic contemplation or absorption into nothingness. Perhaps one reason why Hitler admired him was because of his reference to the Jew as 'the great master of lies'.[7]

Heinrich von Treitschke

Heinrich von Treitschke (1834–1896), German historian, regarded war not only as an inevitability but something to be glorified.

> martial glory is the basis of all the political virtues; in the rich treasure of Germany's glories the Prussian military glory is a jewel as precious as the

masterpieces of our poets and thinkers. War is not only a practical necessity, it is also a theoretical necessity, an exigency of logic. The concept of the state implies the concept of war, for the essence of the state is power ... That war should ever be banished from the world is a hope, not only absurd, but profoundly immoral. It would involve the atrophy of many of the essential and sublime forces of the human soul ... The people which become attached to the chimerical hope of perpetual peace finishes irremediably by decaying in its proud isolation...

Treitschke also affirmed that 'It does not matter what you think, so long as you obey'.[8]

Houston Stewart Chamberlain

Houston Stewart Chamberlain (1855–1927), writer and propagandist, was born in Southsea, Hampshire on 9 September 1855. Aged fourteen, due to poor health, he left England to visit health resorts on the Continent, accompanied by a Prussian tutor, Otto Kuntze, who extolled to him the virtues of Prussian militarism and introduced him to German history, literature and philosophy, including the works of artists and poets such as Beethoven, Schiller, Goethe, and Wagner. Kuntze remained his tutor for four years. At the University of Geneva, Chamberlain embarked upon a three-year study of various subjects, including philosophy, physics, chemistry and medicine.

Having married Anna Horst, a Prussian, Chamberlain and his wife set up home in Dresden where they spent four years, before moving to Vienna in 1889. Here he researched into plant physiology.

Chamberlain began his writing career in January 1892. His *Foundations of the Nineteenth Century*, published in 1899, with an introduction written by the Englishman, Algernon Bertram Mitford (father of the famous Mitford sisters), known as Bertie and who, in 1906, became Lord Redesdale. The book attributes the moral, cultural, scientific and technological superiority of western civilization to the positive influence of the 'Germanic race', which for him included Slavs and Celts.

As far as Christianity was concerned, Chamberlain believed that it had developed into a murderous, totalitarian system because of two factors: the Catholic Church, whose influence relied on terror, and the laws of the Old Testament which he attributed to a Jewish influence. In fact, he opposed any cultural, religious or political system which had global aspirations, such as the Catholic Church, capitalism and socialism.

The *Foundations of the Nineteenth Century* was greeted with rapture by German Kaiser Wilhelm II, who invited the author to his Court. Thus began a lifelong friendship and correspondence between the two of them. 'It was God who sent your book to the German people, and you personally to me,' wrote Wilhelm to Chamberlain.

Chamberlain was, in turn, influenced by the writings of Joseph Arthur, Compte de Gobineau (1816–82) whose *Essai sur l'Inégalité des Races Humaines* made the case for the superiority of Nordics and Aryans, peoples who he, Gobineau, forecast would decline owing to their intermingling with other races.

In 1905, Chamberlain divorced his wife, Anna, and three years later married Eva, the daughter of the late composer, Richard Wagner, who had died in 1883. Chamberlain had first met Wagner and his wife, Cosima, in Bayreuth in 1882 and it was in that city that the couple would settle.

In 1915, Chamberlain, who regarded it as an act of treason that Britain had opposed Germany during the Great War, was awarded the Iron Cross for services to the German Empire; in 1916 he adopted German nationality.

On 30 September 1923, Hitler, who was visiting Wagner's widow, the eighty-six-year-old Cosima at Bayreuth, crossed the road to call on the aged Chamberlain, who was by this time blind, paralyzed and confined to a wheelchair. As Hitler took his leave the old man wept with grief. A few days later, Chamberlain wrote to Hitler.

My belief in the Germans has already been strong although – I confess – it had ebbed. With one stroke, you have changed the state of my soul. That Germany gives birth to a Hitler in the time of direst need is proof of her vitality … may God protect you.[9]

In no way do you resemble the descriptions depicting you as a fanatic. I even believe that you are the absolute opposite of a fanatic … The fanatic wants to persuade people, you want to convince them and to convince only.[10]

On the question of Christianity, Hitler and Chamberlain parted company. Said the former, 'In my view, HS Chamberlain was mistaken in regarding Christianity as a reality upon the spiritual level.' Although 'we have no reason to wish that the Italians and Spaniards should free themselves from the drug of Christianity,' nonetheless, 'let us [i.e., the Germans] be the only people who are immunized against the disease.'[11]

Hitler knew that one day, if he had his way, he would betray Chamberlain's ideals, for it was the latter's wish that no harm should come to the Jews, and had Chamberlain been able to read Hitler's mind, he would doubtless not have been so distraught at their parting.

Chamberlain died on 9 January 1927, aged seventy-one, by which time he had written biographies of German philosopher Immanuel Kant and German poet Johann Wolfgang von Goethe, as well as a biography of Wagner.

Friedrich Wilhelm Nietzsche
Friedrich Wilhelm Nietzsche (1844–1900), German philosopher, scholar and writer, was an admirer of Richard Wagner, regarding that composer's operas as the true successors to Greek tragedy. However, he broke with Wagner in 1876, ostensibly because he believed that the Christian convictions expressed in 'Parsifal' were 'mere play-acting'.

In essays published between 1873 and 1876, Nietzsche repudiated Christian and liberal ethics and democratic ideals, seeing the deeds of the great as being more historically significant than the movements of the masses. Christianity was a 'slave morality', and democracy was a means by which quantity. was made to prevail over quality. As far as nationalism and racialism were concerned, Nietzsche despised them both.

> God is dead, but considering the state the species Man is in, there will perhaps be caves, for ages yet, in which his shadow will be shown. Morality is the herd-instinct of the individual. The Christian resolution to find the world ugly and bad has made the world ugly and bad. Believe me! The secret of reaping the greatest fruit from us and the greatest enjoyment from life is to live dangerously![12]

For Nietzsche the decadent, western, Christian civilization had to be swept away, and the heroic superman who took its place would be above conventional morality. 'A daring and ruler race is building itself up ...,' said he,

> The aim should be to prepare a trans-valuation of values for a particularly strong kind of man, most highly gifted in intellect and will. This man and the elite around him will become the 'Lords of the Earth'.[13]

'I teach you Superman,' said Nietzsche. 'Man is something to be surpassed,'[14] and he described the former thus,

> Such beings are incalculable, they come like fate without cause or reason, inconsiderably and without pretext. Suddenly they are here like lightning: too terrible, too sudden, too compelling and too 'different' even to be hated ... What moves them is the terrible egotism of the artist of the brazen glance, who knows himself to be justified for all eternity in his 'work' as the mother is justified in her child.[15]

When Nietzsche died in 1900, Hitler was only twenty years old. However, two other statements made by Nietzsche, when applied to Hitler, may be considered to be prophetic.

1. *In all great deceivers a remarkable process is at work to which they owe their power. In the very act of deception with all its preparations, the dreadful voice, expression and gestures, they are overcome by their belief in themselves; it is this belief which then speaks, so persuasively, so miracle-like, to the audience.*[16]
2. *He who fights with monsters might take care lest he thereby become a monster. And if you gaze for long into an abyss, the abyss gazes also into you.*[17]

Leopold Poetsch

According to Hitler in *Mein Kampf*, it appears that the concept of racism was first put into his mind by his teacher, Doctor Leopold Poetsch, of the *Realschule* in Linz. In Hitler's words, 'The national fervour which we felt in our own small way was utilized by [Poetsch] as an instrument of our education …'[18]

*   *   *

Is Hitler to be believed when he says that he read – and therefore by implication had a detailed knowledge of – the works of these philosophers and teachers? The fact that so much of their philosophy, but not all, became his philosophy also, lends weight to his assertion.

There were, in addition, other sources upon which Hitler's notions rested, as will be discussed shortly.

Notes

1. Bullock, op. cit., p. 27.
2. Ibid.
3. Hitler, op. cit., p. 64.
4. Ibid, p. 65.
5. Ibid, p. 40.
6. Frank, *Im Angesicht des Galgen*, pp. 46–7.
7. Hitler, op. cit., p. 173.
8. Shirer, op. cit., p. 99.
9. Chamberlain to Hitler, October 7, 1923. American Historical Association, German Records Collection, Roll 4. Microcopy number T84. Folder 8. Frames 3715 to 3721.
10. Briefe (letters) 1882–1924, *Und Briefwechsel mit Kaiser Wilhelm II*, vol. 2, page 124.
11. *Hitler's Secret Conversations, 1941–1944*, The New American Library of World Literature Inc. Speech. December 13, 1941.
12. Nietzsche, *Die Frohliche Wissenschaft* (*The Joyful Wisdom*), pp.3, 18, 116, 130 & 283.
13. Nietzsche, *The Will to Power*.
14. Nietzsche, *Die Begrussung*.
15. Nietzsche, *Zur Genealogie der Moral* (*A Genealogy of Morals*), section 2, para. 17.
16. Nietzsche, *Human, All Too Human*, para. 52, quoted by J.P. Stern, p. 35.
17. Nietzsche, *Jenseits von Gut und Bose* (*Beyond Good and Evil*), 1b, 146.
18. Hitler, op. cit., p. 19.

Chapter 8

The Concept of the 'Aryan'

There were two men who had a greater influence on Hitler's thinking than any others, and they will be discussed shortly. First, however, it is necessary to enquire as to the meaning of the word 'Aryan', for it was on the concept of 'Aryan supremacy' that the Third Reich was founded. Wrote Hitler in *Mein Kampf,*

> If we divide mankind into three categories: founders of culture, bearers of culture, destroyers of culture, [then] the Aryan alone can be considered as representing the first category.
>
> Every manifestation of human culture, every product of art, science and technical skill, which we see before our eye today, is almost exclusively the product of the Aryan creative power. This very fact fully justifies the conclusion that it was the Aryan alone who founded a superior type of humanity. Therefore, he represents the archetype of what we understand by the term MAN. He is the Prometheus of mankind from whose shining brow the divine spark of genius has at all times flashed forth ...
>
> Should he [the Aryan] be forced to disappear, a profound darkness will descend on the Earth; within a few thousand years human culture will vanish and the world will become a desert.'[1]

(Curiously enough, Hitler regarded the inhabitants of the USA as Aryans, even though the time would come when he would plot the destruction of that country.[2]) So who, in Hitler's opinion, were the Aryans, and how had they come into such prominence? In his view,

> Aryan tribes, often almost ridiculously small in number, subjugated foreign peoples and, stimulated by the conditions of life which their new country afforded them, and profiting also by the abundance of manual labour furnished them by the inferior race, they developed intellectual and organizing faculties which had hitherto been dormant in these conquering tribes. Within the course of a few thousand years, or even centuries [Hitler was apparently not quite sure which] they gave life to cultures whose primitive traits completely corresponded to the character of the founders, then modified by adaptation to the peculiarities

of the soil and the characteristics of the subjugated people. But finally the conquering race offended against the principles which they first had observed, namely the maintenance of their racial stock unmixed, and they began to intermingle with the subjugated people. Thus they put an end to their own separate [self-contained] existence; for the original sin committed in paradise has always been followed by the expulsion of the guilty parties.[3]

* * *

In the light of the evidence, it is astonishing that the future leader of a highly literate and cultured country such as Germany should have been so blinkered as to believe that one particular race – of which the Germans were a part – was superior to others. How did he account, for example, for the fact that the Russians – whom he considered to be non-Aryan and therefore inferior – had produced composers of music such as Tchaikovsky, Borodin (who was also a scientist), Glinka and Mussorgsky; poets such as Pushkin and Blok, and writers such as Tolstoy, Dostoyevsky and Chekov, to name but a few. Ironically, as it would transpire, it was Tolstoy who wrote *War and Peace* – arguably the finest novel in world literature – the background to which is French Emperor Napoleon Bonaparte's disastrous military campaign in Russia.

* * *

Was there really such an entity as an Aryan race? According to the *Oxford English Dictionary*, the term 'Aryan' referred to 'the worshippers of the gods of the Brahmans (of the highest Hindu caste)'.[4] 'It also applies to a family of languages (which includes Sanskrit, Zend, Greek, Persian, Latin, Celtic, Teutonic and Slavonic, with their modern representatives', although historically, 'only the ancient Indian and Iranian members of the family are known ... to have called themselves "Aria, Arya or Ariya"'.)

However, J. S. Huxley (English biologist and humanist) stated that 'Biologically, it is almost as illegitimate to speak of a "Jewish race" as of an "Aryan race".'[5] And American historian, Madison Grant, declared that 'the name "Aryan race" must (also) be frankly discarded as a term of racial significance'.[6] Even H. S. Chamberlain admitted that 'It were [i.e., has been] proved that there never was an Aryan race in the past ...'.[7]

Notes

1. Hitler, op. cit.,p. 164.
2. Ibid.
3. Ibid, p. 165.
4. *The Oxford English Dictionary*, 2nd edn 1989, Vol. 1.
5. Huxley, *Race in Europe*, p. 24.
6. Grant, *Passing of Great Race*, 1917, V.62.
7. Chamberlain, *Foundations of the 19th Century*, iv. p. 266.

Chapter 9

Guido von List

Guido von List (1848–1919) was important to Hitler, not only as a primary source of inspiration, but also because he was a formative influence on the man who was to be pre-eminent in providing Hitler with his ideas – namely Lanz von Liebenfels.

List was born in Vienna into a Catholic family on 5 October 1848. His father was a prosperous leather merchant, after whose death List left the family business and became a newspaper journalist. He also contributed articles for periodical magazines and journals, and was a prolific writer of books. He was a staunch supporter of the Habsburg monarchy and imperial dynasty, a sentiment with which Hitler would most certainly not have approved.[1] In the early 1900s he claimed that he was descended from the aristocracy and added the title 'von' to his name.

Elsa Schmidt-Falk told Viennese psychologist, psychotherapist and writer Wilfried Daim that Hitler rated List's work very highly and, above all, his two-volume work, *Deutsch-Mythologische Landschaftsbilder* (*Images of German Mythological Landscapes*). The wife of an SA (Stormtrooper) leader, Schmidt-Falkl was honorary director of the Department of Family Research on the NSDAP's (Nazi Party) Munich-North Executive District Committee and also Honorary Assistant Advisor for Genealogy in the National Socialist Women's Organization. It was Hitler's opinion that List, as author of these two volumes, had provided Austria with such a treasure that other Germanic countries would do well to acquire something similar. Also, he commissioned Schmidt-Falk to make drawings of these aforesaid Bavarian mythological landscapes, which she duly did.[2]

Schmidt-Falk also told Daim that Hitler believed List's reference to the advent of the 'invincible', 'strong man from above' referred specifically to himself.[3] In fact, what List was referring to was his discovery, in 1891, of a prophetic verse in the *Voluspa* (which is contained in a collection of mythological and heroic old Norse poetry, dating from the 12th century and known as the *Edda* – meaning literally, 'The wisdom of the prophetess') which predicted that a messianic figure, the *Starke von Oben* (Strong one from the Skies) would come and set up an eternal order.

As a pan-Germanist (democratic, social-reformist, but anti-liberal and anti-Semitic), List was in favour of promoting German culture and language, and attempted to establish links between modern German place names and the ancient pagan religions. In a speech delivered in 1878, he demanded the 'economic and political union of German-speaking Austria with the German Reich'.[4] In 1911 he predicted war, prophesying that

> the Aryo-German-Austrian battleships shall once more … shoot, sizzling from the giant guns of our dreadnoughts; our national armies shall once more storm southwards and westwards to smash the enemy and create order.[5]

List called for 'the ruthless subjection of non-Aryans to Aryan masters in a highly structured, hierarchical state'.[6] The church, he said, had 'encouraged a deviation from strict eugenics of "the old Aryan sexual morality" …'.[7] According to List,

> The qualification for candidates for education or positions in public service, the professions, and commerce rested solely on their racial purity. The heroic Ario-German race was to be relieved of all wage labour and demeaning tasks, in order to rule as an exalted elite over the slave castes of non-Aryan peoples. Strict racial and marital laws were to be observed; a patriarchal society was to be fostered in which only the male head of the house had full majority, and only Ario-Germans enjoyed the privileges of freedom and citizenship; each family was to keep a genealogical record attesting [to] its racial purity …

List published his ideas in 1911.[8]

* * *

It was List's belief, articulated by him in 1893, that the ancient native Germans, whom he called 'Ario-Germans' – the words 'Aryo' and 'Ario' being interchangeable – once possessed their own language and their own religion – Wotanism (after Wotan, the Germanic god of war).

> The central tenet of Wotanism was the cyclical nature of the universe which proceeded through a series of transformations: 'birth', 'being', 'death', and 'rebirth'.[9]

According to the *Edda*, it was Wotan who first gained an understanding of the runes, which, according to Norse legend, were not only a system of writing but also possessed an inherent, magical power.[10]

The Secret of The Runes was published by List in 1908. He convinced himself that the runes were 'the script of our Germanic ancestors', (i.e., the Aryans)[11] being divided into 'letter-runes' and 'hieroglyph-runes' (holy-signs). The sixth rune embraces the concept of the Aryan tribe or race which 'is to be purely preserved; it may not be defiled by the roots of the foreign tree'. 'Therefore: "Your blood, [is] your highest possession".'[12] The eleventh or *sig* rune ('victory-rune') was, according to List, associated with the 'millenia-old Aryan greeting and battle-cry

... ' (namely, *sal and sig*! – meaning salvation and victory). The message of the *sig* rune is therefore, 'The creative spirit must conquer!'[13]

List declared that the sixteenth (or *Yr* rune) 'plays off against' the seventeenth (or *eh* rune) in that the former warns against frivolous transitory love affairs, whereas the latter – the 'marriage' rune, confirms the concept of lasting love on the basis of marriage as the legal bond between a man and a woman. Marriage is the basis of the *volk* [people] and, according to an ancient legal formula, the 'raw-root of the continuance of Teutondom'. Therefore 'Marriage is the raw-root of the Aryans!'[14]

List classified the 'social levels' of the Aryans into 'provider class', 'teacher class', and 'soldier class'. However, because 'All Aryans or Teutons felt themselves to be one folk,' then 'every individual, be he free man or king, had to belong to the "provider class" in order to prevent this class from being devalued.' In effect, this meant that 'Everyone had, therefore, to be a farmer ...'.[15] 'In the Aryan world,' he said,

> there was no personal ownership of land and soil, only familial estates: the elder governed it for his clan, the members of which only had rights of usage over it. If their number became too great for the ownership of land, then the serfs would have to migrate, never to return. Such migratory expeditions were known as 'colonization efforts' and the resulting Aryan foundations were to be found throughout the whole world ... reaching all the way back into prehistoric times.[16]

It was possible 'to recognize in the old Aryan sexual morality the truly traditional and true wisdom – which must and will lead our folk to salvation'.[17] The 'old Ario-Germanic world view,' said List, 'was that *Wuotanism* [Wotanism] assures those who fall in battle of a heroic heaven with eternal joy in Walhalla [Valhalla – celestial resting place of the souls of fallen heroes].'[18]

* * *

Hitler would certainly have found himself in tune with List's antagonistic feelings towards 'democracy, parliamentarianism, feminism and "Jewish" influences in the arts, press and business'. He would also have concurred with List's prescription for 'a rigid hierarchy of offices, levels of authority and traditional administrative districts [*Gau* – to be administered by *Gauleiters* or regional party leaders.]'[19] Finally, for Hitler, the concept of himself as a new messianic 'strong one from the skies' would clearly have been a difficult one to resist.

Notes
1. Goodrick-Clarke, *The Occult Roots of Nazism*, p. 65.
2. Daim, *Der Mann, der Hitler die Ideen gab*, p. 96.
3. Hamann, *Hitler's Vienna: a Dictator's Apprenticeship*, pp. 212–3.
4. Goodrick-Clarke, op. cit., p. 37.

5. List, *Das Geheimnis der Runen.* 2a., p. 81f. (in Goodrick-Clarke, op. cit., p. 85).
6. Goodrick-Clarke, p. 63.
7. Ibid, p. 68.
8. List, op.cit., 2a. p.70 ff. (in Goodrick-Clarke, op. cit., p. 64).
9. Barker, *Invisible Eagle: The History of Nazi Occultism,* p. 41.
10. Ibid.
11. List, *The Secret of the Runes,* (translated 1988 by Stephen Flowers), p. 42.
12. Ibid, p. 53.
13. Ibid, p. 57.
14. Ibid, p. 63.
15. Ibid, p. 75.
16. Ibid, p. 76.
17. Ibid, p. 98.
18. Ibid, p. 107.
19. Goodrick-Clarke, op. cit., p. 200.

Chapter 10

Jörg Lanz Von Liebenfels

In *Mein Kampf*, Hitler, referring to his sojourn in Vienna (which commenced in December 1908), stated that here 'For the first time in my life, I bought myself some anti-Semitic pamphlets for a few pence'.[1] Wilfried Daim, in his book, *Der Mann, der Hitler die Ideen gab*, (*The Man who gave Hitler his Ideas* – published in 1958), sheds light on what these pamphlets were, and on their authorship.

Daim describes how, in 1951, he was told by a friend, one Dr Erwin von Watersrat 'about the sect of a certain Lanz von Liebenfels. In Watersrat's opinion I ought to meet the people who would interest me, from the psychological standpoint, about the sect'.[2] By coincidence,

> shortly after that, on 27 March 1951, Professor AM Knoll [August Maria Knoll, Professor of Sociology at the University of Vienna] mentioned, in the company of some friends [one of whom presumably was Daim], a certain Lanz von Liebenfels, who in his opinion had given Hitler some decisive ideas. He [Knoll] mentioned the *Ostara*, a journal which Lanz [Daim's preferred name for Liebenfels] had founded in 1905; adding that the ideas propagated in this organ were completely mad.[3]

Professor Knoll possessed six copies of *Ostara* from the years before the First World War, and he had concluded that there was a significant influence (of Lanz von Liebenfels on Hitler) from the ideological congruence between the theories contained in *Ostara* and those of Hitler.

So obvious was the 'identity [i.e., identicalness] of the theories of the *Ostara* journals with those of National Socialism', that Knoll was able to conclude 'that Lanz was Hitler's ideological father'. 'But what interested us above everything was whether Lanz had known Hitler personally,' said Daim.[4]

On being informed by Daim that Liebenfels was still alive, Knoll expressed the opinion that

> one ought to get to know Lanz because he had made world history, and in his effect he was distantly comparable with that of Karl Marx. He [Knoll] said that he had, in his lectures [at the university] between 1934 and 1938 often surprised

the students [the largest number of whom were Nazis] by referring to the *Ostara* as the source of Hitler; for the primitiveness and the madness of these ideas was pretty obvious.

Knoll then asked Daim 'immediately to organize a meeting with Lanz von Liebenfels'. The result was that 'on a rainy morning on May 11, 1951', Daim, Knoll and Watersrat 'looked up Lanz von Liebenfels in his Vienna flat at 32 Grinzingerstrasse'. So who was Lanz von Liebenfels?

* * *

Josef Adolf Lanz (1874–1954) was born in Vienna to a middle-class family; his father being a teacher. In July 1893, when he was aged nineteen, he entered the Cistercian Chapter of the Holy Cross (*Heiligenkreuz* – situated in the Vienna Woods) as Brother George. However, on 27 April 1900, six years after he had been ordained into the priesthood, he left the Order; the Abbey's register recording that this was because of his 'surrender to the lies of the world and to carnal love'.[5]

In 1902, Lanz, in order to disguise the fact that his mother, Katharina, née Hoffenreich, was of Jewish descent, assumed a new identity. He claimed, falsely, that his father was Baron Johannes Lanz de Liebenfels and that he himself had been born in Messina, Sicily in 1872. He also awarded himself a fake doctorate in philosophy and changed his name to the far more impressive Dr Adolf Jörg Lanz von Liebenfels.

In 1905, Liebenfels, as he will now be known, became editor, publisher and contributor to the anti-Semitic monthly journal, *Ostara* (named after the ancient Germanic goddess of Spring), whose logo was the swastika.[6] His writings are appropriately described as 'a potpourri of contemporary theories, most importantly of [Guido von] List's race theories'.[7]

Ostara was dedicated to the 'practical application of anthropological research for the purpose of preserving the European master race from destruction by the maintenance of racial purity'. It was lavishly illustrated with erotic pictures of blonde beauties being seduced by undesirable creatures, referred to by Liebenfels as 'beast-men' or 'ape-people'.

On 25 December 1907, Liebenfels, inspired by the deeds of the Templar Knights (a Christian Order of Chivalry that was in existence at the time of the Crusades), founded his Order of the New Templars (*Ordo Novi Templi*). This was a secret society devoted to his teachings, by which means he hoped that the Aryan 'race' could be salvaged. For its headquarters, Liebenfels chose the ruined castle of Burg Werfenstein, situated on the Danube river between Linz and Vienna. Membership was, of course, restricted to Aryans, one of whom Liebenfels (Lanz) could now pretend to be, having expunged the details of his own Jewish ancestry from the record books!

Titelblatt von „Ostara"-Heft 3, 1906

Ostara 1: Revolution or Evolution? A free conservative Easter sermon for the mastership of the European Race, by J. Lanz Liebenfels. (*Ostara, 1906*)

He was now able to point to the Jews as a dreadful example of what could go wrong in the event of the interbreeding of races. Not only that, but he also blamed the Jews for the death of Christ.

> The Jews – as hybrid beasts of historical and prehistorical races, and from the dross of all fallen cultures – are the living witnesses and testimony of Frauja's (the Lord Jesus Christ's) suffering, the death (Christ's crucifixion) caused by blending of the ancient heroic peoples of venerable manhood.[8]

* * *

Liebenfels, who was undoubtedly influenced by the works of Guido von List, who was twenty-six years his senior, belonged to the Guido von List Society, not merely as an honorary member but also as an actual member. List, for his part, was a member of Liebenfels' Order of the New Templars.[9]

* * *

With reference to his meeting with Liebenfels in May 1951, Daim declared,

> I have to say that the old man, who was at that time not quite 77, made a very sympathetic impression. You could speak quite pleasantly with him; he was kind and conciliatory, even if as Professor Knoll thought he noticed, he was a little nervous, because he was very conscious of his significance with regard to Hitler's ideology.

Liebenfels then proceeded to tell Daim about an encounter that he had previously had with Hitler. Daim recounted how,

> One day in 1909, Hitler visited Lanz [Liebenfels] in his office. Hitler said that he lived in the Felberstrasse (in Vienna) and had regularly bought copies of the *Ostara* in a tobacco/newsagent's kiosk [*Tabac-Trafik*] there. (*Ostara* being the organ of Lanz). He bought it almost [fairly] regularly.[10]
>
> But now he [Hitler] said that a few numbers [copies] were missing and that he wanted to get them all and he asked Lanz for these numbers. Lanz noticed that Hitler seemed to be particularly poverty stricken, and therefore let him have the required copies without charge and, apart from that, gave him a couple of Crowns so that he could travel back home. Hitler was very grateful for this.
>
> In 1908, Hitler abruptly broke off his friendship with Kubizek [August Kubizek, son of a Linz upholsterer and a student of music]. Round about that time, however, he got to know [engineer Josef] Greiner; in fact, if we can believe him, Greiner already knew Hitler at a time when he was still friendly with Kubizek.[11]

Kubizek and Greiner had different attitudes towards Hitler. Whereas Kubizek understands [i.e., believes in] loyalty to one's friend ... even if he [the friend, in this case Kubizek] had an awful lot on his conscience, Greiner is more concerned with showing that he didn't identify himself with all of the ghastly side of Hitler; so that his temporary participation in the National Socialist trend shouldn't be taken the wrong way.[12]

'With Kubizek,' said Liebenfels, 'we can find no reference to *Ostara* or to Lanz.'[13] The most likely explanation for this is that Hitler's interest in them may only have begun after he and Kubizek went their separate ways in 1908. In the light of what Liebenfels had told him, Daim 'sought contact with diploma engineer Greiner ...', and at the ensuing meeting of the two, Daim asked Greiner about *Ostara* and Lanz von Liebenfels.

Greiner immediately knew what I was talking about, and ... told me several things that he had not, because of the editor's wish, put in his book entitled *Das Ende des Hitler-Mythos*. [*The End of the Hitler Myth*, published 1947.] The memories came to him [Greiner] so spontaneously, and the details were so vivid to him, that I have no doubt about the genuineness, at least of the first reminiscences.

He [Greiner] said that in the *Mannerheim* [men's hostel] in the Meldemannstrasse in the north-east district of Vienna, there was, besides Hitler, a certain person called Grill who lived there. His [Grill's] real name was, for Austrian tongues, difficult to pronounce. This Grill was a fallen Roman Catholic priest who was concerned with founding a religion of pure love for one's neighbour without any church apparatus. He was, as he told Greiner in confidence, but not Hitler, the son of a Polish-Russian rabbi who had been brought up in a Catholic monastery.

This Grill talked about several theories, three of which Greiner had written about. Grill, above all, was Hitler's main partner in discussion. From him [Grill] we have many of Hitler's anti-Catholic, in particular anti-Christian, arguments.

In other words, it was Greiner's view that Hitler's opinions on these matters were derived from Grill. Greiner also told Daim that

Hitler possessed a great number of magazines, above all *Ostara* numbers. Greiner thought that there was a pile of them about 25 or 30 centimetres thick. He [Hitler] was very interested in the content and also took the side of Lanz von Liebenfels very enthusiastically in discussions, above all with Grill.

With Grill he unambiguously agreed in the rejection of Christianity, but he did not subscribe to Grill's thesis, [which was] the necessity of a general, 'love one's neighbour'. Instead, Hitler wanted to exclude the Jews, whereas Grill naturally, did not wish to permit that.

Titelblatt von „Ostara"-Heft 10 und 13, 1906

Ostara 2: Anthropology: Primitive man and race in the old literature – selected stories on race, by J. Lanz Liebenfels. (*Ostara, 1906*)

Hitler represented, intensively, the racial standpoint of Lanz. Grill, on the other hand, thought that there were rabbits with blue and red eyes, but they were all rabbits without any particular distinction. Hitler, very emphatically, disagreed with this; he wanted to divide them into better and worse.[14]

Greiner remembered Numbers 2,3 and 4 [of *Ostara*] which portrayed, on its cover, an ascending [astronomical] comet. [The comet was in fact depicted on the front cover of *Ostara*, Issue Number 3, dated 1906.] He remembered exactly that he had seen at least one of these with [in the possession of] Hitler. Also, he well remembered the cover of another copy. Of all the *Ostara* numbers, these had a particularly striking cover [said Greiner] 'so that you do not forget them easily'.[15]

As for the name *Ostara*, Lanz adopted it from the English writer, Beda Venerabilis, or the Venerable Bede (circa AD 673–735), who stated that the ancient English tribes named the month of Easter after the goddess *Eostra*, signifying 'a new beginning'.[16]

*   *   *

These statements indicate that Hitler not only possessed numbers of Liebenfels' *Ostara* journals, but also that he was anxious to obtain more of them. (Amongst the surviving remnants of Hitler's personal library is to be found Liebenfels' *Das Buch der Psalmen Teutsch*, – The Prayer Book of The New Templars – published in 1926.)[17]

However, in order to determine what influence, if any, *Ostara* had on Hitler, it is necessary to compare its sentiments with those expressed by him.

Notes

1. Hitler, op. cit., p. 41.
2. Daim, op. cit., p. 18.
3. Ibid.
4. Ibid, p. 20.
5. Ibid, p. 252.
6. *The Swastika and the Nazis: 14. The Ostara Connection*; www.intelinet.org/swastika14.htm.
7. Hamann, op. cit., p. 217.
8. *Die Priesterschaft St Bernhards von Clairvaux*, II. Teil. Szt Balazs 1930, in Daim, op. cit., p. 196.
9. Daim, op. cit., p. 96.
10. Ibid, p. 25.
11. Reinhold Hanisch, an acquaintance of Hitler, confirms that Greiner was present in a men's hostel in Vienna at the time in question. See Hanisch, Reinhold, *I was Hitler's Buddy*, 5 April 1939, pp. 239–42 (I); 12 April pp. 270–2 (II); 19 April 1939, pp. 297–300 (III).
12. Daim, op. cit., p. 33.
13. Ibid, p. 34.
14. Ibid, p. 37.
15. Ibid, p. 38.
16. Ibid, p. 116.
17. Goodrick–Clarke, op. cit., p. 199, ref 13.

Chapter 11

Ostara

Between 1905 and 1931 a total of 137 *Ostara* pamphlets were published (Series I, II and III – of which 54 were re-issued in the III Series). Of these, all but a handful were composed by Liebenfels himself.

Viennese historian and magazine editor, Friedrich Heer, describes how

> The *Ostara* publications were widely distributed throughout Germany to persons liable to lend a sympathetic ear to its writings. Lanz (i.e., Liebenfels) himself referred to a total circulation of around 500,000 copies. These found their way through to the fanatical agitators in the German theo-political underground ...[1]

Daim states that *Ostara* was distributed free of charge. 'It became more of a secret publication,' no copies of it being kept in the Austrian National Library.[2]

In the beginning, Liebenfels in his publication appeared reasonably well disposed towards the Jews. For example, when a subscriber to a first copy of *Ostara* wrote an anonymous letter complaining to him that 'only a Jew could write your book,' Liebenfels declared, 'I couldn't explain to him that I was not a Jew, though it would not worry me if I were.'[3] In fact, for one particular Jew, Austrian writer, editor, and satirist Karl Krause, Liebenfels was full of admiration, describing him as 'a genius, a genuine genius, for his work is that of a pioneer and creator'. However, as time went by, 'Lanz became progressively more aggressive [to the Jews], the more he published'.[4]

This hardening of attitude by Liebenfels towards Jews was probably the result of a positive decision by him to jump, as it were, onto the bandwagon of increasing Nazi anti-Semitism. This is reflected in the pictures on the jacket covers of the *Ostara* journals. For example, Issue No.1 of Series II, dated 1922, depicts a knight in armour, and in the lower right hand corner, a Jewish face in caricature with the caption 'Who shall lead, who shall be Duke? An Enlightenment through "*Ostara*".' The implication is clear: it is the knightly duke who will lead, not the Jew.[5]

In succeeding editions of *Ostara*, Liebenfels gave his opinion on virtually every aspect of life.

Rückseite des „Ostara"-Heftes 1, Magdeburg 1922

Ostara 3: German: More should lead; more should be dukes. (*Ostara, 1922*)

1. Cultivation of the Land

An early issue of *Ostara* was entitled *The Austro-German Regions of the Alps as Meat and Milk Producers: a Study of the Local Economy*.[6] And according to *Ostara* Series I, Nos. 22–23, 'Only a person who is intimately involved with the soil – the country farmer – is a human being in the real sense. Therefore, the Aryan race prospers only in the cultivation of the land.'[7]

How does this compare with Hitler's ideas? This can be established from his known utterances, for example,

> **Hitler***: No concept, no political theory is sound which is not based on the principle that the existence of the people depends upon its soil and territory. A people which does not find its support in its soil and does not establish an affinity with its soil will perish miserably and wretchedly ...*[8]

2. The Corruption of the Aryan Race

Liebenfels based much of his life's work on the notion that in ancient times, human beings had performed sodomy – copulated with animals – and produced what he described as 'ape-people' or 'Sodom-apelings'. In this way, the pure Aryan race had been corrupted. (This, of course, was in total opposition to English naturalist Charles Darwin's *Theory of Evolution and Natural Selection*.) He elaborated on his views on the first page of the first edition of *Ostara*, published in 1905.

> *Ostara* is the first and only illustrated Aryo-aristocratic collection of publications, which, in both words and pictures, depicts the heroic blond peoples, the beautiful, moral, noble, idealistic, gifted and religious people; the creator and keeper of all knowledge, art and culture; and the main-bearer of divinity. All iniquity and ugliness originates from the cross-breeding of races, in respect of which, for physiological reasons, the woman has always been and remains more submissive than the man. Thus, the arrival of *Ostara* comes at a time when women and the inferior races are taking it upon themselves to procreate and thereby ruthlessly to eradicate the heroic blond race of men, who epitomize all outstanding beauty, truth, ambition and seekers of God.[9]

> **Hitler:** *If nature does not wish that weaker individuals should mate with the stronger, she wishes even less that a superior race should intermingle with an inferior one; because in such a case all her efforts, throughout hundreds of thousands of years, to establish an evolutionary higher stage of being, may thus be rendered futile.*

> *Whenever Aryans have mingled their blood with that of an inferior race the result has been the downfall of the people who were the standard-bearers of a higher culture.*[10]

Nr. 1

Die Oſtara und das Reich der Blonden

Von J. Lanz-Liebenfels

Als Handſchrift gedruckt in 2. Auflage, Wien 1930
Copyright by J. Lanz v. Liebenfels, Wien 1922

Titelblatt des „Ostara"-Heftes 1, 1922, 2. Aufl. 1930

Ostara 4: Ostara and the Empire of the Blondes, by J. Lanz Liebenfels. (*Ostara, 1922*)

3. Eugenics (improving the race by judicious mating)

This philosophy lies at the heart of Liebenfels' teachings, and more articles appear in *Ostara* on this than on any other subject. 'All calamities in the history of the world … have been caused by the liberated woman.'[11] Racial mixing [i.e., miscegenation] is the crime of all crimes, that is the mortal sin.'[12]

Ostara I/47 entitled *The Art of Good Living and in Being Happily Married: a Racial Purity Breviary [instruction manual], for People in Love* discusses a method of preventing conception during intercourse, 'by the use of chemical or mechanical means … for the purpose of breeding a pure race'.[13] 'The perfect man [i.e., the 'Aryan'] has, in accordance with the policy of pure breeding of all Aryan people, the right to put himself forward to several women [i.e., to impregnate them] in order to go on creating numerous people: he is permitted to have more children than those of an inferior race.'[14]

Ostara I/21 introduces the idea of the 'marriage helper', whose 'role is to create sperm for the wife in the place of a person [husband] who is impotent, but Lykurg [Lycurgus – law giver of Sparta, ninth century BC] emphasizes that these marriage helpers must specifically be young, strong and efficient'.[15] 'We must now set up reservations [i.e., breeding colonies] for the blond heroic races in remote, secret places.[16] The breeding mothers are required to live in strict isolation, so there is no temptation for adultery.'[17] In such, 'ecclesia – or communities of the elite for the chosen people, the improvement of mankind will take place. For the time being [however] it is sufficient if we succeed in founding even a small but closed community of highly-bred heroic people, who also can dispose of sufficient wealth, and a milieu [environment] which is appropriate to them'.[18]

Liebenfels even produced a *Rassenwertigkeitsindex* (racial composition index) to enable an individual to assess his degree of Aryanness, awarding twelve points for blue or blue-grey eyes, and minus twelve points for black (dark) eyes. Similar points were awarded or deducted for hair and skin colour, facial features and so forth.[19] In respect of the shape of the skull for example, Liebenfels declared, in *Ostara*, 'The percentage of mad Jews is quite enormous.'[20]

(What Liebenfels, in his ignorance, did not appreciate was that his notion of creating a genetically 'pure' race [if that were ever possible,] precluded the possibility for genetic diversity, on which the evolution of humankind depends.)

Hitler: *What makes a people, or to be more correct a race, is not language but blood.*[21] *A person of mixed blood is not only relatively inferior to a person of pure blood, but is almost doomed to become extinct more rapidly. In innumerable cases wherein the pure race holds its ground, the mongrel breaks down [presumably disintegrates].*[22]

Vienna was described by Hitler as '*the incarnation of mongrel depravity*'.[23] The purpose of the State, he said, was *to preserve and promote a community of human beings who are physically as well as spiritually kindred.*[24] *A folk state* [from the German, *volk*, meaning people] *should in the first place raise matrimony from the level of being a constant scandal for the race. The state should consecrate it as an institution which is called upon to produce creatures made in the likeness of the Lord, and not create monsters that are a mixture of man and ape.*[25] *This triumph* [i.e., of the idea of a People's State] *can be assured only through a militant movement ...*[26]

This pestilential adulteration of the blood, of which hundreds of thousands of our people take no account, is being systematically practised by the Jew today. Systematically, these negroid parasites in our national body corrupt our innocent fair-haired girls and thus destroy something which can no longer be replaced in this world.[27]

4. Euthanasia (putting painlessly to death)
Said Liebenfels in *Ostara*,

what I prophesied thirty years ago, has become true. The hoards of untouchables have eaten up and destroyed all our economic reserves. The insoluble economic chaos is here: the chaos from which civilized and Aryan Christian humanity can save itself only by means of a bloodless and painless destruction and damming up of the dark, untouchable elements.[28]

The first source of sick bodies of inferior races and people incapable of proper work must be destroyed straight away. The modern economy cannot put up any more with these sinister hoards [sic] of people, millions of whom are incapable of work and are simply unsocial, racial curs.[29]

Hitler's similar attitude to such people would shortly be revealed, in all its horror. In fact, the Führer would have his own cousin Aloisia Veit murdered in accordance with this philosophy, as will be seen.

5. Genocide (deliberate extermination of a race)

Ostara: The struggle for nationality made the German-Austrians and other Austrian peoples [both] conscious of their nationality and [also] anti-Semitic.[30] We must therefore, throw away people of inferior race – the monkey people and the primeval people. We must throw away and get rid of it in us, around us and after us.[31] Everywhere, the earth will steam from the blood of the people of mixed race.[32] The basis of all wars is race war.[33] We must join up with [rifle] shooting clubs and armed corps.[34] We will not be able to shoot millions of inferior races with our rapid fire cannons, but a much better means would be to strangle them with rubber.[35]

In *Ostara* III/2, Liebenfels expresses the opinion that

[Lord] Kitchener [British soldier and statesman, 1850–1916], in the time before the [First World] war, was busy with eugenics. He constructed a racially more pure group. By the time he had enough people as reserves capable of fighting, he sent the coloured ones, without any consideration at all, to face the fire of the enemy. If only the Germans had spared their blond racial reserves in this way, and sent the dark, unruly urban mob of untouchables into the Front Line as cannon fodder! If only the Germans had done that![36]

Hitler: *For the good of the German people, we must wish for a war every fifteen or twenty years.*[37] *The new German Empire should have set out on its march along the same road as was formerly trodden by the Teutonic Knights, this time to acquire soil for the German plough by means of the German sword, and thus provide the nation with its daily bread.*[38]

6. Religion
It was Liebenfels' belief that both the Old and New Testaments of the Bible were in favour of racial 'Hygiene' and 'Renewal', viz, *Ostara* journals entitled *Leviticus or Moses as a Racial Hygienist*; *Numeri* (the Book of Numbers) *or Moses as a Renewer of the Race*; and *Racial Mystique: An Introduction to the Aryo-Christian Esoteric Doctrine.*[39] Furthermore, *Ostara* Journal I/59 describes 'Aryan Christendom as a Racial Cult Religion of The Blonds'. Said Liebenfels,

racial purity (care of the race) cannot exist without a religion of the cult of the races, and vice versa – no religion can preserve its purity without the nurturing of the races.[40] Racial breeding and purity of race will be and must be the only religion and church of the future.[41] Therefore our religion must become an ariosophic religion of the cult of races.[42] [Ariosophy meaning 'the combination of German *volkisch* (from the German word *volk*, or in English 'folk', or people) nationalism and racism with occult notions borrowed from the philosophy of Helena Petrovna Blavatsky, and *volkisch* implying something which is anti-democratic, anti-liberal, anti-bourgeois, anti-capitalistic, and promotes a national community of the racially pure.] It must change from a religion which has become distorted by our being gagged. It has been distorted into an altruism, and it must become once more a religion of the superior people, an ariosophic cult religion of racism, which it was right from the beginning. Purity of the race, breeding of the race, cannot be carried out by the state, or by officials, or in a ministerial way, but only through religion and as a sacred idea.[43]

The higher races stem from God: the lower races from Lucifer, a fallen God. The evil must always be under the control of the good, as must the lesser always be under the control of the higher.[44] Through the crushing and destruction of the primitive and inferior human beings, the superior heroic place will rise up out of the grave of racial mix and racial degeneration and will rise up to immortality and divinity and become divine men, both in the seed and the race.[45]

In this holy name and sign we will conquer like our ancestors or, if it has to be, die in the attempt.[46]

These final four words were perhaps the most prophetic to be found in the whole of *Ostara*, in view of what would one day befall the Third Reich.

Hitler [Referring to Jesus Christ and his life]: *Today, 2,000 years later, I recognize with deep emotion Christ's tremendous fight for this world against the Jewish poison. I recognize it most profoundly by the fact that He had to shed His blood on the cross for this fight. As a Christian it is not my duty to permit myself to be cheated, but it is my duty to be a champion of truth and of right.*[47]

7. The 'Aristocratic Principle' (of Governance)
Ostara I/9 is entitled *The People's Thoughts: The Aristocratic Principle of Our Time.*[48] This principle was enunciated by Benedict de Spinoza (1632–77), a Jew of Portuguese origin who was born in Amsterdam. In his book *A Preface To Morals,*[49] Spinoza wrote,

there is an aristocratic principle in all the religions which has attained wide acceptance. It is significant that Jesus was content to leave the governance of the mass of men to Caesar, and that he created no organization during his lifetime beyond the appointment of the Apostles. It is significant because it shows how much more he was concerned with the few who could be saved than with arranging the affairs of the mass of mankind.

Spinoza also believed that the love of God 'involves the love of our fellow creatures'; that 'the State exists to give liberty, not hold in slavery'; and that 'the sovereign in his own interest must rule with justice and wisdom, nor must the State interfere with the freedom of thought'.[50]

Hitler: *The Jewish doctrine of Marxism repudiates the aristocratic principle of Nature and substitutes for it the eternal privilege of force and energy, numerical mass and its dead weight.*[51]

8. Prostitution and Venereal Disease
Ostara I/58[52] is concerned with *The Immoral and Criminal Woman's Lifestyle of Our Times*, and *Ostara* I/76[53] with *Prostitution in Women and Men's Rights: A Judgement.*

Hitler: *The population of our great towns and cities is tending more and more to avail of prostitution in the exercise of its amorous instincts, and is thus becoming more and more contaminated by the scourge of venereal disease.*[54]

The primary cause of syphilis, said Hitler was

to be found in the manner in which love was being prostituted.[55] *To wage war against syphilis means fighting against prostitution ...*[56] *The first remedy [for prostitution] must always be to establish such conditions as will make early marriages possible, especially for young men – for women are, after all, only passive subjects in this matter.*[57]

9. Charity

In *Ostara* I/18, entitled *Race and Welfare Work: A Call for a Boycott of Indiscriminate Charity*, Liebenfels embraces the philosophy 'Everything for the pearls and nothing for the rotten fish. At least one third of diseases are the result of one's own fault or one's own race'. In particular,

> people with mixed parentage have a great tendency towards it (i.e., disease), and often sexual excesses are the underlying reason. All those disgusting skin diseases originate in the East and are really diseases of filth and race. Even those of a higher race will be infected, as modern life (which no longer knows any boundaries between races) forces them to associate with members of lower races.

He now offers the solution.

> If the federal government pursued a racial economy and gently annihilated those families with hereditary impairments, it would be possible to save a considerable part of the nine million Kronen per annum!

'How could it be,' he asks, 'that there were "charitable institutions" for hospitals, foundling [deserted infants of no known parents] hospitals, illegitimate children and fallen girls' when there were 'no such institutions for the preservation of pure and noble blood and for legitimate children?' And yet he believed that 'the old, and those of good Germanic descent, and ... those of true Israeli descent ... should be supported'. The inclusion of the word 'Israeli' would certainly not have pleased Hitler![58] Therefore, the only people worthy of receiving charitable donations, states *Ostara* I/18,[59] were those with

> gold-blond hair, blue (or blue-grey) eyes, a rosy complexion, elongated skulls and elongated faces, high and small straight noses, well-proportioned mouths, healthy white teeth, round chins, a balanced, tall physique, narrow hands and narrow feet.[60]

> **Hitler**: *During my struggle for existence in Vienna I perceived very clearly that the aim of all social activity must never be merely charitable relief, which is ridiculous and useless ...*[61]

What Hitler failed to acknowledge was that his own personal appearance scarcely merited the description of Aryan.

10. Other threats to the Aryan

Ostara I/72, entitled *Race and External Politics*,[62] is concerned with the

> attrition [wearing down] of the heroic Aryans here in Europe, by numerous successive challenges to the Aryan people, through intellectualism, the Press, financial markets, industrialization, overpopulation, through feminism and exploitation, through major capitalism.

11. World Revolution

In *Ostara*, Liebenfels declares 'Greater than the howl of triumph of the untouchables is the terror when [they are] faced with the ario-heroic world revolution'.[63]

12. Culture

Ostara titles include *The Blonds as Creators of Language: A Summary of the Creation of Ancient Languages*[64]; *The Blonds as Creators of Music*.[65] *Race and Poetry*[66]; *Race and Philosophy*[67]; *Race and Painting*[68] and *Race and Architecture in the New Age*[69] also extol the pre-eminent virtues of the 'Blonds'.

> **Hitler**: *Every manifestation of human culture, every product of art, science, and technical skill which we see before our eyes today, is almost exclusively the product of the Aryan creative power. This very fact fully justifies the conclusion that it was the Aryan alone who founded the superior type of humanity …*[70]

> *On this planet of ours, human culture and civilization are indissolubly bound up with the presence of the Aryan. If he should be exterminated or subjugated, then the dark shroud of a new barbarian era would enfold the earth.*[71]

13. Freedom of the Press

> **Ostara**: 'The monkey press has got to be stifled.'[72]

> **Hitler**: *With ruthless determination the state must keep control of this instrument of popular education [the Press] and place it at the service of the state and nation.*[73]

14. Animals

> **Ostara**: 'The superior man is one who is fond of animals.'[74]

Hitler came to possess three German shepherd dogs which he was not slow to chastise if the need arose. However, in one film clip, he is to be seen bending down to embrace one of his dogs, which he kisses. At the same time, his face breaks into a rare smile.[75]

15. The Law and Legal Rights

Ostara asserts that

> the origin of all questions of law has to do with race, and moreover superior races. For those who are plaintiffs, or witnesses, or defendants, the question of their race has to be considered. With a legal right based on race, all other questions are solved by themselves.[76]

> We will famously castrate habitual criminals, and sterilise habitual female criminals.[77]

Hitler would certainly have agreed that the rights of the 'superior' races are paramount.

16. Forced Labour

> *Ostara*: By means of ariosophic running of the economy, the whole problem of unemployment will be solved. All unemployed people who haven't accepted any work by a certain date will have to be organized to become miners.[78]

> It will be assumed that we view work in mines as the sort of work which is unworthy of the heroic type of person. This work should be done only by untouchables, or rather criminals.[79]

One ought to introduce again slavery and castration.[80]
> A culture without slaves is not possible. Therefore, the enslavement of the inferior race is a real and economic demand.[81]

17. Deportation

> *Ostara*: If the untouchables don't want this (to accept working in mines) then away with the stones, and then throw them out into the deserts with the jackals and into the forest of the monkeys, where they will greet gorillas and baboons as comrades and people of a similar race. There, they can put into reality their socialist, Bolshevik, democratic, proletarian state utopia, where everybody has an equal right to vote in secret.[82]

*   *   *

The opinions expressed in the above excerpts quoted from *Ostara* are largely in accordance with those of Hitler, and the way he put them into practice will shortly be seen. However, in other respects, he was not entirely in tune with Liebenfels' teachings. For example, Hitler would have disagreed with Liebenfels' statement that 'Whoever leads Austria will also be the spiritual leader of the world',[83] in that he saw himself primarily as a future leader of Germany. Neither would Hitler have identified with such Ostarian concepts as are embodied in the title of one of its pamphlets, *World Peace as an Achievement and Victory for the Blonds.*[84]

* * *

Is it really possible that Hitler, who was only in his late teens when he first began to read *Ostara*, was actually capable of giving credence to the spiteful, bigoted, and inhuman delusions of Liebenfels, as contained therein? (Delusions being defined as 'erroneous beliefs that usually involve a misrepresentation of perceptions or experiences'.[85]) The answer, unfortunately is yes, for Hitler was just as deluded as his mentor. However, Hitler, unlike Liebenfels, would soon have the opportunity to act on the basis of these delusions.

Modern-day psychiatrists recognize various types of delusional disorder, according to their 'predominant delusional theme'. Of these, the following two appear to correlate most closely with the delusions experienced by Hitler:

Grandiose Type

> Here, 'the central theme of the delusion is the conviction of [the subject] having some great (but unrecognized) talent or insight.'

Persecutory Type

> Here, 'the central theme of the delusion involves the person's belief that he or she is being conspired against, cheated, spied on, followed, poisoned or drugged, maliciously maligned, harassed, or obstructed in the pursuit of long-term goals. Small slights may be exaggerated and become the focus of a delusional system. Individuals with persecutory delusions are often resentful or angry and may resort to violence against those they believe are hurting them.'[86]

For the future leader of Germany, how apt these latter words would one day prove to be.

Notes

 1. Heer, *Der Glaube des Adolf Hitler,* p. 710.
 2. Daim, op. cit., p. 169.
 3. Ibid, p. 12.
 4. Ibid, p. 169.
 5. Ibid., p. 168.
 6. Heer, op.cit., p. 710.
 7. *Ostara*, I/8.
 8. Ibid, I/22–3.
 9. Prange, op. cit., p. 24.
10. Hitler, op. cit., p. 259 (2009 Jaico edition).

11. *Ostara*, I/33.
12. Ibid, I/38.
13. Ibid, I/47.
14. Ibid, I/21.
15. Ibid.
16. Ibid, III/4.
17. Ibid, I/21.
18. Ibid, I/47.
19. Ibid, I/31.
20. Ibid, I/18.
21. Hitler, op. cit., p. 219.
22. Ibid, p. 225.
23. Ibid, p. 79.
24. Ibid, p. 221.
25. Ibid, p. 226.
26. Ibid, p. 257.
27. Ibid, p. 310.
28. *Ostara*, III/4.
29. Ibid, III/4.
30. Ibid, I/72.
31. Ibid, III/4.
32. Ibid, I/70.
33. Ibid, I/10 and I/13.
34. Ibid, I/3.
35. Ibid, I/34.
36. Ibid, III/2.
37. Trevor-Roper, op. cit., p. 55.
38. Hitler, op. cit., p. 87.
39. *Ostara*, I/95, 97, 78.
40. Ibid, III/13.
41. Ibid, III/19.
42. Goodrick-Clarke, op. cit., p. 2.
43. *Ostara*, III/4.
44. Ibid, I/74.
45. Ibid, III/18.
46. Ibid, I/1.
47. Prange, op. cit., p. 71.
48. *Ostara*, I/9.
49. Spinoza, *A Preface to Morals*. Chapter 10, part 2.
50. *Oxford Companion to Literature*
51. Hitler, op. cit., p. 46.
52. *Ostara*, I/58.
53. Ibid, I/76.
54. Hitler, op. cit., p. 142.
55. Ibid, p. 141.
56. Ibid, p. 143.
57. Ibid, p. 144.
58. Liebenfels, *Theozoology*, p. 65.
59. *Ostara*, I/18.
60. Ibid, I/18 (in Hamann, pp. 151–152).
61. Hitler, op. cit., p. 27.
62. *Ostara*, I/72.

63. Ibid, III/13–14.
64. Ibid, I/52.
65. Ibid, I/73.
66. Ibid, I/83.
67. Ibid, I/84.
68. Ibid, I/86.
69. Ibid, I/85.
70. Hitler, op. cit., p. 164.
71. Ibid, p. 216.
72. *Ostara*, I/3.
73. Hitler, op. cit., p. 139.
74. *Ostara*, I/22–23.
75. **Hitler's Mistress Eva Braun*. C 1991. Castle Communications plc.
76. *Ostara*, I/58.
77. Ibid, III/4.
78. Ibid, III/13–14.
79. *Ostara*, III/13–14.
80. Ibid, III/15.
81. Ibid, III/19, in Daim, op. cit., p. 272.
82. Ibid, I/13–14.
83. Ibid, I/83.
84. Ibid, III/4.
85. American Psychiatric Association, *Diagnostic and Statistical Manual of Mental Disorders*, p. 299.
86. Ibid, p.324.

N.B. *Ostara* references (Series I, Nos 1–100); Series II, No.1; Series III, Nos 1–101) are from text in Daim (principally pp.195–207, translated by Martin Clay and Nicholas Dragffy); and from 'Grey Lodge Occult Review' by Manfred Nagl in www.antiqillum.com/glor/glor_005/ nazimyth.htm translated by Sabine Kurth.

Chapter 12

Lienbenfels' Wilder Notions

Other works by Liebenfels, including *Theozoology: or the Tale of the Apelings of Sodom and the Gods Electron*, published in Vienna in 1905, – with which Hitler was no doubt familiar – ascended to even greater heights of phantasmagoric dizziness.

The Gods
According to Liebenfels, the Bible and other ancient religious texts were written in a code which only he could understand.

> Every enquiry concerning the gods explores the old notions and fables, while the ancients concealed their natural ideas, which they preserved ... in parables, and always mixed their enquiries with the fables.[1] The original oriental text and various ancient translations and commentaries of the more ancient Fathers give us the key to this secret language, and from this we may receive the unfathomable wisdom of the ancients.[2] In our search for god, we neophytes (novices) have lost our way because we have forgotten the basic principle of all wisdom of the ancients ..., and because we have forgotten the goal and the beginning of all investigation: the human body.[3]

Liebenfels, therefore, drawing on his knowledge of the Bible, anthropology and ancient Greek and Hebrew texts, together with ancient bas-reliefs and sculptures which he had encountered on his travels, would now make it his business to unlock this 'unfathomable wisdom'. In doing so, he often interpreted the apocryphal stories contained therein literally, and it is therefore not surprising that, in so doing he arrived at the most bizarre conclusions.

Racial Development
His work *'Practical, Racial Metaphysics'*,[4] said Liebenfels was

> concerned with research into the history of the races before their earthly development cycle (pre-terrestrial) ... into the future of the races following their earthly period (post-terrestrial), and finally with research into the extrasensory, extra-terrestrial, cosmic forces that influence racial development in the present.

The race of full-blooded and whole Aryan Man was not the result of natural selection alone. Instead, as the esoteric writings indicate, he was the result of a careful and conscious breeding process by higher and different kinds of being, such as the Theozoa, Elektrozoa, Angels, et sim., which once lived on this Earth.[5]

The *Theozoa, Elektrozoa* etc, from whom Aryan Man developed were

perfect electro-biotic machines, characterized by their supernatural knowledge and power. Their knowledge encompassed everything to be found in the universe and beyond, in the metaphysical spaces of the fourth, fifth and ninth dimensions: they perceived such objects by way of their electro-magneto-radiophotic eye on their forehead, the rudiment of which is the human pineal gland. They had knowledge of all things, and could read past, present and future from the ether (upper air). This is why they performed the office of oracles until well into historical times and live on, even today, in mediums. They possessed supernatural, 'divine' powers, whose centre is located in the lumbar brain. Their bodies exude rays of fire and light, which … materialize on the one hand and dematerialize on the other, breaking down atoms and reconstructing them, cancelling out gravity.[6]

Sodomy (the copulation of mankind with animals)
Liebenfels' volume *Theozoology*, mentioned above and (in the title of less than ten *Ostara* journals) which appeared in the III Series of that publication, 1927–31, revolves entirely around the subject of sodomy, and is concerned with the alleged historical mating of human beings with animals, to produce so-called 'beast-men'.

The original sin of the blond, god-like 'homo sapiens or, more precisely, the homo arioheroicus' women,[7] was in copulating with 'the male anthropo-saurians' [with their 'penis bone'!] and with their descendants, 'the man-animal races,' to whom they were attracted on account of 'the magnitude of the member [i.e., penis]'.[8]

As 'evidence' for this, he used as an example, the so-called 'sea-men', as depicted on a relief 'found in Nimrud, in ancient Kalach' [in the north of present-day Iraq], who were described as 'two-legged beasts about 1.2 metres tall with scaly skin'.[9] He also quotes Roman historian Tacitus' description of

a sodomistic orgy in which 'sea-beasts' took part, such that the lascivious Roman noble women would flock around them [the beasts] in large numbers.

Almost the whole world has succumbed to ape-nature [the offspring of the union of man and beasts], right up to the Germanic countries which have not been fully spared either.[10] All of mankind, including [people in] the Germanic lands, is today dying the sodomistic death …[11]

'Bolshy-Jewish bloodhounds (especially) remind us even today of the horrible faces of antediluvian dragon-monsters' who are the direct 'descendants of … the two-legged dinosaur hominids'.

Rosa Luxemburg, the German Jewish, left-wing revolutionary, who was murdered by government troops in 1919, is described as a 'small, pure-breed Bezah-dwarf ... [Wadi Bezah in Egypt] just like those bred 2,000 years ago in the temple-zoos of Palestine'.[12]

'Our blood, our seed,' said Liebenfels, was 'something divine, the most precious heritage of our fathers.' Although

the blood of each and every one of us is more or less mixed with the water of Sodom ..., from this point forward a halt should be called to this mixing. It followed from many passages in the Bible, that the European white man (in short, the Germanic man) is the Son of Heaven. He is the White Stone, the White Rider who conquers the coloured people ...[13]

Adultery by wives and their quite strange preference for lusty, satyr-like so-called 'interesting men', must be obviated as much as possible ... A precipitin [precipitation] reaction will make it clear to each and every individual how closely or distantly his blood is related to the blood of apes ...[14]

Unilateral woman's rights would make the world into a big brothel in which everything revolves around penises and pussies in a silly and absurd satyrs' 'orgy', and the proper wife, the loyal mother of the house and the healthy, strong troop of children will be mercilessly driven out of the chaste and legitimate home. The adulterous and sensual woman belongs to the whore house, the honour of motherhood is withdrawn from her and her name is blotted out of the book of life. Likewise criminals, the mentally ill, or those with hereditary diseases, should be prevented from reproducing. If we only allow fit persons to reproduce, the hospitals, prisons and the giant criminal justice system will become superfluous.[15]

Dear ladies, tell me honestly, whose wives would you be today if noble men, if god-like Siegfrieds, had not torn you away from the sodomistic monsters, if they had not put you in a warm nest, if they had not defended you, sword in hand, throughout thousands of years, against Slavs, Mongols, Moors and Turks? Choose between us and those sons of Sodom ...[16]

Everybody must begin in himself therefore to carry out the struggle against the Sodom monkeys, and particularly [take care] with the choice of his wife. Only then can he defeat the Sodom ape around himself.[17]

'Woman, still today, loves pleasure–apes and makes the effort to bring humanity downward,' lamented Liebenfels.

Only when we become similar to the electrical god-men physically ... we will again become pure gods. We must take off the dark pelt of the ape and put on the shining breast-plate of the god-man. He who abides in love devoid of the ape-like nature, abides in God, and God in him.[18]

In *The Koran* [Muslim scriptures], said Liebenfels,

it is said that paradise is certain for the whites. The kingdom of heaven will be reached through intervention in the sexual life of man. Those of lesser value must be exterminated in a gentle way; by castration and sterilisation.[19]

For these elements [of the arioheroic people] who have no idea about [i.e., care little about the significance of] race, they deserve to perish, because they are also the enemies of our race. They commit the sin against the Holy Ghost, and this sin will never be forgiven.[20]

Atlantis

In *Theozoology*, Liebenfels asserts his belief in the concept of Atlantis and speaks of how Ludwig Wilser 'in his scientific articles' had 'convincingly proven that the tall, white man emerged from Europe [actually Atlantis]'.[21]

Sacrifice

Bring sacrifices to Fraja [Liebenfels' word for Jesus Christ], you sons of God. Up, up and bring to Him the children of the forest demons and sacrifice them to Jesus. We are not thinking of preaching pogroms because they will occur without any preaching.[22]

'Godman'

If we are striving to bring the angelic men to rulership, we should improve the human body through selective breeding ...[23] Our bodies are the temples of God, they are the members of the future superman which will be formed in us.

- - THEOZOOLOGIE ODER - -
DIE KUNDE VON DEN SODOMS - ÄFFLINGEN UND DEM GÖTTER-ELEKTRON, - - - **EINE**
EINFÜHRUNG IN DIE ÄLTESTE UND NEUESTE WELTANSCHAU-UNG UND EINE RECHTFERTI-GUNG DES FÜRSTENTUMS UND DES ADELS (MIT 45 BILDERN)
~ VON J. LANZ-LIEBENFELS ~
WIEN ~ LEIPZIG ~ BUDAPEST
- - MODERNER VERLAG. - -
PREIS M 2·50 == K 3·—

Theo 1: Theozoology, or the study of the little Aodom-monkeys and the gods electron, by J. Lanz Liebenfels.

Through conscious and goal-oriented influencing of the secreting glands, we shall be able in the coming two centuries to rebuild atoms and cells of all living beings and ... finally to create a new human race, which will develop out of the arioheroical one.[24]

Everywhere and always, we must protect the institution of marriage, for it is the secure refuge of the race, the warm nest of the young phoenix, and the future

God-Man ... Marital fidelity must be required of all women in all circumstances ... but marital fidelity on the husband's part is also necessary.[25]

The technology [of creating a new human race] ... [and] all higher scientific wisdom ... is to remain the secret knowledge of a numerically small, pure-bred, heroic-Aryan ruling elite.[26]

Robotic Machines

A newly bred slave being with crude nerves and strong hands whose mental potential has been carefully limited ... will perform for us all those jobs for which we have not invented machines ... The proletariat [those without capital, who were dependent on being hired as labourers] and the under-humanity cannot be improved or saved or made happy. They are the work of the Devil and must simply be, of course humanely and without pain, eliminated. In their place, we will have biological machines, whose advantage over mechanical machines will be that they repair and procreate themselves ... This 'robot' will be the key to the future since his existence will solve not only the technological but also the social and racio-economic problems – and thereby all political problems that beset us. Total equality is nonsense! The social question is a racial question and not an economic one ... Who can say where the equality of rights should stop? Why should it stop with the Australian Aborigine? Gorillas, chimpanzees and bats have exactly the same claim to socialist 'human rights'.[27]

Liebenfels' Concept of Divinity

'If I were asked what I understood divinity to be,' said Liebenfels, 'I would say: by that I understand the living beings of the ultra-violet and ultra-red forces and world. In former times they were embodied and moved about in complete purity. Today they live on in human beings. The gods slumber in bestialized human bodies, but the day is coming when they will rise up again. We were electric, we will be electric, to be electric and to be divine is the same thing!'[28]

* * *

In 1932, the publisher of a new work by Liebenfels entitled *The Book of Psalms in German: The Aryosophes, Racial Mystics, and Anti-Semites Prayer Book* sent a copy to Hitler, together with a dedication.[29]

In that year, on the occasion of his (alleged) sixtieth birthday, Liebenfels required that his guests toast him with the words 'The pioneer of National Socialism is the modest, simple monk, Jörg Lanz Liebenfels'.[30]

However, at his meeting with psychologist Wilfried Daim in 1951, Liebenfels described how, from the year 1938, Hitler had banned him from writing 'obviously to hide his sources from foreign countries – you know, other people'. More plausible reasons, however, were firstly that Hitler would have preferred that people did not discover that he himself had lifted, as it were, his ideas straight from the pages of Liebenfels' *Ostara*, instead of thinking them out for himself, and secondly he may have feared being held up to ridicule if it became known that he had associated with a man whose more extravagant ideas might be described in modern terms as a mixture of 'science fiction' and 'horror movie!'[31]

Liebenfels also confided to Daim 'that he had rejected National Socialism as it eventually developed'. Can this be true, bearing in mind the intensity and fervour of his *Ostara* and other works? No. The truth is more likely to lie in the fact that National Socialism, which had brought ruin on the German people, had been utterly defeated and, now, six years after the end of the war, Liebenfels felt it would be unfashionable to continue to support a lost cause.

* * *

Hitler therefore, cherry-picked those aspects of Liebenfels' philosophy which suited his purpose, while discarding or ignoring those which did not. In Daim's words 'Hitler tried to avoid some of the more comical and extreme of the Lanz (Liebenfels) writings.'[32]

Nonetheless, many of Liebenfels' more outlandish theories were to find strong resonances in the policies adopted by Hitler and his Nazi Party, when time and again, the mad monk's notions were embraced and put into practical effect.

To summarize: many, if not the majority of the core tenets of the philosophy of Nazism were lifted (by Hitler) straight from the pages of the works of Lanz von Liebenfels, and from *Ostara* in particular. And thanks to Hitler, catch phrases of Liebenfels such as 'Racial Purity', 'Inferior Races', 'Race War', 'Selective Breeding', 'Sterilization', 'Deportation', 'Pogroms' and 'Extermination' would echo loudly along the corridors of power of the Third Reich.

It should also be remembered that Hitler shared Liebenfels' interest in astrology – the study of the position and motion of celestial bodies as having an influence on human affairs – for as Angela Raubal said to Bridget of her [Angela's] half-brother 'He never does anything without consulting the astrologers.'[33]

Notes

1. Liebenfels, op. cit., p. 65, p. 9.
2. Ibid, p. 9.
3. Ibid, p. 10.
4. *Ostara*, I/80.
5. Liebenfels, *Bibliomystikon*, Vol.II. p. 158 (in *Occult Sciences and Nazi Myths*, by Manfred Nagl; www.antiqillum.com/glor/glor_005/nazimyth.htm
6. Ibid, Vol. III. p. 40.
7. Ibid, Vol. I. p. 90.
8. *Ostara*, I/21, (in antiqillum, op.cit.).
9. Liebenfels, *Theozoology*, op. cit., pp. 65, 23.
10. Ibid, p. 53.
11. Ibid, p. 61.
12. *Ostara*, I/13–14 (in antiqillum, op. cit.).

13. Liebenfels, *Theozoology*, op.cit, p. 66, A reference to the Bible: Book of Revelations.
14. Ibid, p. 67.
15. Ibid, p. 68.
16. Ibid.
17. *Ostara*, III/101.
18. Liebenfels, *Theozoology*, op. cit., pp. 69–70.
19. Ibid, p. 67.
20. *Ostara*, III/4.
21. Liebenfels, *Theozoology*, op. cit., p. 51.
22. *Ostara*, III/3.
23. Liebenfels, *Theozoology*, op. cit., p. 62.
24. *Ostara*, III/15, 19 (in antiqillum, op. cit.).
25. Liebenfels, *Theozoology*, op. cit., p. 67.
26. *Ostara*, I/75 (in antiqillum, op. cit.).
27. Ibid, I/19.
28. Liebenfels, *Theozoology*, op. cit., p. 44.
29. Krause, *Die Fackel*, pp. 6ff.
30. Becker, *Zur Geschichte der Rassenhygiene: Weige ins Dritte Reich*, p. 384.
31. Daim, op. cit., p. 182.
32. Ibid.
33. Unger, op. cit., p. 161.

Chapter 13

Germany Again in Crisis

Hitler's rise to power must be seen against a backdrop of a depressed economy and high unemployment. The Great War had left a legacy of bitterness, anger, and hardship, and he offered a solution to what the German people saw as otherwise insuperable problems. And to win them over, he first made it clear that he absolutely identified with them in their view of the Treaty of Versailles as an 'instrument of unrestricted oppression'.[1]

In 1923 the value of Germany's currency fell and, as it did so, the government responded by printing more and more money, in order that employers and factories could meet their obligations to their workers and to their suppliers respectively. However, this merely served to increase the upward spiral of inflation. Soon, a situation arose where the banks successively overprinted say, a one Reichsmark banknote, first with the number 10, then 1,000 and finally, 1,000,000 or more. In other words, the currency was rendered virtually valueless; savings accounts also became worthless, and foreigners were able to purchase German land, property and businesses at knock-down prices.

On 22 December 1923, forty-six-year-old Dr Hjalmar Schacht, formerly head of the German National Bank, was appointed President of the Reichsbank even though he was not a member of the Nazi Party. Of Danish descent, Schacht had been brought up in New York City, where his father was a merchant. He now proceeded to establish a gold reserve and travelled to London in order to peg the Deutschmark to a gold standard.

On 21 January 1924, Schacht declared that German reparations – the legacy of the Great War – would in future be paid only in kind, through German exports. However, French Prime Minister, Raymond Poincaré, insisted that they be paid in cash. Nevertheless, in that year the German economy recovered to the extent that inflation was reduced to single figures. The Weimar government had achieved this by borrowing money from the Americans and using it to pay the French and British the reparations due to them under the terms of the Treaty of Versailles. In other words, the recovery was based on short-term credit.

Under a plan put forward by an Allied committee led by American Charles Dawes, and ratified by the Reichstag on 29 August 1924, Germany achieved some amelioration of the harsh terms of the Treaty of Versailles. Also, the French agreed to end their occupation of the Ruhr. Germany now came to the attention of Americans anxious to invest in the German State and in every possible German business and municipality.

However, by 1924 the Nazis had, as yet, failed to make any significant impact on the German political scene. Not only that, but a potential rival to Hitler had emerged in the form of Captain Ernst Röhm, Commander of the SA, whose ambition was for his men to take over the role of the army, with himself as commander-in-chief.

On 26 April 1925, Field Marshal Paul von Hindenburg was elected President of the Republic, following the death of Friedrich Ebert. On 16 October the Treaty of Locarno, or the so-called Rhineland Security Pact, signed in London, guaranteed Germany's existing frontiers with France and Belgium. The following year, Germany was admitted to the League of Nations and normal relations with the Western Powers were restored.

Meanwhile Hitler, on his early release from prison in December 1925, set about reforming the SS, which had originally been created to form his personal bodyguard, enlarging it by creating, in each German city, a core of Nazis whose loyalty to himself would be total and unquestioning.

*   *   *

In the 1928 election, the Nazis won only twelve seats in the Reichstag (seat of the democratic German government) with just 2.6 per cent of the vote. At the same time, a sudden drop in agricultural prices brought poverty to the countryside.

At an international conference held in February 1929 in Paris under Owen D. Young, American lawyer and Chairman of the General Electric Company, the question of German reparations was again discussed. The result was that, on 7 June, the Young Plan was accepted by the Germans: a new Bank for International Settlements would be opened in Basel in Switzerland into which Germany would be required to pay reparations until the year 1988. Payments would increase annually for the first thirty-six years, but annual instalments would never exceed 660 million Deutschmarks. For Germany, this arrangement was a considerable improvement.

On 29 October of that year, the New York Stock Market crashed. This was followed by the Great Depression of 1929–30. Many German businesses now failed as American investors in Germany went bankrupt, and America withdrew its short-term loans.

On 7 March 1930 a discouraged Hjalmar Schacht resigned as President of the Reichsbank. He then embarked on a lecture tour of America, where he argued that Germany was unable to pay her reparations under the Young Plan, and that these reparations should therefore be suspended for fear of their being a 'menace to world peace and stability'.[2]

On 27 March 1930, following the collapse of Germany's so-called 'Great Coalition Government', a minority government of centre and right-wing parties was formed under Heinrich Brüning. However, national elections called by Brüning on 14 September, left the Great Coalition unable to form a majority, and Brüning was forced to rely upon President Hindenburg's powers of rule by emergency decree.

In that year, Heinrich Himmler, a Nazi Party member from 1923, was made head of the SS, which, under his leadership, effectively became the Party's police force. In the September elections the Nazis increased their percentage of the vote, winning 170 seats (compared with the communists seventy-seven, and the coalitions of middle parties which held the remainder) out of a total of 560 seats.

In 1931 the five major German banks crashed, more than 20,000 German businesses failed, and the unemployment figure rose to 5.5 million. Increasingly desperate Germans now turned to the Nazi Party. However, the communists also gained support, and there followed a period of civil unrest.

Reinhard Heydrich now joined the SS and proceeded to use it to gather intelligence on Hitler's rivals. Soon, this organization would become a vehicle for the perpetration of state terror as a means of achieving total political and social control of the country through its network of informants in every walk of life.

Throughout that summer the German press contained stories of homosexual behaviour and sleaze among the higher echelons of the Nazi Party. This applied particularly to the SA whose leader, Ernst Röhm, was openly homosexual. At first, Röhm and his henchman were tolerated by the Nazis, Hitler stating that as far as SA leaders were concerned 'their private lives cannot be an object of scrutiny, unless it runs counter to vital principles of National Socialist ideology'. However, to the Nazis, the excesses of the SA were soon to become an embarrassment.

Christabel Bielenberg, a British writer who had married a German lawyer, described the Germany which she knew in 1932, where one German in three was out of work out of a workforce of 30 million[3] and there was great social unrest:

> Every weekend political marches took place in Hamburg, and the Nazis used to march through the communist districts. The communists then answered by coming into the other parts of the town and there were fights, deaths, and shooting practically every weekend.

The political situation was such, she said, that

> People wished that some strong man would clean up the place. We've got to get out of what we're in. Anything is better than this situation that we're in at the moment.[4]

Emil Klein, a Nazi Party member from 1921 to 1945, said subsequently that he had once paid four billion Reichsmarks for a sausage and bread.

It really was a collapse. People said, 'It can't go on like this.' Then the debate began about the need for a strong man, and the call for a strong man became louder and louder, because democracy achieved nothing.[5]

Jutta Rudiger (Nazi Party member 1931–1945) described the

desperation and poverty caused by the mass unemployment … It was really terrible …[6] In this situation, Hitler seemed to be the bringer of salvation. He said, 'I will get you out of this misery if you all join in.' And everyone understood.[7]

In the election of July 1932 the Nazis captured 37.3 per cent of the vote, making them, with 230 seats, the largest party in the Reichstag, even though they still lacked an overall majority. On 13 August, Hitler demanded of the eighty-five-year-old President von Hindenburg, that he (Hitler) be made chancellor. Knowing only too well what Hitler's intentions were, Hindenburg was horrified. Was democracy in Germany to be snuffed out after a mere fourteen years? However, a group of businessmen, together with Hjalmar Schacht, President of the Reichsbank from 1923 to 1930, argued that Hitler should receive the chancellorship for the good of the country.

In another election, held in November 1932, the Nazi vote fell back slightly, to 33.1 per cent. The Party was also in some difficulty, being acutely short of funds. Now, former Chancellor, Franz von Papen, proposed that Hitler could become chancellor provided that he, von Papen, was appointed Vice-Chancellor, and that the number of National Socialist (Nazi) Party members in the cabinet was restricted to two.

This was accepted, and on 30 January 1933, Hitler was duly sworn in by President von Hindenburg) as chancellor of a coalition government, at forty-three, the youngest chancellor in Germany's history. That same evening, the Nazis held a torchlight celebration parade through the streets of Berlin.

Notes
1. Hitler, op. cit., p. 347.
2. Weitz, *Hitler's Banker*, p. 114.
3. Ibid, p. 11.
4. *World at War: Hitler's Germany: the Only Hope, 1933–1936*.
5. *The Nazis: A Warning from History, Part 1*.
6. Ibid.
7. Ibid.

Chapter 14

The 'Saviour' Cometh

One of Hitler's constant themes was that he had been chosen to lead the German people:

> I can give expression to my deepest feeling only in the form of humble thanks to Providence who called upon me and vouchsafed to me, once an unknown soldier of the Great War, to rise to be the leader of my people so dear to me.[1]

Hitler's Message

Hitler's message to the German people was a blunt one. They must make themselves completely subservient to him, and he would destroy their enemies. And in his message, the threat of violence was unmistakable, for, as he had already stated in *Mein Kampf* (a book which was a best-seller in Germany, the royalties from which made Hitler an extremely wealthy man),

> whoever wishes to win over the masses, must know the key that will open the door to their hearts. It is not objectivity, which is a feckless attitude, but a determined will, backed up by force, when necessary.[2] The soul of the masses can be won only if those who lead the movement for that purpose are determined not merely to carry through the positive struggle for their own aims, but are also determined to destroy the enemy that opposes them.[3] The masses are but a part of Nature herself ... Their wish is to see the stronger side win and the weaker wiped out, or subjected unconditionally to the will of the stronger.[4]

In July 1932 he reinforced his message in an election speech, in which he made no secret of the fact that his Nazi Party intended to impose a dictatorship. He asked,

> is it typically German to have thirty (political) parties? We are intolerant. I have given myself one goal – to sweep these thirty political parties out of Germany. We have one aim and we will follow it fanatically and ruthlessly to the grave.[5]

As for his German National Socialist Labour Party (GNSLP), 'It was imperative from the start to introduce rigid discipline into our meetings and to establish the authority of the chairman absolutely',[6] because only by violence and terror could 'a new regime be created by means of constructive work'.[7] In the chambers or senate, said Hitler, anticipating the situation that would pertain should his party come to power, 'the right of decision belongs exclusively to the president, who must be entirely responsible for the matter under discussion'.[8] He then went on to describe, with unconcealed delight, how his Storm Troopers had launched an attack on their opponents.[9] (In fact, Hitler devoted a whole chapter to the 'Nature and Organization of the Storm Troops'.)

However, apart from stressing the need for obedience, Hitler was deliberately vague about his party's policies. When asked 'What is your detailed programme?' his reply was,

> I can only answer: after a government with your [the Weimar coalition's] kind of economy, with your kind of administration, your decay, the German people have to be rebuilt from top to bottom. We do not want to lie, we do not want to cheat. Therefore I have refused ever to appear in front of these people and make cheap promises.[10]

Therefore, for the time being, rhetoric would have to suffice.

The Importance of Propaganda

Hitler quickly realized that, by his words, he was able to influence people, so much so that he made a deliberate study of what is now referred to as 'body language' in order to achieve maximum effect. As Emil Klein observed,

> face to face with Hitler, I was never that enthusiastic about him and his moustache. But he could enthuse me through the power of his speeches. He also convinced me – and everyone else.

And, referring to the addressing of mass meetings, Hitler himself declared,

> thought is eliminated. And because this is the state of mind I require, because it secures to me the best sounding-board for my speeches, I order everyone to attend the meetings, where they become part of a mass, whether they like it or not ...[11] I am conscious that I have no equal in the art of swaying the masses, not even [Joseph] Goebbels [*Reichsminister* for Propaganda].[12]

He encouraged his audiences to take a pride in themselves,

> the German people is no longer a people of dishonour, a people of shame, of self-destruction, of faint-heartedness, and lack of faith. No Lord, the German people has become strong again, in its spirit, strong in its will, strong in its persistence, strong in endurance of every sacrifice. Lord, we will not desert you. Now bless our struggle and our freedom, and thus our German people and fatherland.[13]

Hitler's speeches, in which he clenched and shook his fist and contorted his face in an agonized way, in order to give the impression that the same problems which concerned his audience also concerned him, had an electrifying effect. Hitler's powers of oratory cannot be denied. However, they were not arrived at spontaneously. Paul Devrient, born in 1890 in Wandsbeck, was a successful German operatic tenor, and in his book *Mein Schuler Adolf Hitler*, published in 2003, he reveals that, from 1929 to 1933, he acted as a paid tutor to Hitler. In the year 1932 in particular, Devrient accompanied Hitler on his Nazi Party campaign trail – which took them to more than a hundred German towns – in the course of which the former gave the latter lessons in oratory.

Nevertheless, Hitler used the same phrases over and over again, delivering them in a hostile, snarling voice, or with agonized hand-wringing and breast-beating. His vocabulary was limited and his speeches, though strong on rhetoric, lacked substance. For example, 'And we know before us lies Germany, within us marches Germany, and behind us comes Germany'[14] or this, when he addressed the first Party rally at Nuremberg.

> The most precious possession we have is our people, and for our people, and on behalf of our people, we want to struggle, and we want to fight, and never weaken, and never weary, and never doubt, and never despair. Long live our Movement! Long live the German nation!

In the creation of his new regime, said Hitler, propaganda would be of the utmost importance.[15] He had already devoted no less than fourteen pages to this subject in *Mein Kampf*. The function of propaganda, he said

> does not lie in the scientific training of the individual, but in calling the masses' attention to certain facts, processes, necessities, etc, whose significance is thus for the first time placed within their field of vision. The whole art consists in doing this so skilfully that everyone will be convinced that the fact is real, the process necessary, the necessity correct etc. But since propaganda is not, and cannot be the necessity in itself … its effect for the most part, must be aimed at the emotions and only to a very limited degree at the so-called intellect …[16]

An example of Hitler's propaganda is his attempt to convince the German people that they would not have lost the war, had their leaders not capitulated. He claimed that,

> As far as England is concerned, the war was really won when Germany was destroyed as a colonial and commercial power, and was reduced to the rank of a second-class state.[17] The stigma of shame incurred by a cowardly submission can never be effaced.

Here, he was quoting the Prussian general and author, Karl Philip Gottlieb von Clausewitz.[18] Hitler now offered the German people what they sought – a solution to their problems.

> Today you must stand before the world, with me, and behind me, and solidly declare, we want nothing but peace, we want nothing but calm, we want only to devote ourselves to our duties, we also want nothing but equal rights, and we will not allow anyone to take away our honour.

Although it is clear with hindsight that Hitler was being disingenuous when he spoke of wanting nothing but peace and calm, this was a message with which war-weary Germans readily identified.[19]

Pageantry
As a devotee of the late operatic composer, Richard Wagner, Hitler was conscious of the power which drama and pageantry could exert over an audience. Those who attended the Nuremberg Party Rallies of the mid-to-late 1930s, can scarcely deny that Hitler held his enthralled audiences in the palm of his hand, so to speak, and that they would have followed him, almost without exception, to the very ends of the earth. The rallies were best described by Sir Nevile Henderson, the then British Ambassador to Germany,

> the hypnotic effect of thousands of men marching in perfect order, the music of the mass bands, the forest of standards and flags, the vast perspectives of the stadium, the smoking torches, the dome of searchlights.* The sense of power, of force and unity was irresistible, and all converged with a mounting crescendo of excitement on the supreme moment when the Führer himself made his entry. Paradoxically, the man who was most affected by such spectacles was their originator, Hitler himself, and, as Alfred Rosenberg, German Nazi politician, remarks in his memoirs, they played an indispensable part in the process of self-intoxication.[20]

Since early 1920, Hitler had been concerned with the design of a flag for his Party (the NSDAP).

> I, as leader, was unwilling to make public my own design, as it was possible that someone else could come forward with a design just as good, if not better, than my own. As a matter of fact, a dental surgeon from Starnberg submitted a good design very similar to mine, with only one mistake, in that his swastika with curved

---

* The 'dome' effect was achieved by making the beams of the searchlights intersect high up in the sky, giving the auditorium a cathedral-like appearance.

corners was set upon a white background. After innumerable trials, I decided upon a final form – a flag of red material with a white disc, bearing in its centre a black swastika ... The new flag appeared in public in the mid-summer of 1920.[21]

Although Hitler did not mention him by name, the dentist referred to was a Doctor Friedrich Krohn.

A ritual, first established in the July 1926 Nazi Party Rally held at Weimar, was the Blood Banner Ceremony, where Hitler consecrated in excess of 300 huge flags by touching each one with the tattered remnants of a bullet-ridden, blood-stained Party banner which had been held by a dying Nazi during the failed *Putsch* of 1923. In the four days between 31 August and 3 September at the 1938 Party Rally held at Nuremberg, Hitler took the salute of a million men, and addressed some 60,000 or so Hitler Youth.

Appearances however, were deceptive, because behind the serried ranks and precision marching of the Storm Troopers lay a disorganized system of government in which Hitler, for his part, often delegated the same tasks to two or more of his minions at the same time. Confusion was compounded by his obsequious henchmen, whose principal desire was to please him rather than to act for the benefit of their country.

The Nazis were also anxious to connect Germany to its past, to the glorious days of the Teutonic Knights. With this in mind, Hitler and his Party attempted to recreate this medieval era by staging elaborate pageants, with knights on horseback wearing chain mail and flamboyant swastikas emblazoned on their breast, and comely maidens attired in long, white, flowing dresses.

With God's Help ...

Hitler, in his speeches, often invoked the imagery of Christianity: 'The German people have become strong again. May the Lord God bless our struggle and our German people and Fatherland,'[22] said Hitler in *Mein Kampf*:

> Everybody who has the right kind of feeling for his country, is solemnly bound, each within his own denomination, to see that he is not constantly talking about the Will of God merely from the lips, but that in actual fact he fulfils the Will of God and does not allow God's handiwork to be debased. For it was by the Will of God that men were made of a certain bodily shape, were given their natures and their faculties. Whoever destroys His work wages war against God's Creation and God's Will. Therefore, everyone should endeavour, each in his own denomination of course, and should consider it as his first and most solemn duty to hinder any and everyone whose conduct tends, either by word or deed, to go outside his own religious body and pick a quarrel with those of another denomination.[23]

As for his Nazi Party, it was to be 'the selecting ground for German political leaders. Its doctrine will be unchangeable. Its organization will be as hard as steel. Its total image however, will be like a holy order'.[24]

The *Volk*

Since Hitler was anxious for the people of the countryside not to feel excluded from the activities of his Nazi Party, he arranged for his Brownshirts to attend the annual harvest celebrations, where country people recreated the image of the *Volk* (community of pure blood and race), by dressing in national costume. In this, Hitler displayed a certain cynicism, in that while he would have approved of the idea of the German *Volk* as a means of maintaining German culture and identity, for him, it was the future which was all important.

The Hitler Youth

Hitler was also anxious to extend his Party's appeal to young people. 'We believe that the German youth must be lean and agile; fleet as a greyhound, tough as leather, and as hard as Krupps steel,' he said.[25]

In 1931, twenty-four-year-old Baldur von Schirach, son of the director/manager of a theatre, became Reichs Youth Leader. Two years later, the Nazis took over all Germany's youth organizations. Ten-year-old boys were conscripted into the organization of young German people; at fourteen they joined the Hitler Youth, which Schirach had founded and become leader of in the same year, and at eighteen they joined the Nazi Party. Girls joined the League of German Girls, the BDM or *Bund Deutscher Mädel*, which taught domestic skills rather than encouraging intellectual pursuits.

Although membership of the Hitler Youth and BDM was ostensibly voluntary, in practice any child who opted out would find him or herself disadvantaged when it came to choosing a school or, later, in choosing a career. Furthermore, at the Nuremberg Party Rallies the Hitler Youth were obliged to swear their allegiance to Hitler.

Addressing the Hitler Youth, Hitler embarked, in his mendacious way, upon his usual theme: 'We want our people to be peace-loving but also courageous. You must be peace-loving.'[26] 'We can look proudly on our German youth. You are our life blood ... , our own flesh.' However, he added the rider: 'Nothing is possible unless one will commands ... and the others visibly obey. German boys and German girls, we want our people to be obedient. You must practise obedience.'[27]

For all Hitler's talk of peace, his intentions were quite the opposite, for, in the words of Hans Fruhwirth, ex Hitler Youth, 'Now there was paramilitary training ... small-bore rifle shooting, and marches using a map and compass'.[28] With hindsight, the inference was obvious: when the time came, Schirach would be able to deliver his willing recruits directly to the armed forces. Sure enough SS *Reichsführer* Heinrich Himmler subsequently came to an agreement with Schirach whereby the Death's Head units of the SS would recruit directly from the Hitler Youth. Wearing their black uniforms they would be trained to be willing executioners. The Hitler Youth therefore, had become in essence, a pre-military training unit.

The Role of Women

German women who were not married were encouraged to attend elite bridal schools – of which there were five – where they were trained to become 'perfect housewives', i.e., to manage a household, become proficient in cookery and learn about motherhood. At the end of such a course at bridal school, the woman would be presented with a diploma indicating that she had now qualified as a 'master housewife'.

For a woman to marry, she first had to obtain permission from the state. Proof of her racial and medical purity was required and, having married, she and her husband were required to testify to this on their marriage certificate. As a married woman, it was now her duty to produce as many children as possible, for which, according to the results of her labours, she would receive the Motherhood Cross in gold, silver, or bronze!

Workwise, women were excluded from certain professions, and married women, in particular, were disallowed from joining the Civil Service and from attaining other positions of power and authority. It was made clear to them that their duty was in the home, looking after the husband and children – which had the added virtue of reducing the level of unemployment. Women were barred from attending the annual Nuremberg Rallies. However, they were encouraged to participate in cross-country runs and communal physical training, in order to foster a sense of community spirit.

Hitler summed up his idea of the contented woman thus,

> charm, grace, and rhythm unite to form a happy picture and a positive approach to life. They [women] have no longing for public office or the parliament. A happy man, and a host of happy children are dearer to them.[29]

As for himself, he believed that as a single man, his appeal to women was greater than it would have been, had he been married – although he appears to have ruled marriage out right from the beginning.

Putting Germany back to Work

When Hitler became Chancellor on 30 January 1933, the first action of the Reichsbank was to inject the sum of one billion Deutschmarks into the housing and construction industries, then to finance the first of the autobahns (2,500 miles of superhighway linking the major cities), which would cost another 600 million Deutschmarks. Although Hitler claimed credit for the *autobahnen*, they had actually been planned long before he came to power. There now commenced an urgent programme of public works, together with covert re-armament, so that Hitler was soon able to say, with justification, that, during his first year in power, over 2.7 million unemployed had been brought back into the labour force.[30]

Germany and her Neighbours

During the 1930s, Hitler told a pack of outrageous lies in respect of his future intentions with regard to his fellow European countries, while at the time he tightened his grip on his own country, and covertly built up, with hostile intentions, a massive war machine. In October 1930 he was at pains to emphasize his desire for Germany to live in peaceful coexistence with her neighbours.

Plate 1

Plate 2

Plate 3

Plate 4

Plate 5

Plate 1: Adolf Hitler. A 1933 portrait by the artist B. Jacobs.
Plate 2: Jörg Lanz von Liebenfels.
Plate 3: Liebenfels as a monk of the Order of the Holy Cross.
Plate 4: Liebenfels as a prior of the Order of New Templars.
Plate 5: Liebenfels as a country gentleman.

Plate 6   **Plate 7**

Plate 8

Plate 6: Grail ceremony in the cavern chapel at Staufen.
Plate 7: The ruins of the castle of Werfenstein, circa 1840.
Plate 8: A drawing by Hitler, then a soldier at the front, of a military store in Fournes, France.
Plate 9: Hitler in custody in the Fortress of Landsberg in 1924.

Plate 9

Plate 10

Plate 10: Reich President Paul von Hindenburg and Reich Chancellor Adolf Hitler.

Plate 11: At the 'Rally for Freedom', Hitler inspects a guard of honour formed by the company of his personal bodyguard, or *Leibstandarte*.

Plate 12: Hitler consecrates the banners at the 'Rally for Freedom'.

Plate 13: Hitler talks to a Nazi party member, the widow of one of the fallen of 9 November 1923, on 9 November 1935 in Munich. In the background may be seen the Brown House, the national headquarters of the Nazi party.

Plate 11

Plate 12

Plate 13

Plate 14

Plate 14: A model of the
proposed convention hall
for the Reich Party in
Nuremberg.

Plate 15: Hitler and Rudolf
Hess, the deputy Führer,
inspect progress on the
construction site of the
'Führer houses' in Munich.

Plate 16: Hitler at
Obersalzberg.

Plate 15

Plate 16

Plate 17

Plate 17: An historic meeting: Hitler meets Britain's Anthony Eden, Lord Privy Seal, and Sir John Simon, the Foreign Secretary, on 6 March 1935.

Plate 18: An official 47th birthday photograph of Hitler, 20 April 1936.

Plate 19: Hermann Göring, Minister President, visits Hitler at Obersalzberg.

Plate 18

Plate 19

Plate 20

Plate 21

Plate 22

Plate 23

Plate 24

Plate 20: Day of rest: Hitler with a small girl, Helga Goebbels, daughter of Dr Goebbels.

Plate 21: Hitler, Professor Leonhard Gall and Architect Albert Speer witnessing the construction of the Museum of German Fine Art in Munich.

Plate 22: 'Good news'

Plate 23: At the opening of the first section of the *Autobahn* from Munich to the Austrian border.

Plate 24: Hitler surrounded by children with Baldur von Schirach on the right.

Plate 25

Plate 25: Hitler Youth members on a visit to Obersalzberg.

Plate 26: The opening of the Frankfurt–Darmstadt *Autobahn*: (from left to right) Werner von Blomberg, Reichs Minister for War; Hitler; Dr Fritz Todt, General Inspector; Dr Hjalmar Schacht, President of the Reichs Bank; Dr Julius Dorpmüller, Director of Reichs Transport; Dr Goebbels, Reichs Minister.

Plate 27: On board a Kriegsmarine warship, Hitler visits a Norwegian fjord.

Plate 28: Hitler's cousin Aloisia Veit, a hospital patient in 1932 and later murdered with Hitler's assent.

Plate 26

Plate 27

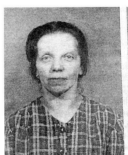

Plate 28

Plate 29

Plate 30

Plate 29: Aloisia Veit's certificate of birth and baptism.

Plate 30: Aloisia Veit's resident's permit for the district of Vienna, dated 28 January 1931.

Plate 31: Steinhof Asylum, where Aloisia Veit was a patient, showing one of the patients in a wire cage in 1938.

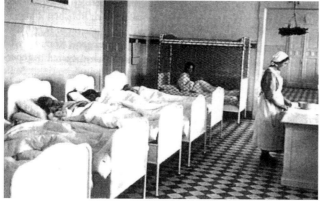

Plate 31

I think I can assure you, that there is no one in Germany who will not with all his heart approve any honest attempt at an improvement of relations between Germany and France. My own feelings force me to take the same attitude ... the German people has the solemn intention of living in peace and friendship with all civilized nations and powers ... and I regard the maintenance of peace in Europe as especially desirable and at the same time secure, if France and Germany, on the basis of equal sharing of natural human rights, arrive at a real inner understanding ... the young Germany that is led by me and that finds its expression in the National Socialist Movement, has only the most heartfelt desire for an understanding with other European nations.[31]

Our boundless love for, and loyalty to our own national traditions makes us respect the national claims of others and makes us desire from the bottoms of our hearts to live with them in peace and friendship.[32] Before the entire world I declare: we are ready to offer the French people a hand of reconciliation.[33]

The world must know that my love of peace is a longing for peace of the entire German people.[34] When did the German people ever break its word?[35] The German government is ready at any time to participate in the system of collective cooperation for safeguarding European peace ...[36]

The assertion that it is the intention of the German Reich to coerce the Austrian state is absurd and cannot in any way be substantiated or proved ... Germany neither intends nor wishes to interfere in the internal affairs of Austria, to annexe Austria, or to unite Austria.[37] It is my wish to solve the great differences among the nations in precisely the same way in which I solved our domestic problems – according to the principles of justice, fairness, and understanding.[38]

The German government has assured Belgium and Holland that it is ready to recognize and to guarantee these states as neutral regions in perpetuity.[39] Without taking the past into account, Germany has concluded a non-aggression pact with Poland.* This is more than a valuable contribution to European peace, and we shall adhere to it unconditionally.[40] Germany had no intention of attacking other peoples.[41] None of the Scandinavian statesmen, for example, can contend that the German government or that German public opinion has ever made a demand which was incompatible with the sovereignty and integrity of their state.[42]

And the most classical lie of all was, 'We have no territorial demands to make in Europe!'[43]

*   *   *

---

* A reference to the German–Polish Pact of 26 January 1934.

Not everyone was taken in by Hitler's rhetoric, and those of the intellectual elite who voted with their feet and left Germany, following Hitler's accession, included tenor Richard Tauber (born in Austria), German novelist and Nobel Prize winner Thomas Mann, and German-Jewish mathematical scientist Albert Einstein.

Even Dr Hjalmar Schacht, President of the Reichsbank, had no illusions about Hitler for, when he heard, in September 1938 that British Prime Minister Neville Chamberlain was about to visit Berlin his reaction was, 'Imagine! The Prime Minister of this world power [Britain] comes to visit this gangster!'[44]

Notes
1. Prange, op. cit., p. 94.
2. Hitler, op. cit., p. 191.
3. Ibid, p. 192.
4. Ibid.
5. *The Nazis: A Warning from History, Part 1.*
6. Hitler, op. cit., p. 269.
7. Ibid, p. 254.
8. Ibid, p. 252.
9. Ibid, p. 280–281.
10. *The Nazis: A Warning from History, Part 2.*
11. Rauschning, op. cit., p. 211.
12. Ibid, p. 210.
13. *Hitler: a Profile. The Blackmailer.*
14. *The Nazis: A Warning from History, Part 2.*
15. Hitler, op. cit., Ch.XI.
16. Ibid, Vol.1, Chapters 6 and 12.
17. Ibid, p. 370.
18. Ibid, p. 368.
19. *Hitler: a Profile: The Blackmailer.*
20. Henderson, Sir Nevile, *Failure of a Mission*, p. 71.
21. Hitler, op. cit., p. 276.
22. *Nazis: The Occult Conspiracy.*
23. Hitler, op. cit., p. 310.
24. *Nazis: The Occult Conspiracy.*
25. *Hitler's Henchmen: Schirach, the Corrupter of Youth.*
26. *Hitler: a Profile: The Seducer.*
27. Ibid.
28. Ibid.
29. *Hitler's Women.*
30. *World at War: Hitler's Germany: the Only Hope, 1933–1936, Part 1.*
31. *Der Volkischer Beobachter,* 26 October 1930.
32. Prange, op. cit.,17 May 1933, Berlin, p. 161.
33. Ibid, 24 Oct. 1933, p. 191.
34. Ibid, 26 Oct. 1933, Köln, p. 159
35. Ibid, 11 Nov. 1933, Berlin, p. 179.
36. Ibid, 21 May 1935, Berlin, p. 183.
37. Ibid, 21 May 1935, Berlin, p. 184.
38. Ibid, 12 March 1936, Karlsruhe, p. 167
39. Ibid, 30 Jan. 1937, Berlin, p. 186.
40. Ibid, 30 Jan. 1939, Berlin, p. 189.
41. Ibid, 1 April 1939, Berlin, p. 182.
42. Ibid, 28 April 1939, Berlin, p. 185.
43. Ibid, p. 181.
44. Gisevius, *Bis zum Bitteren Ende*, p. 356.

Chapter 15

A New 'Holy Order'

In *Mein Kampf*, Hitler treated the subject of religion somewhat gingerly, but his inference was obvious. The House of Habsburg, he said, had attempted to transform his homeland, Austria, into a Slav state, and to this end, they had appointed 'parish priests of Czech nationality ... in purely German districts'. It was his opinion, therefore, 'that the Catholic clergy ... were grossly neglecting the rights of the German population'.[1] As for Protestantism, it too 'fails the moment it is called upon to defend national interests which do not belong to the sphere of its ideals ...'.[2]

When Hitler met his nephew, William Patrick Hitler, in August 1929, he made it clear that traditional Christian religion would, in Nazi Germany, be nothing more than an irrelevance:

Germany is too small for religion *and* the [Nazi] Party ... There will be no place for religion in the future. First we will get rid of the Jews. They are the weakest. And then we must rule out Catholicism. The Catholics are too well-organized. In a few generations no one will ever know that a Jew called Jesus ever existed, and no German will be ruled by a man in a robe [i.e., a priest]. Germany will be our religion.

As for the present 'Germany is chained, thanks to the Jews and the Catholics', declared Hitler.[3]

A decade later, in 1934, Hitler's sister, Paula, told her half-brother Alois's former wife, Bridget, that the former, as newly-appointed Chancellor, was arranging for priests everywhere 'to be thrown into prison on the slightest pretext ...'.

It is Adolf's insatiable vanity that has led him into this madness. What man in his right senses can believe himself [to be] the reincarnation of our saviour, as Adolf does? That's why he hates the Church, because it will not tolerate his sacrilegious attempts to beatify himself. He would have had himself declared god by now, if it were not for the strength of the Catholic church. Already, he has established Hitler churches. A painting of my brother, the Anti-Christ, hangs before their altars. On each side burn unholy candles. *Mein Kampf* is their bible ... They mean to discredit Christianity and bring back to Germany the pagan beliefs of two thousand years ago. This year they made the *Sonnenwendfeuer* (midsummer) at the beginning of summer, and in a few days there will be another heathen holiday when it ends. All throughout the length and breadth of Germany they hold meetings.[4]

Paula was understandably furious that her brother had renounced the family's Catholic faith, his mother Klara having been a devout worshipper. However, whether he believed himself to be a god is a matter for conjecture. As far as the unholy rituals described above are concerned, these were largely the brainchild of Heinrich Himmler, commander (*Reichsführer*) of the SS, Hitler's personal bodyguard, and also commander of the German police.

Himmler was the son of devout Catholic parents whose father, a school teacher, had once been tutor to the Crown Prince of Bavaria. Whilst studying agriculture in Munich, he had joined the right-wing militia, or Free Corps. It was he who had carried the flag through the streets of Munich for the Nazis in the failed coup of 1923. In 1935, the one-time chicken farmer, Himmler, declared,

> I, as leader of the SS and as a farmer born and bred, want to make it clear here today that the idea of 'blood', which has been upheld in the SS from the very beginning, would have been worthless if it were not inexorably linked to the belief in the sanctity of the soil.[5]

And just as Hitler enjoyed planning his expansionist wars, so Himmler was anxious to make a link between German history and Nazi ideology.

The SS (Schutzstaffel)

Up until 1935, recruits to the SS were hand-picked by Himmler in person; great importance being attached to eye and hair colour (blue and blond respectively being the colours of choice), and to the shape of the skull, as defining a person's degree of Aryanism.

The SS were regularly indoctrinated with theories of Aryan superiority. According to Father Gereon Goldmann (SS Police Division), SS men were told that 'We are the race that must rule the world … and all other races must be subordinated to the Aryan race. They are no more than slaves. We rule the whole world'. There was 'not a word about religion. Their religion was simply the Aryan race, which was what they took as their creed'.[6]

As for Hitler, his obsession with racial purity led him to require the SS to keep a genealogical register of its members. The discovery of a Jew in his ancestry any time after the year 1750 would result in the swift removal of an SS officer from his post.[7]

The SS and the Teutonic Knights

'When world history later proclaims Adolf Hitler not only the greatest German leader, but also the greatest Aryan,' said Himmler, 'then they will say that we, his closest followers, his chosen knights, were loyal, obedient believers, that we were steadfast and worthy of being his heroic champions.'[8]

And to SS officers stationed at the Dachau concentration camp,

> Never forget we are a knightly order from which one cannot withdraw; to which one is recruited by blood, and within which one remains, body and soul.[9]

Perhaps in this, Himmler had in mind the Order of Teutonic Knights, founded by Heinrich Walpot von Bassenheim in 1198 and originally established to care for crusader knights who had been wounded, or who had fallen ill during the Crusades. An exclusively Germanic Order, it was instrumental in the thirteenth century in expanding German domination over Prussia and the Baltic states. However, on 15 July 1410 the Teutonic Knights were defeated by a combined force of Poles, Lithuanians and Mongols at the Battle of Tannenberg, and their power was broken. And Himmler, like Hitler, undoubtedly drew inspiration from Liebenfels, and his Order of the New Templars, founded in 1907, upon whose ethos the SS was based.[10]

Wewelsburg Castle

Just as Liebenfels selected Austria's Burg Werfenstein castle to be the headquarters for his Order of New Templars, so, in 1934, Himmler renovated the ruined mountain fortress of Wewelsburg near Paderborn in Westphalia, which would now become the headquarters of the SS. And in the manner of Arthur, the legendary sixth-century King of the Britons, Himmler installed in the banqueting hall a huge, round conference table with thirteen seats, to accommodate himself and his twelve most senior commanders – *Obergruppenführeren*. Hitler saw the image of the Nazi Party as being like a holy order. The Order of New Templars, however, was undoubtedly an order, but anything less holy can scarcely be imagined, to judge by the results.

Karl-Maria Wiligut-Weisthor (1866–1946)

Wiligut was a professional soldier who had seen service on the Russian and Italian Fronts during the First World War. He claimed to be a clairvoyant and a possessor of extra-sensory powers who could recall the time 'around 228,000 BC, when there were three suns in the sky and the earth was populated with giants, dwarfs and other supposedly mythical beings'.[11] In September 1933 he had been recruited by Himmler to the SS and appointed head of its Department of Pre- and Early History within the Race and Settlement Headquarters, based in Munich.

Wiligut used a runic alphabet which, according to Nordic legend, was given to mankind by Odin, the supreme god of Norse mythology. Members of the SS were taught about the runes, each of which had a special meaning. Also, by throwing them, like dice, fortunes could be told, magic powers invoked, and spells cast.

In November 1924, Wiligut was committed to the Salzburg mental asylum and declared to be insane.[12] Nevertheless, the single *sig* rune (single letter 'S') became the logo of the Hitler Youth.

King Heinrich

Himmler was fascinated by the Saxon King Heinrich, regarded as the protector of Germany from the eastern hordes. On 2 July 1936 at Quedlinburg Cathedral, he delivered a eulogy on Heinrich, to mark the one thousandth anniversary of his death, and afterwards laid a wreath on the king's tomb.

According to Heinz Müller, an eye witness at Quedlinburg, Himmler genuinely believed that he was the reincarnation of Heinrich. 'He [Himmler] was the Aryan type [which] he presumed Heinrich to be, and in his mind [he] believed he was his descendant.'[13]

Guido von List
Das Geheimnis
der Runen

Titelblatt einer Schrift von Guido von List aus dem Jahre 1908

Runes 1: Guido von List and the origins of the runes. (*1908*)

The Ahnenerbe

In July 1935 in a villa in a suburb of Berlin, Himmler created the SS *Ahnenerbe* (Society for the Research and Teaching of Ancestral Heritage). Its remit included the performing of medical experiments on human beings, the checking of blood lines for purity, and the resurrection of ancient occult and pagan practices.

The official *Ahnenerbe* teaching was based on the theories of Viennese engineer and technician Hans Horbiger and expounded by him in his book *Glazialkosmogonie*, published in 1913. Horbiger believed that the Earth repeatedly traps planets from outer space into its orbit, which finally crash into the Earth. In his view, it was the result of just such a collision that caused the Great Flood and the destruction of the island of Atlantis, named after the Greek god Atlas, original home of the master race.[13]

Atlantis

According to ancient myth, Atlantis (mentioned by the Greek philosopher Plato in the fourth century BC) was an extensive island in the Atlantic Ocean and 'said to have been a powerful kingdom before it was overwhelmed by the sea'.[14]

A forceful proponent of the notion of Atlantis was Ukrainian-born theosophist Helena Petrovna Blavatsky (1831–91). According to Blavatsky's 'Secret Doctrine', there lived in Atlantis a race of 'super beings' who had fallen from grace through evil and vice. When the floods came, however, not all the Atlanteans perished, for certain priests escaped by boat to India and, in particular, to Tibet. This race of

Tibetans eventually made its way to Northern Europe where its descendents became the Nordic or Aryan race. Lanz von Liebenfels was another firm believer in the concept of Atlantis.

In 1884, Blavatsky was accused, by the Indian press, of concocting fictitious, spiritualist phenomena. The following year, the Hodgson Report, commissioned by the London Society for Psychical Research, declared her to be a fraud.

The *Ahnenerbe*, in its quest to discover the origins of the Aryan race, sent expeditions to Iceland, the Middle East, North Africa, the Caucasus and Venezuela. An expedition to Amazonia was led by SS 'researcher' Edmund Kiss, who was, by profession, a popular playwright. Dr Ernst Schäfer, an SS scientist who led one such expedition in April 1938, later described to his post-war US Army interrogator a meeting that he had once had with Himmler. It was Himmler's belief that the Nordic race did not evolve, but came directly down from Heaven to settle on the Atlantic continent (Atlantis) and that, after Atlantis became submerged under the sea, ancient immigrants from Atlantis had founded a great civilization in Central Asia.[15]

Wherever the expeditions went the accompanying Nazi scientists convinced themselves that the edifices and ruins which they found were vastly superior to anything which could have been built by the indigenous population. Instead, they must have been built by a former superior Aryan civilization, and this included the Great Pyramids of Egypt.[16]

Several *Ahnenerbe* expeditions were dispatched to Tibet at enormous expense, the last being in the winter of 1938–39. Here, Nazi researchers proceeded to inspect the bemused Tibetans for typical Aryan traits, such as narrow foreheads, long limbs, and angular features. For this, detailed measurements were taken using metal callipers. Even the shades of eye and colour of skin were recorded, using colour-code charts. Liebenfels, it will be remembered, was a strong advocate of using physical features to determine the degree of 'Aryanness', one of his journals being entitled *Character Assessment relative to Skull Shape: an Elementary Racial Phrenology*.[17]

By such methods, Himmler hoped to prove that the ancestors of these Tibetans, whom he believed were also the ancestors of the Nazis, were gods and, having done so, it should then be possible to recreate a new race of Aryan 'godmen' through selective breeding. As for the breeding stock, this would consist of Himmler's highly selected SS men, all of whom must be at least five foot nine inches tall, and be able to prove their German ancestry back to the year 1750. This was entirely in keeping with Liebenfels' notion that

Gods and goddesses with hair like the sun, and with eyes like the blue sky, with rosy cheeks, with eternal health and eternal youth, they will sing the praises of their suffering breed mothers, as the women who created them.[18]

* * *

Himmler was clearly deluded, and architect and Nazi Party member Albert Speer for one, was in no doubt as to what he thought of Hitler's *Reichsführer* SS.

> Himmler … obviously was going his absurd way, which was compounded of beliefs about an original Germanic race, a brand of elitism, and an assortment of health food notions. The whole thing was beginning to assume far-fetched pseudo-religious forms.

And it was obvious that, even for Hitler, Himmler had gone a step too far, for Speer went on to say,

> Goebbels, with Hitler, took the lead in ridiculing these dreams of Himmler's, with Himmler himself adding to the comedy by his vanity and obsessiveness. When, for example, the Japanese presented him with a Samurai sword, he at once discovered kinships between Japanese and Teutonic cults and called upon scientists to help him trace these similarities to a racial common denominator.[19]

It is therefore hardly surprising that the Führer never visited Wewelsburg Castle, the epicentre of Himmler's activities, of which he was openly scornful.

> What nonsense! Here we have at last reached an age that has left all mysticism behind it, and now he wants to start all over again. We might just as well have stayed with the Church. At least it had tradition. To think that I may some day be turned into an SS saint! Can you imagine it? I would turn over in my grave …[20]

This remark, of course, confirms that Hitler had discarded Christianity – if indeed he had ever embraced it, which is doubtful. As for Himmler's archaeological excavations, he regarded them as an embarrassment.

> Why do we call the whole world's attention to the fact that we have no past? Isn't it enough that the Romans were erecting great buildings when our forefathers were still living in mud huts? Now Himmler is starting to dig up these villages of mud huts and enthusing over every potsherd [fragment of pottery] and stone axe he finds. All we prove by that is that we were still throwing stone hatchets and crouching around open fires, when Greece and Rome had already reached the higher state of culture. We really should do our best to keep quiet about this past. Instead, Himmler makes a great fuss about it all. The present day Romans must be having a laugh at these relegations.[21]

* * *

Despite all, Hitler was evidently prepared to tolerate the eccentric peregrinations of his *Reichsführer* SS, just so long as they remained harmless. The fact was, that the Führer had other, and more important fish to fry.

Notes

1. Hitler, op. cit., p. 109.
2. Ibid, p. 112.
3. Unger, op. cit., pp. 58–9.
4. Ibid, pp. 168–9.
5. *Secret History: The Nazi Expedition.*
6. *The SS: Himmler's Madness.*
7. Lumsden, *SS Regalia: A Collector's Guide to Third Reich Militaria*, p. 66.
8. *The SS: Himmler's Madness.*
9. *Nazis: The Occult Conspiracy.*
10. Barker, op. cit., p. 54.
11. Goodrick-Clarke, op. cit., p. 181.
12. Ibid, p. 182.
13. *The SS: Himmler's Madness.*
14. *Brewer's Dictionary of Phrase and Fable.*
15. *Nazis: The Occult Conspiracy.*
16. *Secret History: The Nazi Expedition.*
17. *Ostara*, I/37.
18. *Ostara*, I/21.
19. Speer, *Inside the Third Reich*, p. 183.
20. Ibid, p. 147.
21. Ibid, p. 148.

Chapter 16

Nazism in Practice: Echoes of *Ostara*

Having embraced the philosophy of arguably the most pernicious racist of all time, namely Jörg Lanz von Liebenfels, German leader, Hitler, would now proceed to put the latter's ideas into practice.

Germany and her Neighbours

With Hitler now in power, the question was, who would Germany choose as her allies, and who would she see as her enemies? An indication of this was given by him in *Mein Kampf*, written almost a decade previously, in 1924.

Referring to the period prior to the Great War, Hitler had

thought it would have been better if Germany had abandoned her senseless colonial policy and her naval policy, and had joined England in an alliance against Russia, therewith renouncing her weak, world policy for a determined European policy with the idea of acquiring new territory on the Continent.

And as regards the present time, 1924,

The Russia of today, deprived of its Germanic ruling class [a reference to the fact that since the days of Tsar Peter the Great 1672–1725, the princes of some of Germany's lesser reigning Houses, such as Hesse-Homburg, had served in the Russian administration][1] is not a possible ally in the struggle for German liberty …

From the purely military viewpoint, a Russo-German coalition, waging war against Western Europe, and probably against the whole world on that account, would be catastrophic for us [because] the struggle would have to be fought out, not on Russian, but on German territory …[2]

France, he described as

the mortal enemy of our nation [who] deprives us … by holding us in her grip and pitilessly robbing us of our strength. Therefore we must stop at no sacrifice in our effort to destroy the French striving towards hegemony over Europe.[3]

This was a reference to what Hitler considered to be the grossly unfair terms of the Treaty of Versailles. On the other hand, he considered 'England and Italy as the only countries with which it would be worth while for us [Germany] to strive to form a close alliance …'.[4] Regarding Italy's leader, Benito Mussolini, Hitler declared that he had 'conceived a profound admiration for the great man beyond the Alps, whose ardent love for his people inspired him not to bargain with Italy's internal enemies, but to use all possible ways and means in an effort to wipe them out'. What placed Mussolini 'in the ranks of the world's great' was 'his decision not to share Italy with the Marxists, but to redeem his country from Marxism by destroying internationalism [i.e., the spread of communism internationally]'.[5] 'The colossal Empire in the East [Russia],' said Hitler ominously, 'is ripe for dissolution.'[6] §

*   *   *

By February 1933, Hitler's National Socialists included no less than 400,000 SA (Storm Troopers) – their numbers would soon rise to 3 million – who would swear an oath of allegiance to their leader, Ernst Röhm, rather than to Hitler. The smaller SS, on the other hand, was a better disciplined force, commanded by Heinrich Himmler.

On the night of 27 February 1933 the German parliament building – Reichstag – was partially destroyed by fire. Hitler immediately announced that this was the result of a communist plot, and issued an emergency decree which President von Hindenburg countersigned, giving Hitler the authority to crush the communists. This decree also enabled Hitler to suppress newspapers, search premises without a warrant, and imprison people without trial, he being accountable only to Hindenburg himself. In fact, according to Hermann Rauschning, politician and President of the Danzig Senate until 1934, it was Hermann Göring 'who ordered the Reichstag building to be burnt at Hitler's command'.[7]

In a new election called by Hitler on 5 March 1933 the Nazis achieved 43.9 per cent of the vote. Together with the Nationalists, they were now able to form a majority in government, the communist deputies having been either arrested or forced underground.

The state opening of Parliament was on 21 March 1933, which Hitler proclaimed as a 'day of national unity'. Now came a torrent of propaganda, terror and intimidation, orchestrated by Joseph Goebbels. Storm Troopers began incarcerating so-called enemies of the state in concentration camps, the first being Oranienburg near Berlin. Another, Dachau, was opened near Munich. These so-called enemies included communists, social democrats, liberals, religious dissidents and Jews. After a year, most were released after suffering beatings and psychological torture. The first step had been taken to identify and isolate those whom Hitler's mentor, Lanz von Liebenfels, had already identified in *Ostara* as being enemies of the state.

Two days later, the passing of the Enabling Act granted Hitler's cabinet full legislative powers without its having to obtain the consent of the Reichstag. Now, all political parties other than the Nazis were forcibly disbanded and censorship was imposed.

In April 1933, Hermann Göring founded the Gestapo, the political police force of the Third Reich, which he based on the Prussian Secret State Police Force. May Day was proclaimed Labour Day by Hitler. However, the truth was that trade unions had no place in the German society which he envisaged. They would therefore be abolished. On 10 May students at universities throughout Germany lit bonfires to destroy tens of thousands of books which the Nazis considered to be 'un-German'. On 21 May a non-aggression pact was agreed between Britain, Italy, Germany, and France.

In the summer of 1933 the Nazis superimposed on the Federation of German Sovereign States, which had constituted the old Weimar Republic, regional Nazi Party leaders, *Gauleiters*, who received their instructions directly from Berlin. This was precisely the administrative structure advocated by Guido von List, with whose works, as previously stated, Hitler was familiar. A new, supreme People's Court was created against which there was no appeal, except to Hitler himself. This, too, was dominated by the Nazis. All political parties were abolished fully, apart from the National Socialist Party.

On 20 July 1933, Reichschancellor Franz von Papen, a Roman Catholic, made a treaty with the Vatican whereby it was agreed that if the Nazis refrained from interfering with the Church, then the Church, in turn, would not complain about the way in which the country was being run.

There now developed a power struggle between, on the one hand, Hitler, big business, the army, and Heinrich Himmler, head of the SS, and, on the other, Captain Ernst Röhm, head of the SA. Röhm desired that his Storm Troopers be integrated into the regular German army, but the army saw this as an attempt by him to take over the armed forces and become their minister. Hitler, however, realized that the expertise of the armed forces would be vital for the future battles in which he planned to engage. A deal was therefore struck: in return for Hitler eliminating Röhm, each and every member of the armed forces would undertake to swear this oath of allegiance to Hitler, 'I swear by God, this Holy Oath, to the Führer of the German Reich and the German people, Adolf Hitler.'[8]

Hitler now decided to stage his National Socialist (Nazi) Party Rallies in Nuremberg, instead of Weimar as hitherto, where vast complexes of stadia would be built for the purpose. The rallies would hereafter be held every September.

On 14 October 1933, Germany withdrew from the League of Nations and from the Geneva Disarmament Conference. Both were events of great significance in the light of what is now known about Hitler's warlike intentions. In the elections of 12 November the Nazis won 92 per cent of the seats, and the votes of those who dissented were declared invalid. By the end of the year unemployment had decreased by about 2 million.

In order to fund the government's contracts for armaments, estimated to be worth approximately 21 billion Deutschmarks, Hjalmar Schacht, President of the Reichsbank, founded the Metallurgical Research Company – MEFO – confining its bond issues in equal parts to Germany's four leading industrial companies: Krupp, Rheinstahl (steel), Gutehoffnungshutte (coal) and Siemens. As for Hitler, he did not trouble himself with the minutiae of economic detail.

I have never had a conference with Schacht to find out what means are at our disposal. I restricted myself to saying, 'This is what I require and this is what I must have.'

On 6 January 1934, in what later came to be seen as a supreme irony, the Nazis signed a non-aggression pact with Poland.

By the spring of 1934 the Hitler Youth and BDM movements were well established, with communal singing, night hiking, organized games, and parades and marches, all ostensibly intended to engender a new spirit of community and hope. Soon their numbers would rise to 3.5 million.

At the so-called Transfer Conference, convened in Berlin in April 1934, Schacht told Germany's foreign creditors that on 1 July the country would have to declare itself bankrupt unless they accepted more of Germany's exports.

In April, Himmler, Commander of the SS, took over from Göring both the control of the Gestapo, *Geheime Staatspolizei*, or State Secret Police, and the supervision of the concentration camps.

When it was reported that Ernst Röhm, head of the SA and its 3 million Storm Troopers, was planning a 'massive insurrection',[9] Hitler decided to make his move, taking personal charge of the operation in order to avoid any subsequent split in the Nazi Party. First, he persuaded Röhm to take a holiday. Then, on 30 June 1934 in an operation code-named *Hummingbird*, he employed his SS to imprison and summarily shoot leaders of the SA throughout Germany, eighty-five in all. This was the so-called 'Night of the Long Knives'. Hitler personally arrested Röhm, by bursting into his hotel room brandishing a pistol and screaming, 'You are a traitor!'

Röhm was imprisoned in Munich, but it was only after two days of intense pressure from Himmler that Hitler finally agreed to Röhm's execution by the SS. Röhm had previously been offered a pistol and given the opportunity to commit suicide, an offer which he declined. By then, dozens of SA leaders had been arrested, tortured and executed.

Hitler's SS was now given orders to crush all his opponents. They included Gustav von Kahr, who had put down Hitler's beer hall *Putsch* and who was murdered in the vicinity of Dachau concentration camp; General Kurt von Schleicher, the last Chancellor of the democratically elected Weimar Republic, who was likewise murdered, along with his wife. Gregor Strasser, an early rival of Hitler for the leadership of the Nazi Party, suffered the same fate and Karl Ernst, Head of the Berlin Storm Troopers, was murdered whilst on his honeymoon. The death toll ran into hundreds and possibly thousands.

Two weeks after Röhm's death, Hitler addressed the German parliament to tell its members that the Nazi Party had now been purged of these 'degenerate' homosexuals. For his action he received warm applause, even though thirteen of those killed in his purge of the SA had themselves been Members of Parliament. The SS now replaced the SA as the dominant force, its membership reaching a quarter of a million by 1939. Von Hindenburg and the army generals were both delighted and relieved.

In an effort to eradicate homosexuality from the SS, Himmler now required that all new recruits sign a statement saying that they understood that the practice of this would incur the death penalty. Nonetheless, some homosexuals were subsequently shot while others were dismissed from their posts or sent for counselling.[10]

According to army officer Ewald von Kleist, many people, including some army generals, were murdered without trial. Their deaths were announced in the newspapers which stated, quite openly, that the Government had been obliged to shoot each one on the grounds that it was an 'Emergency Case'.

Schacht was relieved when, on 1 July 1934, Britain offered Germany a moratorium on all debts, after which the United States followed suit. Instead, payments were to resume through bonds. By now Schacht had turned the economy round to such an extent that he was able to encourage fifty-one German banks, of which fifteen were still under Jewish management, to float a new, German Reichsbond, to be sold abroad at 4 per cent interest.[11]

On 27 July 1934, Hitler invited Schacht to be his economics minister, in addition to being President of the Reichsbank, an appointment which he took up on 2 August. German policy was now to pay for foreign goods with so-called 'blocked' German Deutschmarks, i.e., ones that could only be used in turn for the purchase of German goods. Germany soon found, however, that other countries were quick to retaliate with similar forms of financial self-protection. Czechoslovakia, for example, decided to cease trading with Germany altogether, thus depriving the 'Fatherland' of a major source of iron ore, machinery, coal, weapons, automobiles, and shoes.[12]

President von Hindenburg died on 2 August 1934 at the age of eighty-seven, after which the office of president was promptly abolished. Hitler would henceforth be known as Führer and Reichschancellor. On 18 September the Soviet Union was elected to membership of the League of Nations, a reflection of international concerns over Nazi Germany.

In 1935 Himmler was given overall charge of the SS into which the Gestapo had now been absorbed. When, on 2 October 1935, Mussolini, known as *Il Duce*, (The Leader), invaded Abyssinia, now Ethiopia, the Führer lent him his full support, the quid pro quo being that the Italian dictator would withdraw his protective hand from Austria, a target for Hitler's expansionist plans.

In 1936, Hitler's former acquaintance from Vienna, Reinhold Hanisch, committed his memories of Hitler to paper and attempted to find a publisher for his work. He was promptly arrested, charged by the Nazi regime, and imprisoned for tampering with, and falsifying, some watercolour paintings made by Hitler during their time together in the men's hostel. Hanisch, according to the official report, died in prison after a sudden attack of pleurisy which had lasted for three days.[13]

* * *

In order to guarantee the success of the Aryan race, it was necessary for as many Aryan babies to be born as possible. To this end, Heinrich Himmler, in December 1935, created an organization known as the *Lebensborn*, 'spring of life', which provided homes where unmarried German mothers could give birth to pure, Aryan children. He also encouraged the practice of eugenics (defined as: 'pertaining to race improvement by judicious mating ... [thereby] helping the better stock to prevail)'.[14] 'No longer shall it be left to chance that healthy people make the correct and successful choice of spouse,' he said, 'so help your own race as best you can and then you shall belong to the best race.'[15] Members of the SS were ordered to have at least four children. Whether this was in or out of wedlock did not matter, though bachelors were encouraged to marry. SS men who were childless were penalized by being paid less. This order was enshrined in writing but was to be kept secret. However, in the face of opposition from the SS, many of whose members were Roman Catholics, it was revoked on Hitler's command. These policies of *Lebensborn* and eugenics were a practical demonstration of the doctrine put forward by Liebenfels in *Ostara*.

Later, in 1941, Himmler would demand that any strong, healthy, blond orphans found in Poland were to be sent to the Reich for forcible adoption and Germanization. The children were separated into groups, for example: ultra-Aryan 'Group 1A' children were only allowed to be adopted by Nazi Party members who had a university degree. Eye colour and skull shape was meticulously measured, and checks were made of their general health. Finally, children not only from Poland, but also from Russia and the Ukraine were imported into Germany: over 200,000 of whom were adopted by German families.[16]

* * *

In 1936, Himmler was appointed Reichs Chief of Police. Now, in addition to the SS and the Gestapo, he commanded the SS's own security service, or *Sicherheitdienst* (the SD), the Criminal Police, and the ordinary uniformed police of town and country. In the same year, the SS created an autonomous combat element known as the *Waffen*, 'armed', SS. By now, two million girls, aged from fifteen to twenty-one, had joined the BDM, thereby dedicating themselves to 'comradeship, service, and physical fitness for motherhood'. On 7 March, Hitler repudiated the demilitarization clauses of the Treaties of Versailles and Locarno by marching his troops into the demilitarized Rhineland. As he had calculated, the Allies took no action.

That summer, Hitler's foreign affairs advisor, Joachim von Ribbentrop, was sent to Britain to replace German Ambassador Leopold von Hosch, who had died in London on 10 April. It was Ribbentrop who, in June 1935, had negotiated the Anglo-German Naval Agreement, whereby Britain would allow Germany to fix her naval tonnage at 35 per cent of the size of her own fleet, and would also concede a 45 per cent maximum for submarines. Now, Hitler hoped that Ribbentrop would bring the same techniques of persuasion to bear on Britain as he had done on his customers in his former life as a champagne salesman, with a view to creating a formal Anglo-German Alliance.

Ribbentrop's objective was to strike a bargain. As Germany did not control the seas, Hitler believed that it was not in Germany's interests to acquire overseas colonies. Therefore, he would agree not to interfere with Britain and her Empire, provided that Britain, in turn, gave him a free hand on the continent of Europe.

For Hitler, the opportunity for European adventurism arrived on 17 July 1936 when civil war broke out in Spain, a republic since 1931, between supporters of Spain's Second Republic (moderates, socialists, communists, and Catalan and Basque regionalists) on the one hand, and nationalist insurgents (monarchists, conservative Catholics, and *Falangists* or fascists), led by General Francisco Franco, on the other. The German leader assisted Franco by sending him tanks and technicians and also the Condor Legion of the Luftwaffe, the aircraft of which provided transport for Franco's forces. Meanwhile, Italy sent 75,000 troops to assist Franco, while Russia, for her part, sent supplies, but no troops, to support the Republic. Hitler now, as a prelude to his own forthcoming adventures in Europe, had the satisfaction of helping a fascist dictator overthrow a democratic, albeit corrupt, Spanish government, though the process would take almost three years.

The Olympic Games of 1936 took place in Berlin, where Hitler was aghast to see African-American sprinter, Jesse Owens, win a total of four gold medals. Meanwhile, only sixty kilometres from the city, slave labourers co-opted by the Nazis were demolishing the old Oranienberg concentration camp and replacing it with a new one, to be named Sachsenhausen. That September at the Party Rally, Hitler announced a new four-year plan which would be administered by Hermann Göring. In a programme of *autarky* (self-sufficiency), Germany would obtain her fuel, textiles, rubber and other industrial necessities, through reopening mineral and coal mines inside the Reich's borders, and through new technology.[17] Schacht, however, believed that the high cost of raw materials produced in this way would raise prices to such an extent that German products would become uncompetitive. However, it was not with world trade that Hitler and Göring were primarily interested, but rather aircraft, tanks and guns for their own particular agenda.

On 25 October 1936, Germany signed a treaty with Italy, thus cementing the Rome-Berlin Axis. Hitler would now give Italy a free hand in Africa and the Mediterranean, in exchange for being given a free hand in Central Europe himself. On 30 October, Ribbentrop submitted his credentials as German Ambassador to Great Britain, to the new king, Edward VIII. The new ambassador, however, was not regarded as a gentleman, and committed a serious faux pas by giving the King a Nazi salute. Such behaviour led to him being referred to by the British, not as Herr Ribbentrop but as 'Herr Brick-en-drop'. He, for his part, was anxious that King Edward, whom Germany saw as potentially a powerful ally, might be forced to abdicate on account of his love affair with Wallis Simpson, a twice-divorced woman.

Japan was under the same pressure as Germany, if not more so, to provide living space for her growing population, and to produce raw materials for her industries. On 25 November 1936, Germany and Japan signed the Anti-Comintern Pact

(*Comintern* being an acronym for Communist International), whereby both countries agreed to take steps to combat communism. The Pact also contained a secret protocol, whereby both parties agreed to refrain from making any political treaties with the Soviet Union.[18] Hitler made it clear that he would dearly have liked Britain to join also.

> Ribbentrop, bring me England into the Anti-Comintern Pact. That is my greatest wish! However, if all efforts come to nothing, well then I am prepared for war, though I'd regret it a lot, but if it has to be ... But I believe it would be a short war, and I'd offer generous terms to England, an honourable, mutually acceptable peace.[19]

On 30 January 1937, Hitler guaranteed the neutrality of Belgium and the Netherlands – a cynical act, bearing in mind what was to come. On 27 April the Spanish market town of Guernica, near Bilbao, which was of no military significance, was bombed by the Luftwaffe, an atrocity which cost approximately 1,000 lives.

On 10 March 1937, Hjalmar Schacht's presidency of the Reichsbank was renewed for another four years. However, it now became apparent that Schacht and Hermann Göring were not seeing eye-to-eye over the economy and, on 6 October, Schacht was summoned to the Berghof by Hitler in an attempt to iron out the difficulties. Interference from Göring was making life impossible, said Schacht, and he tendered his resignation as Minister of Economics. This came into effect on 26 November.

At a secret meeting in early November 1937, Hitler informed his generals that Germany must expand to survive, that its problems could only be solved by the use of force, and that Austria and Czechoslovakia were to be the first targets.[20] On 9 November, Japan invaded China.

On 4 February 1938, Joachim von Ribbentrop replaced Konstantin von Neurath as Germany's Foreign Minister, so putting an end to the Nazi-Conservative alliance. On the same day, Hitler dismissed two of his top military commanders, namely Defence Minister Field Marshal Werner von Blomberg and Commander-in-Chief of the German Army General Werner von Fritsch: both had voiced objections to his expansionist plans.

In January 1939 in a speech to the Reichstag, Hitler complained that

> Amongst the accusations which are directed against Germany in the so-called democracies is the charge that the National Socialist state is hostile to religion. In answer to that charge I should like to make before the German people the following declaration: '*No one in Germany has in the past been persecuted because of his religious views, nor will anyone in the future be so persecuted ...*'[21]

Germany's Catholic bishops, however, took a different view. For, two years earlier on 22 January 1937 they had complained, in a pastoral letter, of Nazi Party interference in the conduct of church affairs. German theologian and resistance figure Martin Niemoller, for example, who was arrested in 1937, spent a total of eight years in concentration camps and it is estimated that subsequently, as many as 4,000 priests, mainly German, were murdered by the Nazis.[22]

Within two years however, Hitler's rhetoric would change completely with statements like

> National socialism and religion cannot exist together ... The heaviest blow that ever struck humanity was the coming of Christianity. Bolshevism is Christianity's illegitimate child. Both are inventions of the Jew.[23] The reason why the ancient world was so pure, light and serene was that it knew nothing of the two great scourges: the pox and Christianity. [24]

'The Party,' said Hitler, 'must be an Order, that is what it has to be – an Order, the hierarchical order of a secular priesthood.'[25]

Surely here, Hitler had in mind the ritualistic and virulently racist Order of New Templars, founded by Liebenfels in 1907.

Notes

1. Vorres, *The Last Grand-Duchess*, p. 85.
2. Hitler, op. cit., pp. 361 & 363.
3. Ibid, p. 367.
4. Ibid, p. 366.
5. Ibid, p. 374.
6. Ibid, p. 361.
7. Rauschning, op. cit., p. 85.
8. *The Nazis: A Warning from History, Part 2.*
9. Weitz, op. cit., p. 165.
10. *The last Nazi Secret.*
11. Weitz, op. cit., p. 163.
12. Muhlen, *Schacht: Hitler's Magician*, p. 118.
13. Hanisch, *I was Hitler's Buddy*, 5 April 1939, pp. 239–42 (I); 12 April, pp. 270–72 (II); 19 April, 1939, pp. 297–300 (III).
14. *Chambers English Dictionary.*
15. *The SS: Himmler's Madness.*
16. Ibid.
17. Weitz, op. cit., p. 208.
18. Shirer, op. cit., p. 299.
19. Michalka, *Ribbentrop und die deutsche Weltpolitik, 1933–1940*, p. 155.
20. Toland, op. cit., p. 421.
21. Speech in Reichstag. 30 Jan. 1939.
22. Fourier, *Lexikon der Papiste.*
23. Trevor-Roper, op. cit., Speech, 11/12 July 1941.
24. Ibid, Speech, 19 October 1941.
25. Rauschning, op. cit., p. 237.

Chapter 17

Private Life and Family

The Berghof

From the summer of 1925, Hitler, now in his mid-thirties, and in receipt of royalties from the sales of his newly-published and highly successful book, *Mein Kampf*, enjoyed holidaying at the mountainside resort of Obersalzberg in the German province of Upper Bavaria. Below the resort was the small market village of Berchtesgaden. In July the following year he first rented and then purchased an alpine house there known as *Haus Wachenfeld*. After Hitler became Chancellor of Germany in 1933, this would be turned into a huge complex known as the Berghof.

Instrumental in effecting the transformation was Martin Bormann who, in 1935, extended the Berghof to create a building three storeys in height with thirty or so rooms, including conference room and terrace. It also contained a suite, reserved exclusively for his companion Eva Braun when she came to visit. Also, land was acquired in the vicinity, to make an estate occupying six square miles in area.

Hitler's routine, when at his Obersalzberg retreat, was to rise in late morning and, after luncheon, take a fifteen-minute afternoon walk to the nearby *Mooslahnerkopf* Teahouse. He neither smoked, drank, nor ate meat, affirms Hermann Rauschning.[1] He would select a different person each day to walk beside him; the remainder of the party – including Eva, and often her sister, Gretel, and some of her friends – staying behind at a respectful distance.

One of Hitler's absorbing pastimes was to study the plans – made by architect Albert Speer – for the new buildings which were to grace the Third Reich. Herbert Döhring, a member of Hitler's SS bodyguard from 1936 to 1943, states, tongue-in-cheek, that he spent more time doing this than governing the country! 'He always had his building plans in mind, even when he was travelling.'[2] They included the new Reichs Chancellery, which was built in 1938.

In the evenings Hitler would watch films, the choice of which demonstrated his affection and admiration for Britain and her Empire, which, according to Herbert Döhring, was unbounded. He would talk admiringly about 'this huge English Empire' and would wonder at how 'such a relatively small people could establish and manage something like this, and keep it in order'.[3] His favourite film was *The Lives of the Bengal Lancers* (1935), set in India, Britain's so-called 'Jewel in the Crown'. Hitler also loved to watch English romantic, comedy films such as *A Hopeless Case* (1939).

Paula Hitler

From the time of his mother's death in December 1908, Hitler went to live in Vienna, and Paula heard nothing from her brother until the early 1920s.

Alois Hitler

'During most of the 1930s, Alois kept a small inn in a Berlin suburb, but in 1937, basking in the reflected glory of his half-brother, he opened a new café-restaurant in Berlin's fashionable West End.'[4]

Angela Hitler

After the First World War, Angela, a widow since 1910, moved to Vienna and became manager of *Mensa Academia Judaica* – a boarding house for Jewish students and an astonishing fact, in view of what was to follow. Between 1908 and 1919, as with Paula, Hitler failed to maintain contact with her. In 1928, she and her daughter Geli moved to Obersalzberg where she became Hitler's housekeeper. She was subsequently made manager of the household at the Berghof. However, when Eva Braun became virtually a full-time resident there in 1936, Angela found her presence irritating, so she moved out and relocated to Dresden. In that year, she married German architect Professor Martin Hammitzsch.

Eva Braun and her 'Home Movies'

A former photographer's assistant, Eva was adept with a movie camera, and it is thanks to her that a great deal of colour film, albeit silent, depicting the life of Hitler and of his inner circle at the Berghof, exists for posterity. Sceptics will argue that Eva's filming is stage-managed, and there is no doubt that, for most of the time, Hitler is aware that he is being filmed. On the other hand, neither he nor Eva would ever have dreamt that the footage would be seen by the outside world.

Hitler always appears smartly dressed, either in military uniform, or in suit and tie. He is courteous and attentive to the wives of his colleagues, and holds earnest conversations with their menfolk. Although the films are silent, it has recently been possible to decipher what he is saying with the aid of computer technology. As for their children, he is content to take their hands and take them for a promenade around the Berghof's extensive terrace, talk animatedly to them, and sometimes even embrace them. He clearly loves his three German shepherd dogs, and in one clip is to be seen kissing one of them on its head. Now, for once, what his sister described as his 'morbid mask'[5] of a face slowly softens into the ghost of a smile.

The more discerning observer, however, will realize from the film that this is not the whole story. This man is overly formal – even to the extent of giving a military-style salute to the children of his former junior school! He is ill at ease, with mouth invariably turned down at the edges and hands clasped together, sometimes in front of his body but more often behind – the attitude of one who is striving desperately to exercise self control. He is defensive, with cap pulled well down over his forehead, and arms frequently folded in front of him. He is part of the group, and yet the tense atmosphere which he generates indicates that he is not part of it. Often he stands alone, content to stare at the distant view. It is particularly noticeable how, in the Führer's absence, the atmosphere rapidly improves and everyone, including the Nazi wives who congregate together, become jolly again.

Even the dogs are naturally playful and exuberant again for in their master's presence they crouch down, terrified and submissive with ears held back, and when he beckons them, they wriggle towards him on their bellies, knowing that if they misbehave he will whip them savagely. For this is a man whom they dare not cross, a person who likes to be in complete control.

Paradoxically, it is at his Nazi Party rallies, rather than at the Berghof that, like an exploding volcano, all Hitler's inhibitions release themselves as he rants and raves, shouts and snarls, and gesticulates wildly and aggressively, as his normally mask-like face contorts itself with hatred.

Notes
1. Rauschning, op. cit., p. 66.
2. *The Nazis: A Warning from History, Part 3.*
3. Ibid.
4. Unger, op. cit., pp. 11–12.
5. Ibid, p. 154.

Chapter 18

William Patrick Hitler

William Patrick Hitler, son of Bridget and Alois and nephew of the Führer, was probably the only person in the world whom Hitler feared, for reasons which will soon become clear. Not only that, but when William confronted his uncle it was he who came off best.

In August 1929 the eighteen-year-old William, who was then working for an engineering company in London, spent a two-week vacation in Germany, where he met with his father Alois, who since 1916 had been remarried, to Hedwig, in Berlin. On a subsequent visit to his father that same summer, the two attended the National Socialist Party Congress in Nuremberg.[1] In 1930, William paid a second visit to Germany where he was introduced to Hitler, his uncle, for the first time.

In the same year, 1930, Bridget received a telegram from Angela Hitler, informing her that Angela's brother, Alois, Bridget's former husband and William's father, was dying. In fact, Alois was perfectly fit and well, and this was a ruse, perpetrated by Hitler, to lure William back to Germany.

Hitler was furious with William who had been giving interviews to the Press, as a result of which the New York office of Hearst Newspapers had made a telephone call to the Führer, asking if he had a nephew in London who 'was an authority on the Hitler family'. Hitler told William that,

> My personal affairs are being discussed. Anyone can say who I am, where I was born, what my family does for a living. They mustn't learn about this stupid bigamy [i.e., that committed by Alois]. I can't have it. No one must drag my private affairs into the newspapers. I'm being attacked from every side. I have to stand before them [presumably the Party and the Press] without the slightest stain, the slightest blemish. The shadow of a suspicion would be enough to ruin me.[2]

But there was something else which terrified Hitler even more. A hatred for the Jews was a cornerstone of his philosophy. If an investigative journalist were to discover the presence of a Jew in his family tree (no evidence has ever been uncovered that this was the case), then this would be catastrophic for his standing as the leader of his country.

William, until now, did not know that his father, Alois, and his uncle, Hitler, were the offspring of the same father – Alois senior. And when he discovered the fact it was his turn to be furious, because Hitler had denied the fact that he, William, was his nephew.

In October 1933, William left England for Germany where he took up a position in a Berlin department store. He was subsequently summoned to meet Hitler, now Chancellor of Germany, who gave him the sum of 500 Deutschmarks until he could find a better position. This he did, finding employment at Berlin's *Reichskreditbank* for a period of ten months, before commencing work with the Opel motor car company.

In June 1934, during the infamous 'Blood Purge', William was arrested by the authorities and released only after an appeal to the British Consulate, he being a British citizen. William was dissatisfied with the salary offered to him at the bank and, on 29 November, he wrote to Hitler asking permission to return to England, where, he said, he intended to make a statement to the English Press.[3] Hitler declined, saying, 'I don't believe it would be desirable for you to go just now'.[4] In other words, William was a virtual prisoner in Germany. Nevertheless, the Führer did arrange for William's salary to be doubled.[5]

In 1937, Bridget travelled to Germany, where she met with Hitler at the Berghof, and then to Salzburg, Austria, where she met with Hitler's sister, Paula. When she expressed her concern to Paula about the safety of her son William, Paula replied,

Don't worry, I'll make Adolf understand that your son is under my protection. If any harm comes to him, I have enough proof of the things I say that if I wanted to make them public it would ruin Adolf.

'But what would happen if …?' asked Bridget. 'What would happen if Adolf should get me into his power?' said Paula, finishing the sentence for her,

You don't have to think about it. I'm taking care of myself, and so are the Vienna police. Still it is better to be prepared for anything when you are fighting a madman.[6]

Paula was not the first person to describe her brother as 'a madman', nor would she be the last.

In 1938, Hitler summoned William to the Berghof and demanded that he relinquish his British nationality and become a German citizen. William declined to do so. He managed to escape by subterfuge to England when, according to his mother, he presented her with the key to

our safe-deposit box at the [English] bank, in which we locked all our documents, letters and information we had gleaned on the Hitler family and their activities.[7]

To Bridget's horror, William announced his intention of returning to Germany which he did for reasons which she did not find altogether convincing. She subsequently became more and more concerned about him until finally, in desperation, she made contact with an intermediary, whom she calls 'Fenton', to whom she made an offer. She would hand over all the documents in the bank, provided that her son was permitted to return to England. Bridget did not complete her diary of subsequent events, but the outcome was that, in 1938, William did return to England and, in March 1939, he and his mother emigrated to the USA.

There can be little doubt that, had it not been for Hitler's fear that either William or Bridget would reveal some unpalatable truth about his ancestry, Hitler would have had his nephew William eliminated.

Notes
1. Unger, op. cit., pp. 52 & 55.
2. Ibid, pp. 64–7.
3. Gardner, op. cit., pp. 128–9.
4. Ibid, p. 130.
5. Unger, op. cit., p. 98.
6. Ibid, pp. 173–4.
7. Ibid, p. 185.

Chapter 19

Hitler's Relationship with Women

The Office of Strategic Services (OSS) was a US secret intelligence organization headed by General 'Wild Bill' Donovan, a veteran of the Great War. In 1943, Donovan asked psychoanalyst Dr Walter C. Langer, of Harvard University, for his help in attempting to understand the workings of Hitler's mind. To this end, Langer interviewed refugees, émigrés, and high-ranking defectors from Nazi Germany, no less than 269 people in all, in order to establish a psychological profile of Hitler. The outcome, particularly in relation to Hitler's relationship with women, would surprise everybody.

Renate Müller
One interviewee was American film-director Arnold Zeissler who had made moving pictures in Germany in the early 1930s. Zeissler told Langer that Hitler had often requested that actresses be sent to him at the Reichs Chancellery. Hitler would then regale them with stories of mediaeval torture methods. One, Renate Müller, became a firm favourite of his.

Langer, in his report to Donovan, states that Zeissler described to him how, one morning, he (Zeissler) found Müller, who had spent the previous evening with the Führer, in a troubled state. She

> had been sure that he [Hitler] was going to have [sexual] intercourse with her; that they had both undressed and were apparently getting ready for bed when Hitler fell on the floor and begged her to kick him. She demurred, but he pleaded with her and condemned himself as unworthy, heaped all kinds of accusations on his own head, and just grovelled in an agonizing manner. The scene became intolerable to her, and she finally acceded to his wishes and kicked him. This excited him greatly, and he begged for more and more, always saying that it was even better than he deserved and that he was not worthy to be in the same room with her. He became more and more excited.[1]

Hitler then, allegedly, masturbated in front of her, and then thanked her.[2] Needless to say, this, for a woman was a personal insult of devastating proportions!

On 1 October 1937, Müller's body was found in the courtyard of a Berlin clinic, beneath a window from which she had apparently jumped to her death.

Geli Raubal

Ernst Hanfstaengl was a political and personal confidant of Hitler who also entertained him by playing the pianoforte. After a power struggle with Goebbels, however, he fell from grace and, in 1937, in fear of his life, he fled Germany and went to Virginia, USA, where he offered his services to Allied intelligence. In the spring of 1943, Langer visited Hanfstaengl and talked to him at length. 'Hitler is shy when trying to win a woman's affection,' Hanfstaengl told Langer. His favourite phrase is, 'If you go to a woman, don't forget your whip.' Hitler was in the habit of carrying a riding whip – as his father had done before him.[3] Photographs of him attest to this fact, and show that the whip was about three feet long and therefore capable of doing serious damage. Then, they discussed Hitler's affair with his half-niece, Geli Raubal.

Geli, whose full name was Angelika Maria, was the daughter of Hitler's half-sister Angela and Leo Raubal, an official in the tax bureau in Linz, who had died in 1910. Geli spent her childhood in a small village in Austria and, according to her school-friend Anna Gruebl, she was blonde, friendly and beautiful. She was also a fine sportswoman and an excellent swimmer. In 1928, Hitler invited the widowed Angela to be housekeeper at his home, *Haus Wachenfeld*, in the Obersalzberg. She accepted and duly arrived, bringing her two daughters, Elfriede and Geli. The latter, who was then aged twenty, subsequently enrolled as a medical student at the University of Munich.

Ernst Hanfstaengl suggested to Langer that Hitler probably beat Geli with his riding whip and derived sadistic pleasure from it.[4] When Geli fell in love with Hitler's chauffeur, Emil Maurice, Hitler was furious and forbade the couple to meet, except in his company. From then on Hitler and Geli became almost inseparable, Hitler persuading her to abandon her medical studies in favour of becoming a singer.[5]

Otto Strasser was another high-ranking Nazi defector to be interviewed by Langer. He told Langer that, by 1931, Hitler's relationship with Geli had become obsessional. Geli herself told Strasser that Hitler would make her undress, and that he would lie down on the floor. Then she would have to squat down over his face, where he would examine her at close range and this would make him very excited. When the excitement reached its peak, he demanded that she urinate on him, and that gave him his sexual pleasure.* The whole performance was extremely disgusting to her.[6]

Hanfstaengl also told Langer about a scandal that had been concealed in 1930 when the treasurer of the Nazi Party had been forced to buy someone off for trying to blackmail Hitler. That person had come into possession of a folio of

---

* Urophilia is defined as deriving sexual pleasure from urine and urination, and there is currently no consensus of opinion as to the origin of this condition. It is one of a group of unconventional forms of sexual behaviour known as paraphilias.

pornographic drawings which Hitler had made: they were 'depraved, intimate sketches of Geli Raubal with every anatomical detail'.

In the State Archives of Munich, capital city of Bavaria, is the suicide register for 1931. It shows that, in that year, 334 citizens took their own lives, one of these being Hitler's niece Geli. An account of the circumstances of Geli's death, which has been the subject of speculation ever since it occurred, is given by Hitler's half-brother Alois's former wife Bridget.[7] According to her, on 17 September 1931, Hitler was at his Munich apartment – where he had installed Geli – having dinner with her and her mother Angela, his half-sister. When Geli told her uncle that she wished to go to Vienna and he asked her why, she replied, 'I want to see Aunt Paula.' Hitler did not believe her. 'It is to see that filthy Jew, the one who claims to be a singing teacher. Is that it?' But Geli insisted, saying, 'I have to go to Vienna, Uncle Alf [Adolf] because I am going to have a baby.'

That evening, after Angela had left for Berchtesgaden, the housekeeper at the apartment, Josephine Bauer, heard shouting and Geli threatening to shoot herself. Bauer then 'claimed to have heard the swish of a whip and Geli began to scream ... she was sure Adolf was beating Geli'. Just before Hitler left, Geli said, 'Uncle Alf [Adolf], I ask you once more. Will you let me go to Vienna?' And again the answer was no.

Next morning, when Bauer arrived at Geli's apartment it was 'full of men.' They told her that Geli was dying. Having received the news Hitler returned first, followed by Geli's mother, Angela, who was prevented from seeing her daughter. 'Geli lived for some hours more. Only Adolf and Dr Brandt remained with the dying girl.' Angela herself was not allowed to see her dying daughter. Finally, Adolf emerged to say, 'She's dead, she's dead and I am her murderer.'[8] Whereupon Göring, who was also present, remonstrated with Hitler and urged him to tell 'Frau Raubel [Geli's mother, Angela] the truth, that Geli committed suicide'.

According to Bridget, however, Hitler's sister Paula was convinced that her brother, who feared a scandal in the family, had murdered Geli. Paula also believed that the 'fiction' of Geli's pregnancy was 'circulated by Göring to establish a possible motive for suicide'.[9]

Mimi Reiter and others
Not only did Geli Raubal and Renate Müller, female acquaintances of Hitler, come to an untimely end but, for example, in 1926, eighteen-year-old Mimi Reiter, his first acknowledged girlfriend, almost succeeded in hanging herself. And two other women alleged that Hitler had made attempts on their lives.

Unity Valkyrie Mitford
Unity, the daughter of Lord Redesdale, was an English socialite. Her sister was Diana, who in 1936, married British politician and founder of the British Union of Fascists (BUF) Sir Oswald Mosley. Both Unity and Diana joined the BUF.

In 1933, the two sisters travelled to Germany. They visited the Brown House, the Nazi Party's new and impressive headquarters in Munich, and attended the first

Nuremberg Party Rally of the Nazi era. Subsequently, Unity became determined to meet Hitler in person and, having discovered that he was in the habit of dining, when in Munich, in the *Osteria Bavaria* restaurant, she waited for him here, day after day, until finally she was successful.

In August 1936, the Olympic Games, held in Berlin, were attended by both Diana and Unity, who were accommodated by the Goebbels family at their nearby country house just outside Berlin. Hitler called Unity by her middle name, 'Valkyrie' (a goddess of Scandinavian mythology), and referred to her as his 'ideal of the Germanic woman'.[10] Both sisters were tall and blonde. Diana, he described as an 'angel'. The Führer was equally impressed that their grandfather, Baron Redesdale, was a devotee of the author and diplomat Houston Stewart Chamberlain, whom he himself admired enormously. And he was gratified to learn that their father, Lord Redesdale, was a friend of the family of the late German composer, Richard Wagner, someone to whom he was equally devoted.

In September 1936, the sisters again attended the Nuremberg Party Rally, as they did the following year, this time accompanied by their brother Tom. In August 1938, Unity became seriously ill with pneumonia whilst attending the annual Bayreuth Festival, where the operas of Richard Wagner were performed, as Hitler's guest. He responded by sending her flowers.

August 1939 found the sisters again at the Bayreuth Festival as Hitler's guests where they socialized with the Wagner family and other Nazi leaders. On the final day, 2 August, Hitler and the sisters attended a performance of Wagner's *Gotterdammerung (Twilight* – or ultimate defeat by evil – *of the Gods'.*) To Diana this was a bad omen. She wrote,

> Never had the glorious music seemed so doom laden. I had a strong feeling … that I should never see Hitler again, that the whole world was crumbling, that the future held only tragedy and war.[11]

As for Unity, she declared that 'if there is war between England and Germany, I'm going to go and shoot myself'.[12] And on 3 September 1939, two days after war did break out, Unity handed over an envelope to Adolf Wagner, *Gauleiter* of Munich. It contained her Nazi Party badge, a signed photograph of Hitler, and a letter from herself to the Führer. Then, in the *Englische Garten* (English Garden), she shot herself in the temple with a small, automatic pistol. With the bullet lodged in her brain she was taken to hospital in Munich – still alive. Hitler visited her on several occasions and, when her speech returned after six weeks, the Führer gave her the option of staying in Germany or going back to Britain. She chose the latter. She died, as a result of her injuries, on 28 May 1948 aged thirty-three.

Eva Braun

Born in Munich in 1912, Eva was twenty-three years younger than the Führer and he first met her in early October 1929 when she was employed as receptionist and model at the studio of his personal photographer, Heinrich Hoffmann. By all accounts, she was a fun-loving person who loved parties and dances.[13] She was also fond of swimming, skiing and cycling. However, as with Hitler's other female relationships, this one was equally problematical.

In November 1932, having been ignored for weeks on end by Hitler, Eva shot herself in the neck but sustained no serious injury. On 28 May 1935 she made another suicide attempt, this time by taking an overdose of tablets. According to Eva,

> He has so often told me that he is madly in love with me, but what does that mean when I haven't had a good word from him in three months?

Hitler, for his part, described Eva as 'cute, cuddly, and naïve'. But as far as marriage was concerned, it was out of the question. 'I am married to Germany,' he said.

From 1936, Eva resided with Hitler at the Berghof. Here, she was known as Fräulein Braun, and portrayed by the Führer as one of his many secretaries.

'Home movie' cinematographic films, taken by Eva and others, probably with her camera, reveal that on the occasions when he and she are in one another's company, rather than showing her any demonstrable signs of affection, he is usually seen with his arms folded, and often with his back to her. Even when he speaks to her he usually stands aloof, with hands held behind his back. For Eva, her dog and her rabbit gave her more affection than he did; or so it seemed.

According to Hitler's telephone operator, Rochus Misch, although at the Berghof Hitler and Eva had separate accommodation, their rooms were linked by a passageway. Nonetheless, Herbert Döhring, Administrator of the Berghof and married to Hitler's personal cook, Anna, was certain that their relationship was not of a sexual nature. He recalled that,

> My wife … often did Hitler's washing, and the first thing she always did was to check if there had been any sexual activity. But there was never any evidence. My wife checked the sheets, but there were no signs of any sexual activity, none.

This fact, he said, was confirmed by the other servants.[14]

Eva's cousin, Gertraud Weisker, described Eva as

> a really depressed person. She had to cover up her depression all the time by doing sport, or buying new clothes. She was trying to distract herself from things that depressed her. She could not concentrate on anything either …[15]

There is no doubt, therefore, that as a result of her unfulfilled relationship with Hitler, Eva suffered considerably. 'I'm just a prisoner in a golden cage,' said she, pathetically.

Notes

1. Langer, op. cit., p. 171.
2. *Sex and the Swastika: The Making of Adolf Hitler.*

3. Olden, *Hitler the Pawn*, p. 235.
4. *Sex and the Swastika: The Making of Adolf Hitler.*
5. *Sex and the Swastika: The Making of Adolf Hitler.*
6. Ibid.
7. Bridget was told the story by her son, William, who learned it from Hedwig, who learned it from Geli's housekeeper, Josephine Bauer. In Unger, op. cit., pp. 75–6.
8. Unger, op. cit., pp. 75–6.
9. Ibid, pp. 172–3.
10. *Hitler's Women.*
11. Dalley, *Diana Mosley: A Life*, p. 236.
12. *Betrayal: Oswald Mosley, the English Führer.*
13. *Eva Braun.*
14. Ibid.
15. *Hitler's Women.*

Chapter 20

Lebensraum

In 1924, Hitler wrote in *Mein Kampf,*

> The annual increase of population in Germany amounts to almost 900,000 souls.
> The difficulties of providing for this army of new citizens must grow from year
> to year and must finally lead to a catastrophe, unless ways and means are found
> which will forestall the danger of misery and hunger.[1]

He decided therefore, that in order to create more living space –*Lebensraum* –
Germany needed to expand her frontiers. He had considered another alternative,
which was to artificially restrict the number of births – following the French
example – but had rejected this on the grounds that such a policy 'robs the nation
of its future'.[2]

* * *

Swedish Professor Rudolf Kjellen (1864–1922) was the first person to use the term
'geopolitics', which is concerned with the relationship between the geographical
morphology of a particular country and its politics.

Friedrich Ratzel (1844–1904) was a graduate of Heidelberg University who, in
1880, was appointed Professor of Geography at Munich's Technical High School.
He became particularly interested in the reasons why human populations tend to
become distributed in a particular way, influenced as they were by the physical
topography of the areas in which they found themselves – mountains, lakes etc – as
well as by religion, language and ethnicity.

It was Ratzel who, in 1897 in his work *Politische Geographie*, developed the
concept of *Lebensraum*. Whereas Charles Darwin's *Theory of Evolution by Natural
Selection* referred to living organisms, Ratzel, for his part, regarded the nation as a
living thing, and subject to the same Darwinist pressures as living creatures in its
quest for survival: hence the expression 'social Darwinism'. Each nation had a
dynamic of its own: it was born, it grew and matured, but it could also die. If it were
to survive, it would require the land and space to do so.

Ratzel believed, therefore, that it was natural for the state to seek to increase its
size, and inevitable that, if the state's neighbours were weak, a strong state would

expand at their expense. However, in order to achieve this, he was in favour of colonization rather than piecemeal takeovers, such as the Nazis were shortly to inflict on their neighbours.[3]

As for 'racism', Ratzel was opposed to it, being quick to point out the *advantages* of the admixing of people of different origins, and the extra vitality which this would bring as exemplified by countries such as the USA. He also believed that what moulded a nation was its people's relationship with the land and the space it occupied, rather than genetic factors.

As always, however, it was Liebenfels' *Ostara* which was Hitler's 'Bible', and the Führer's forthcoming invasions of the territories of his neighbours were entirely in accordance with the mad monk's philosophy. Said Liebenfels, as already mentioned, 'The evil must always be under the control of the good, as must the lesser always be under the control of the higher,' and he referred to 'the crushing and destruction of the primitive and inferior human beings ...'

*   *   *

It was Hitler's intention to implement the policy of *Lebensraum* and thereby acquire more territories in the east. First, however, his homeland, Austria, must be incorporated into the Fatherland. Even though he was by birth an Austrian, he always harked back to the time when Austria was part of the German Empire; hence, his choosing to champion the cause of a greater German Reich.

Austria

Prior to the *Anschluss*, the incorporation by Hitler of Austria into Germany, Austrian Nazis, funded by the SS, conducted a campaign of terror directed at such strategic targets as railways and power stations.

When Engelbert Dollfuss became Chancellor of Austria in 1932 he was faced with having to deal with violence between the socialists and the Nazis. He responded by raising a private army and ruling as a dictator. He therefore deprived himself of the support of those who might later have supported him against the Nazis.

On 25 July 1934 in a *Putsch* code-named Operation *Summer Festival*, a force of 150 Austrian Nazis, attired in the uniforms of the Austrian army, forced their way into the Austrian Chancellery and shot Chancellor Dollfuss to death. They then announced, over the radio, that the Chancellor had 'resigned'. Meanwhile, back in Berlin, the German News Bureau (DNB) declared, 'The inevitable has happened. The German people in Austria have risen against their oppressors, gaolers, and torturers.'[4] Despite this, however, the *Putsch* was quelled.

In 1935 when Mussolini invaded Abyssinia, Hitler gave the Italian dictator his tacit support. Now, in return, Mussolini would himself turn a blind eye to Hitler's annexation of Austria.

The French hoped to contain Germany in the east by forming an anti-Nazi bloc to include Poland, the Soviet Union and Czechoslovakia. To this end, on 2 May

1935, France and the Soviet Union signed a mutual assistance pact. Hitler, however, at a conference with his military chiefs on 5 November 1937, declared that his first objective was to seize Czechoslovakia and Austria as a means of securing his eastern and southern flanks. Not only would this ensure abundant food supplies for the Reich, but it would also mean 'shorter and better frontiers' and 'the freeing of forces for other purposes'.[5]

On 11 February 1938, Austrian Chancellor Kurt von Schuschnigg, who had replaced the murdered Dollfuss, travelled to the Berghof to meet Hitler who warned him that 'Perhaps you will wake up one morning in Vienna to find us [the Germans] there – just like a spring storm'. However, the Führer 'would very much like to save Austria from such a fate because such an action would mean blood'.[6] When Schuschnigg protested that such an invasion of his country would probably lead to war, Hitler declared that in his opinion, nobody – neither Italy, England, nor France – would lift a finger to save Austria. Then Ribbentrop showed Schuschnigg a prepared draft agreement: Germany would support Austria's sovereignty provided that all Austrian National Socialists, including those who had been imprisoned for the assassination of the former Chancellor Dollfuss, were set free, and all those National Socialist officials who had been dismissed were reinstated. Furthermore, Artur von Seyss-Inquart, leader of Austria's Pan-German faction, was to be appointed Minister of the Interior with complete control of the nation's police forces; another Austrian Nazi was to be made the new Minister of Defence. When Schusschnigg refused to sign what was in effect an ultimatum, Hitler sent for General Keitel, Chief of the High Command of the German armed forces. Faced with such intimidation, Schuschnigg gave way.

However, Hitler was still not content. On 20 February, in a speech to the Reichstag, he accused Austria of mistreating its 'German minority'. It was

> intolerable for a self-conscious world power to know that at its side are co-racials, who are subjected to continuous suffering because of their sympathy and unity with the whole German race and its ideology.[7]

This was seen by the Austrian Nazis as a green light for them to commence demonstrations throughout the country.

Hitler now made further demands on Schusschnigg: a Nazi was to be appointed as Minister of Economics; the ban on the Nazi newspaper *Der Volkischer Beobachter* was to be lifted, and within three weeks National Socialism was to be recognized and legalized in Austria. By this time there was turmoil throughout the country with frequent clashes between the Nazis and the State Police. Schuschnigg responded by declaring that a plebiscite would be held whereby the nation would be asked the question: 'Are you in favour of a free and German, independent and social, a Christian and united Austria?' This was the last thing that Hitler wanted, and it forced his hand. 'I am now determined to restore law and order in my homeland and enable the people to decide their own fate, according to their judgement, in an unmistakeable, clear and open manner,' he wrote, in a letter to

Mussolini.[8] On 11 March 1938, Schuschnigg resigned as Chancellor of Austria, and in the Austrian elections held on 9 April 1938, 99.02 per cent of the population voted in favour of the union of Austria with Germany.

On 12 March 1938, Hitler issued a proclamation.

> Since early this morning, soldiers of the German armed forces have been marching across the Austro-German frontiers. Mechanized troops and infantry, German airplanes in the blue sky, summoned by the new Nationalist Socialist Government in Vienna, are the guarantors [that] the Austrian nation shall, at an early date, be given the opportunity to decide its own future by a genuine plebiscite.[9]

In the event, the Nazis encountered no resistance. Mussolini telegrammed to Hitler, 'I congratulate you on the way you have solved the Austrian problem.'[10]

On the same day, Hitler crossed the border at his birthplace, Braunau am Inn (Inn river), for a triumphal procession into Austria which included a visit to Linz, his former home town. Dr Eduard Bloch, who had not seen Hitler for thirty years, remembers the Führer's motorcade passing along the street beneath the windows of his consulting rooms, the very rooms where 'he [Hitler] had gone as a boy to have his minor ailments attended to'.[11]

At the time of the *Anschluss* there were, according to Dr Bloch, 700 Jews residing in Linz. The 'homes, shops and offices of all these people were marked with the yellow, paper banners, now visible throughout Germany – JUDE [JEW].' However, after the evacuation order there were but seven members of this race left in Linz. (This referred to the expulsion of Jews from the city to the armaments factories, to be used as forced labour, or to concentration camps.)

Now, after thirty-seven years of active work, Dr Bloch's practice was at an end. He would, however, receive favourable treatment at the hands of the Nazis, but only, presumably, because of his previous connections with Hitler. Despite his hatred for the Jews, the Führer was apparently unable to banish from his mind the previous kind and devoted attentions of the good doctor to his mother and his family. Bloch believes that he was the only Jew in all of Austria who was allowed to keep his passport. He was 'even given a ration card for clothes – something generally denied Jews'. Finally, he was permitted to leave Linz for America. He wrote,

> It would be impossible for me to take my savings with me. But the Gestapo had one more favour for me. I was to be allowed to take 16 Marks from the country, instead of the customary 10![12]

* * *

Referring to Linz, Hitler said,

If Providence once called me forth from this town to lead the Reich, then it must have given me a mission. That mission can only have been to restore my dear homeland to the German Reich.[13]* This country and this people are not entering the Reich in a humiliating role. I myself am leading you there.

With the occupation of Austria, Hitler secured 60 million pounds of gold, and access to the Erzberg, a mountain rich in iron ore. The new Reich now contained over eighty million citizens (of whom, by this time, nine million had joined the Hitler Youth Movement). In April 1938, Britain formally recognized Italian sovereignty over Abyssinia, yet another milestone on the road of appeasement by her of the Axis powers.

Czechoslovakia

Three million Germans lived in the adjacent Sudeten region of Czechoslovakia, a country that was to be Hitler's next target.

I would rather have the war when I'm 50, than when I'm 55 or 60. Ahead of us is the last problem which must and will be solved. [he followed this up with the most notorious lie of all] *It (the Sudetenland) is the last territorial demand I have in Europe ...*[14]

For three years prior to 1938, Hitler had been secretly supporting the Sudeten Nazi Party of Konrad Henlein whom, in March 1938, he named as his personal representative.

Having discussed the invasion of Czechoslovakia with Mussolini, Hitler, on 19/20 May, began mobilizing his troops on the Czech borders. This prompted Czech President Edvard Beneš to order a 'partial mobilization' of his own forces, which promptly moved in to protect the Sudetenland. On 28 May, Hitler told his military leaders, 'It is my unshakeable will to wipe Czechoslovakia off the map ...'[15] This would eliminate any threat which Czechoslovakia might be to the rear, when Hitler's forces made their drive to the east to implement his policy of *Lebensraum*.

Just as he had done previously in Austria, Hitler now portrayed the German Czechs as an oppressed minority, and gave vent to his feelings in a speech he made on 12 September 1938 at the Nuremberg Rally. 'The Germans in Czechoslovakia are neither defenceless, nor are they deserted, and people should take notice of that fact.'[16] True to form, the Sudeten Germans took this as a signal to commence demonstrations and, in the ensuing mêlée, the death toll quickly rose to twenty-one. The Sudeten Germans now went on strike and refused to pay their taxes,

---

* By this, he was presumably referring to the First Reich, or Holy Roman Empire (AD 800–1806). The Second Reich referred to the unified post-1871 Germany, and the Third Reich to the enlarged Germany envisaged by Hitler.

whereupon the Czech government declared martial law and further lives were lost as it continued, forcibly, to put down the rebellion.

On 15 September 1938, British Prime Minister, Neville Chamberlain, went to Germany for a meeting with Hitler at the Berghof: now aged sixty-nine, this was the first time he had flown in an aircraft. After a three-hour discussion, Hitler agreed to give Chamberlain time to consult with his colleagues back in England over the Sudeten question. On 18 September, Premier Édouard Daladier, who was visiting England as head of a French delegation, agreed with Chamberlain that 'friendly pressure' might persuade the Czechs to surrender some portions of Sudeten territory to Germany.[17]

Czech President Beneš, having been informed of the Anglo–French decision, was now assured by Moscow that the Soviets would support Czechoslovakia in the event of an attack by Hitler. Despite this, however, Beneš received an ultimatum from Britain's Foreign Secretary, Lord Halifax, to the effect that he must accept the proposal 'without reserve and without further delay, failing which His Majesty's Government will take no further interest in the fate of the country [i.e., Czechoslovakia]'.[18] Beneš had, therefore, no choice but to agree.

On 21 September 1938, Chamberlain again left for Germany, this time to meet Hitler at Bad Godesberg on the Rhine river. To his surprise, however, Hitler told him, 'I am exceedingly sorry Mr Chamberlain, but I can no longer discuss these matters. This solution [to the Sudeten question], after the developments of the last few days, is no longer practicable'. He then demanded that the British and French accept his decision to occupy the Sudetenland forthwith.[19] On the 23rd, Hitler upped the ante by demanding the withdrawal of all Czech forces and the ceding of the Sudetenland to Germany, this to take place within the space of five days. The Czechs responded by mobilizing a million men.

Chamberlain had refused Hitler's request that President Beneš be presented with a document in which the Nazi demands were stated. However, to please Chamberlain, Hitler would make a small concession and 'agree to 1 October as the date for evacuation'.[20] Chamberlain now flew back to England to discuss matters with his Cabinet. 'Herr Hitler,' he said, 'would not deliberately deceive a man [i.e., Chamberlain] whom he respected and with whom he had been in negotiation.' It would, therefore, be a tragedy if 'the opportunity of reaching an understanding with Germany on all points of difference between the two countries' were to be lost. Nevertheless, the leader of the French delegation, Daladier, was adamant that France, which had already ordered a partial mobilization of forces, did not recognize Hitler's right to seize the Sudetenland.

Chamberlain then decided to write Hitler a personal letter, suggesting that a joint commission be appointed to determine how the proposals already accepted by the Czechs were to be put into effect. 'If the letter fails to secure any response from Herr Hitler,' said Chamberlain, 'then Sir Horace Wilson [Chamberlain's confidential advisor] should be authorized to give a personal message from me to the effect that, if this appeal was refused France would go to war, and if that happened, it seemed certain that we should be drawn in.'[21]

When Wilson duly presented Hitler with Chamberlain's letter, the Führer flew into a rage. 'He now holds the decision in his hand,' said Hitler, in reference to Benes. 'Peace or war! Either he will now accept this offer and at last give Germans their freedom, or we will take this freedom for ourselves!'[22]

In a press statement, Chamberlain, referring to a guarantee made by Britain that the Czechs must keep their promise to evacuate the Sudetenland, declared that this guarantee was conditional on the Germans abstaining from the use of force. Whilst he was aware that Germany had the support of Italy's fascist leader, Mussolini, he was 'of the opinion that it would be wise to accept the British proposal, and begs you [Hitler] to refrain from mobilisation'.[23]

Hitler responded by inviting Chamberlain, Mussolini and Daladier to Munich for a meeting which took place on 29 September 1938. When Chamberlain enquired as to how the Czechs were to be compensated for losing their property in the Sudetenland, Hitler said angrily, 'Our time is too valuable to be wasted on such trivialities!'[24] At 1.30am the following morning, it was formally agreed that the evacuation of the Sudetenland by the Czechs would begin on 1 October. As for the Czech representatives, they were aggrieved that they had not been included in the discussions during which the fate of their country was being decided.

Chamberlain returned to England where, to cheering crowds outside No. 10 Downing Street, he said, 'Here is a piece of paper which bears his [i.e., Hitler's] name upon it as well as mine. I believe it is peace for our time'.[25] This was greeted with wild applause.

Shortly afterwards, according to Manfred von Schroeder, German diplomat and Nazi party member from 1933 to 1945, Hitler was heard to say, 'They have cheated me out of my war.'[26] This was confirmed by Schacht who later reported Hitler as saying, 'That damned Chamberlain had spoiled my parade into Prague.'[27] After this so-called Munich Agreement, Czech President Edvard Beneš resigned and went into exile. On 1 October 1938, German forces duly moved into the Sudetenland and within twenty-four hours Hitler himself was paying a triumphant visit to the Czech capital. The region would supply ample quantities of 'brown' coal from which Hitler was able to produce synthetic petrol for his air force and motorized armies.

On 21 January 1939, Hitler increased his pressure on Czechoslovakia when he informed that country's Foreign Minister, František Chvalkovský, that Germany would not give guarantees to a state which did not eliminate its Jews.[28] In February 1939, Goebbels launched a propaganda campaign against the Czechs, declaring that ethnic German citizens were being terrorized, and that Czech troops were massing along the Sudeten border. In an all too familiar scenario, nationalists in the Slovak province of eastern Czechoslovakia now demanded their independence.

On 9 March 1939, the British Ambassador to Germany, Sir Nevile Henderson, showed just how Hitler had duped him when, in a letter to Halifax, he said,

Hitler himself fought in the [First] World War, and his dislike of bloodshed, or anyway of dead Germans, is intense. I can find no justification for the theory that he is mad, or even verging on madness. I am of the opinion that he is not thinking today in terms of war.[29]

That evening, Emil Hácha, the newly appointed President of Czechoslovakia, gave Hitler the excuse he was waiting for by dismissing the Slovak government, ordering his troops to prepare to move into Slovakia and declaring martial law. Meanwhile, Soviet leader Stalin was telling his Eighteenth Party Congress that, although his country was an ally of Czechoslovakia, their Soviet-Czech Mutual Assistance Pact, signed in 1935, required them to act against Germany only after France had intervened against Germany first.

Hitler now increased his campaign of intimidation when, accompanied by five German generals, he crossed the Danube river and disrupted a meeting of the Slovak Cabinet in their regional capital, Bratislava, and ordered it to proclaim the independence of Slovakia. In his mind was the fact that this region was of great strategic importance as a base for future Nazi operations against the Soviet Union.

Karol Sidor, named by Hácha as the new premier of the autonomous Slovak government in place of its former prime minister, Josef Tiso, declared that before acceding to Hitler's wishes, he must first discuss the situation with the government in Prague. However, in a snub to both Hácha and Sidor, Hitler invited Tiso to meet him in Berlin, where on 13 March, the German leader declared,

> Tomorrow at midday, I shall begin military action against the Czechs … Germany does not intend to take Slovakia into her *Lebensraum*, and that is why you must either immediately proclaim the independence of Slovakia, or I will disinterest myself in her fate.[30]

In the face of this bullying, the Slovakian parliament was forced to accept a declaration of independence, drafted by Ribbentrop, whereby a new Slovakia came into existence.

On 14 March 1939 the ageing Czech President, Hácha, was invited to Berlin for talks. Having kept him waiting till 1.15am, Hitler informed him that his country would now be invaded by German troops. The order for Czechoslovakia to be incorporated into the Third Reich had already been given, and the army would enter Czechoslovakia at 6.00am on 15 March. Hácha was asked to sign a document which placed the fate of the Czech people in the hands of the Führer. In the event of a refusal, Hitler threatened that the Czech capital, Prague, would be destroyed by bombing within a few hours. Hácha had no choice but to sign.

Tiso now sent a telegram to Berlin proclaiming Slovak independence and requesting German protection. Hitler's troops duly moved into Slovakia to guarantee its newly-won independence. The province of Ruthenia, however, being of no interest to the Nazis, was ceded to Hungary, whom Hitler wished to appease. On 16 March 1939, Hitler, now in Prague, laid claim to the Czech provinces of Bohemia and Moravia which now became a Reich protectorate. The Nazi occupation of Czechoslovakia was complete.

Meanwhile, back in Britain the patience of Prime Minister Chamberlain had run out. It would be a great mistake he said, in reference to a possible future invasion of Poland by the Nazis, for Germany to suppose that Great Britain 'had so lost its fibre that it would not take part to the uttermost of its power in resisting such a challenge, if it were made'. Hitler had unilaterally broken the Munich Agreement. He was therefore, not to be trusted; there would be no more appeasement.

On 31 March 1939, Britain together with France, gave military guarantees to Poland, Romania, Greece and Turkey and initiated political and military talks with the Soviet Union.

Poland

Although Hitler has been criticized – quite rightly – for his expansionist policies, the other side of the coin is that, following the First World War, the Allies, with the aim of weakening any future German potential for aggression, had allowed the Poles to incorporate the larger portion of the German territories of West Prussia and Posen into their country. Also, in order to give Poland access to a seaport, namely Danzig, a city populated almost entirely by Germans, the Allies had sanctioned the establishment of the so-called 'Polish Corridor'. On 25 January 1932, Poland signed a treaty of non-aggression with the Soviet Union. On 26 January 1934, Hitler in his typically disingenuous way, signed a ten-year, non-aggression pact with Poland.

Following the Munich Agreement of September 1938, however, Germany requested that Danzig be returned to her, and that she be permitted her own corridor – to link East Prussia with the larger part of the Reich. In return, the Poles would be allowed to use Danzig as a free port and their existing borders would be guaranteed.

In the spring of 1939 the Nazis reverted to their usual tactics of accusing the Poles of persecuting the German minority in that country. In other words, those who were to be the victims of the aggression, would be blamed for initiating it. Polish Foreign Minister, Colonel Józef Beck now warned the Germans that any action which 'clearly threatens Polish independence' would be resisted. Furthermore, on 31 March 1939, Chamberlain gave an undertaking to Poland that if that country's independence was threatened then 'His Majesty's [i.e., King George VI's government] and the French government would at once lend them [the Poles] all the support in their power'. And in a speech to the House of Commons he warned Hitler that 'If an attempt were made to change the situation by force in such a way as to threaten Polish independence, why then that would inevitably start a general conflagration in which this country would be involved'.[31] A fortnight later, similar guarantees were given to Romania and Greece.

Hitler chose to ignore these warnings, and on 3 April 1939, issued his senior commanders with a 'Most Secret' war directive: 'Since the situation on Germany's eastern frontier has become intolerable, and all political possibilities of peaceful settlement have been exhausted, I have decided upon a solution by force.' On 28 April he declared that the 1932 Polish-German Non-aggression Pact was to be cancelled since it had been, 'unilaterally infringed' by the Poles. As for England, he was dismissive of her military capability, saying 'How could the English picture a modern war, when they can't even put two fully-equipped divisions in [to] the field?'[32]

On 23 August 1939, Foreign Minister Ribbentrop of Germany was in Moscow signing the Nazi-Soviet Pact with Soviet Commissar for Foreign Affairs Vyacheslav Molotov. The pact declared that each country would observe a benevolent neutrality towards the other in the event of either one being attacked. In this way, Hitler hoped he would avoid having to fight a future war on two fronts. The pact contained a secret protocol whereby the two countries agreed that, in the event of war between Germany and Poland, Finland, the Baltic States and Bessarabia would fall within the Russian sphere of influence. It was also agreed that, once Hitler had invaded Poland, Soviet leader Josef Stalin would have a share in the spoils. However, in retrospect it is clear that Hitler's objective was to lull the Soviets into a false sense of security prior to his planned invasion of their country also.

At the time the pact was being signed in Moscow, Hitler was standing on the terrace of his Berghof retreat, staring out at the mountains. A Hungarian female member of his entourage said to him, 'My Führer, this augurs nothing good. It means blood, blood, blood and again blood. Destruction and terrible suffering, blood and again blood.' To this, Hitler replied, 'If it has to be, then let it be now.'[33]

* * *

In order to make the Poles appear responsible for the German invasion, Hitler arranged for German SD (*Sicherheitsdienst*) elements, disguised as Polish soldiers, to create disturbances in the border areas the night before it took place. And to prove that a skirmish had taken place, bodies would be scattered on the ground, but unbeknown to the outside world, these bodies would be those, not of Germans or Poles, but of murdered inmates from concentration camps.

On 1 September 1939, Hitler declared, 'Last night Poland opened fire on our own territory using regular army troops for the first time. Since 5.45am we have been returning fire'.[34] The Nazis now invaded Poland – a country rich in coal and agricultural products – with a force of 1.25 million men. Immediately prior to the attack on Poland, and with typical duplicity, Hitler had sent Ribbentrop to Warsaw to lay a wreath in memory of the dead of the Great War, and to reassure the Poles that there would be no attack. Two days later, Britain and France declared war on Germany.

* * *

Meanwhile, Hitler derived encouragement from the success which the nationalist insurgents were having against the incumbent Spanish Republican regime for, on 28 March 1939, Spain's capital city, Madrid, had fallen to the Nationalist forces of General Franco. The Spanish Civil War had given Hitler the opportunity to test his military equipment and to improve his military capabilities – a dress rehearsal for what was shortly to come.

To Hitler's satisfaction, Franco now established a fascist dictatorship in Spain, replacing approximately 50,000 school teachers with *Falangists* (the Spanish fascist group) whose job it would be to inculcate in their pupils the values that 'will create the new empire which the people want'.

Under the Franco regime Spanish children were taught how Spain had seven enemies: liberalism, democracy, Judaism, masonry, Marxism, capitalism, and separatism, which had all been 'defeated in the Great Crusade, although not annihilated. They hide like venomous insects, continuing to poison the air from the shadows'. And from newly revised text books, Spanish children were also taught that 'Jews drank Christian blood' and were 'spies, political conspirators who lived in secret friendship with the Moors', and that human liberty leads to anarchy. [35]

* * *

The picture emerges of Hitler as a selfish and scheming bully, and a warmonger who would stop at nothing to pursue his stated policy of *Lebensraum*, at whatever cost. He had no respect for treaties, nor for the sovereignty of his neighbouring countries.

Notes

1. Hitler, op. cit., p. 82.
2. Ibid, p. 83.
3. Mills, Hist. 203, 16, *Fascism Part II*: http://www.husky1.stmarys.ca/-mills/course203/16_Fascism_2.html
4. Toland, op. cit., p. 353.
5. Ibid, p. 421.
6. Ibid, p. 434.
7. Ibid, p. 437.
8. Ibid, p. 443.
9. Ibid, p. 450.
10. Ibid, p. 453.
11. Bloch, op. cit., Vol. 1, 15 March, pp. 11, 35–9; and 22 March, pp. 69–73.
12. Ibid. p. 72.
13. *Hitler: a Profile: The Betrayer.*
14. *Hitler: a Profile: The Blackmailer.*
15. Toland, op. cit., p. 464.
16. Ibid, p. 473.
17. Ibid, p. 476.
18. Ibid, p. 477.
19. Ibid, p. 479.
20. Ibid, p. 482.
21. Ibid, p. 483.
22. Ibid, p. 484.
23. Ibid, p. 487.
24. Ibid, p. 490.
25. *Churchill, Part.1. Renegade and Turncoat.*
26. *The Nazis: A Warning from History, Part 1.*
27. Fest, *Hitler*, p. 840.

28. Toland, op. cit., p. 510.
29. Ibid, p. 513.
30. Ibid, p. 514.
31. *Hitler's Henchmen: Ribbentrop, the Puppet.*
32. Toland, op. cit., p. 527.
33. *The Nazis: A Warning from History, Part 3.*
34. *Hitler: a Profile: The Seducer.*
35. Foca Ediciones. *La Historia Que Nos Ensenaron, 1937–1975.* ('The History They Taught Us. 1937–1975'.)

Chapter 21

Marxism: a Threat to Germany?

According to Hitler in his book, *Mein Kampf*, written in 1924, it was during his time in Vienna (1907–13) that he realized the 'terrible significance for the existence of the German people' of 'Marxism and Judaism'.[1] For him, the two were irrevocably entwined and, furthermore, he was of the opinion that 'a Jew can never be rescued from his fixed notions', even though he himself

> talked to them until my throat ached and my voice grew hoarse. I believed that I could finally convince them of the danger inherent in their Marxist follies. But I achieved only the contrary result.[2]

So who was Marx, and was Hitler correct in perceiving the doctrine of Marxism as a threat?

Born in Trier in Germany in 1818, Karl Marx was the son of a lawyer and the grandson of a Jewish rabbi named Mordeccai. Having studied history and philosophy at the universities of Bonn and Berlin, he was influenced initially in his political beliefs by a Communist-Zionist named Moses Hess, founder and editor of the newspaper *Die Rheinische Zeitung*, which was the main vehicle of leftist thought in Germany.

In 1843, Marx and his wife, Jenny, moved to Paris where the following year he met German philosopher Friedrich Engels, whom Moses Hess had previously converted to communism. Engels was the son of a wealthy textiles magnate who was later to subsidise Marx with profits from his factories in Britain and Germany. In 1845, Marx moved to Brussels, having been expelled from France for his political activities.

In 1848, Marx returned to Germany with Engels and took part in the unsuccessful revolutionary uprisings in the Rhineland. This was the year in which he wrote his famous *Communist Manifesto* in which he declared that

> The proletariat [poorest labouring class], during its contest with the bourgeoisie [middle class], is compelled by the force of circumstances, to organise itself as a class ... by means of a revolution, it makes itself the ruling class, and, as such, sweeps away by force the old conditions of production.[3]

The proletariat will use its political supremacy to wrest, by degrees, all capital from the bourgeoisie, to centralise all instruments of production in the hands of the state, i.e., of the proletariat organized as the ruling class; and to increase the total of productive forces as rapidly as possible.[4]

After the Paris revolution of 1848, which established the Second Republic, Marx transferred to Cologne to resume editorship of *Die Rheinische Zeitung* but, when the newspaper closed the following year, he moved to London, where he would remain for the rest of his life.

Marx was a leading figure in the creation in London, in 1864, of the 'First International', an abbreviation for 'International Working Men's Association'; its objective was to promote international cooperation between socialist, communist and revolutionary groups.

In 1867, Volume 1 of Marx's magnum opus, *Das Kapital*, was published. As for Engels, he would devote the remainder of his life to editing and translating the works of Marx, including Volumes 2 and 3 of *Das Kapital*, published in 1885 and 1894 respectively, after his death. The volumes were 'printed abroad and circulated ... secretly in Russia'.[5]

* * *

So yes, Hitler was correct in believing that Marx envisaged his brand of communism – where the 'bourgeoisie' were to be replaced by 'a new, classless, communist society' – as being applicable to all countries, Austria and Germany included. Furthermore, Marx was quite prepared for new communist regimes to be installed by force, if necessary. Hence, the statement with which he ended his Communist Manifesto of 1848: 'The workers have nothing to lose but their chains. They have a world to win. Workers of all lands, unite!'

In *Mein Kampf*, Hitler refers to 'the Jew, Karl Marx'. Prejudiced as he was against the Jews, whom he could only see in terms of their ethnicity – i.e., from the viewpoint of a racist – he failed to mention that Marx's family had converted from Judaism to Protestantism, or that Marx himself had no time for any type of religion, Christianity included.

There was, however, common ground between Marx and Hitler, as the former reveals in his essay *On the Jewish Question*, where he scornfully described 'the secular basis of Judaism' as being characterized by 'practical need' and 'self interest'. The 'secular cult' of the Jew, said Marx, was 'haggling', and his 'secular god' was 'money', and he elaborated on his theme as follows,

We therefore recognize in Judaism, the presence of a universal and contemporary anti-social element whose historical evolution – eagerly nurtured by the Jews in its harmful aspects – had arrived at its present peak, a peak at which it will inevitably disintegrate. The emancipation of the Jews is, in the last analysis, the emancipation of mankind from Judaism.

In other words, it was Marx's view that the Jews would be well advised to abandon their historical faith. Nevertheless, at the same time, Marx saw no reason why Jews should be denied the same equal status as any other citizens.[6] Unlike Hitler, therefore, he can in no way be described as a racist.

Marx had a rival in the First International. He was Michael Bakunin, a Russian exile and an anarchist. Whereas Marx's wish was for the Jews to be freed from what he described as the tyranny of Judaism, Bakunin demanded no less than their entire annihilation. 'In all countries the people detest the Jews,' he wrote, 'They detest them so much that every popular revolution is accompanied by a massacre of Jews: a natural consequence ...' Marx countered by issuing, in June 1872, a pamphlet entitled *The Fictitious Splits in the International*, which he admitted was 'undergoing the most serious crisis since its foundation'. He accused Bakunin of inciting 'racial war' and organizing secret societies as part of his anarchistic master plan to wreck the working class movement. Marx now forced the expulsion of Bakunin from the First International.[7]

Marx died in London in March 1883 and is buried in Highgate Cemetery. In the same year the first Russian Marxist organization, the Emancipation of Labour group, was created in Geneva by Georgi V. Plekhanov who 'had been obliged to take refuge from the persecution of the tsarist government for his revolutionary activities'.[8]

* * *

As previously indicated, Hitler shared many of the delusions of Lanz von Liebenfels. Did Hitler also embrace Liebenfels' deluded attitude towards Karl Marx? The answer is yes, as will now be demonstrated.

In *Ostara*, Liebenfels describes Marx as a 'dark, inferior mongrel'[9] and goes on to say,

> In the course of its further development, the Talmudic-Tachandalic Empire* succeeded in harnessing the intelligence of the Aryan Christians to its purposes by way of the ... secret society of Free-Masons. This society of obscurantists is responsible for the so-called 'Enlightenment' – the various revolutions, liberalism, socialism and materialism in the Nineteenth Century – and for the Bolshevism in the Twentieth ... During the Middle Ages ... there was no proletariat and no proletarian problem. This class only came into being through the daemonic efforts of modern Free-Masons and their false doctrines of the so-called 'Enlightenment'.[10]

---

* Talmud – the sacred writings of Orthodox Judaism; Tachandalic – pertaining to the original race of inferior humans.

The conceptual manure-heaps, the mental excrement that is materialistic-rationalistic-social democratic-bolshevist-tachandalic philosophy and science of the modern period will not be of even historic interest in future generations.[11]

Bolshevism, Marxism, Sovietism, communism, socialism, democratism ... are offshoots ... of these primaeval, base, and inferior racial origins.[12]

And finally, and most menacingly,

The socialistic-bolshevistic primitive race has given us notice. Fine, we will give them notice that we've given up charity and humanity. They want class warfare, they shall have race warfare, race warfare from our side until the castration knife.[13]

Hitler: *Bolshevism is Christianity's illegitimate child. Both are inventions of the Jew.*[14] [An obvious reference to Karl Marx.] *To be sure, our Christian Cross should be the most exalted symbol of the struggle against the Jewish–Marxist–Bolshevik spirit.*[15]

Notes

1. Hitler, op. cit., p. 22.
2. Ibid, p. 44.
3. Marx, *The Communist Manifesto: Selected Works*, Eng. edn., vol. 1, pp. 227–8.
4. Ibid.
5. *History of the Communist Party of the Soviet Union: Bolsheviks*, p. 9.
6. Wheen, *Karl Marx*, p. 54.
7. Ibid, p. 341.
8. *History of the Communist Party of the Soviet Union: Bolsheviks*, op. cit., p. 9.
9. *Ostara*, I/61.
10. Ibid, III/13–14 (in Grey Lodge Occult Review, *SF, Occult Sciences and Nazi Myths*, by Manfred Nagl, 1974; www.antiquillum.com/glor/glor_005/nazimyth.htm
11. Ibid, III/15 (in antiquillum, op. cit.).
12. Ibid, I/13–14 (in antiquillum, op. cit.).
13. Ibid, III/4, in Daim, op. cit., p. 30.
14. Trevor–Roper, op. cit., p. 37.
15. Prange, op. cit., p. 88.

Chapter 22

'International Communism'

In *Mein Kampf* Hitler wrote that,

> In Russian Bolshevism, we ought to recognize the kind of attempt which is being made by the Jew in the Twentieth Century to secure dominion over the world.[1]

So what was Bolshevism, and was this statement true? If so, was it by force that the Bolsheviks aimed to achieve their ends?

The Bolshevik Party was in the vanguard of the proletarian movement which advocated revolutionary socialism, together with democratic centralism. Founded by Vladimir Ilyich Ulyanov – otherwise known as Lenin – it was a faction within the Marxist Russian Social Democratic Labour Party (RSDLP).

Lenin was born in 1870 into a middle-class family in Simbirsk in Russia. His father was a provincial school superintendent, his mother, the daughter of a doctor. From 1892, Lenin practised as a lawyer in Southern Russia. It was he who, using the teachings of Marx, would provide the impetus for the Russian Revolution of October 1917, which must be seen against a background of centuries of oppression of the Russian people by that country's rulers, the tsars.

In 1894, the year that Nicholas II became Tsar, Lenin moved to St Petersburg, renamed Leningrad in 1924, where he organized the illegal and revolutionary Union for the Liberation of the Working Class. Also, he wrote a book entitled *What the Friends of the People Are* in which 'for the first time', he 'advanced the idea of a revolutionary alliance of the workers and peasants [i.e., the proletariat] as the principal means of overthrowing tsardom, the landlords, and the bourgeoisie [capitalists]'.[2] To this end, between 1894 and 1900, Marxist organizations were created in Moscow, Siberia and Transcaucasia,[3] and 'in October 1897, the Jewish General Social Democratic Union – known as the *Bund* – was founded in the western provinces of Russia'.[4]

In November 1895, Lenin wrote a leaflet aimed at fomenting political agitation amongst 500 striking textile workers at a factory in St Petersburg. The secret police now clamped down on clandestine cells in the country and, the following month, Lenin was arrested by the tsarist government and exiled to Siberia for three years, along with fellow revolutionary Nadezhda Krupskaya, whom he subsequently married. Following his release from exile in 1900, Lenin lived in various countries, including Switzerland, Germany (Munich) and Finland.

In February 1904, Russia became involved in a disastrous war, this time with Japan. That winter brought soaring inflation with hunger and hardship. On 22 January 1905 striking demonstrators marched to the Tsar's winter palace demanding a representative government, workers' rights, and peace with Japan. There was a massacre in which some 500 people were shot and many injured, despite the demonstration being a peaceful one. When, in May 1906, the *Duma*, the elected assembly, demanded radical reform, Nicholas responded by dissolving it. Four years were to pass before it was reinstated. The year 1908 marked 300 years of Romanov rule in Russia, making this the longest serving dynasty in Europe.

In the summer of 1914, following a dispute between Austria-Hungary and Serbia, an ally of Russia, the Russian Empire clashed with both the German and Austro-Hungarian Empires. This temporarily united the Russian people, fifteen million of whom now fought for their country in the Great War, with over half of that number being either killed, wounded, or captured within the next two and a half years. With the advance of the Russian imperial armies, Lenin was obliged to leave Poland and return to Switzerland. In the summer of 1915, Tsar Nicholas left the capital to lead his troops at the Front.

By early 1917 inflation had made the Russian rouble all but worthless, and there were food queues and starvation. On 23 February there were riots – the so-called February revolution (March, by the Western calendar) – and regiments of the army mutinied. On 16 March, Tsar Nicholas abdicated. A month later, Lenin, after twenty years in exile, returned home to Russia from Zürich. Now, the First Provisional Government was established under Russian politician Prince Georgi Lvov; he was replaced in July by Russian revolutionary leader, Aleksandr Kerensky.

Lenin's Bolshevik Party, however, was opposed to the Provisional Government, under whom, said Lenin 'the people would secure neither peace, nor land, nor bread ...'.[5] However, a Bolshevik uprising in July 1917 was crushed by Kerensky, who was persuaded by the western powers to continue the war with Germany, whereupon further military defeats only led to greater unrest.

* * *

The night of 25 October 1917 (7 November, by the western calendar) was a turning point in the history of Russia when 'revolutionary workers, soldiers, and sailors, took St Petersburg's Winter Palace by storm, and arrested the Provisional Government [which had taken refuge there]'.[6] When the Second All-Russian Congress of Soviets opened that same evening, the Bolsheviks secured an overwhelming majority over 'the Mensheviks,* Bundists, and Right Socialist Revolutionaries'.[7]

---

* Anti-tsar, pro-middle class, liberal reformists.

For Lenin, the first step had been taken towards the fulfilment of Karl Marx's dream – in Russia, at any rate. On 8 November 1917, the Congress elected him Chairman of the Council of People's Commissars, the Bolshevik Government's highest governing authority.

*   *   *

Without question, Lenin's aim, in the early period of his leadership, was to expand soviet influence beyond Russia, and by force if necessary. 'Without a world revolution,' he said, 'we will not pull through.'[8] However, whatever his dreams for the internationalization of communism may have been, his ambitions were soon to be tempered with harsh reality. The country remained at war; the majority of those who had gone to fight were peasants, and there was therefore a shortage of manpower, which in turn led to a shortage of food. Also the emergence of the *kulaks* – a middle class of peasant whose philosophy was more akin to capitalism than communism – was a problem that had not been foreseen.

On 5 December 1917 an armistice was signed between Russia and Germany. However, by this time the central powers (Germany and Austria-Hungary) had overrun Russian Poland, most of Lithuania, Serbia, Albania and Romania. Furthermore, even within Russia there was to be no peace, for in the same month, a civil war broke out which was to last for three years, with the Bolsheviks being opposed, principally, by former tsarist generals who were supported by forces from Britain, France, the United States, Japan and Canada.

When, in January 1918 the Constituent Assembly, the democratically elected body whose function was to write a constitution for Russia, failed to legitimize his new government, the exasperated Lenin promptly dissolved it. His action, he said, was the abandonment of 'formal democracy' in favour of 'revolutionary dictatorship'. In the same month, the fragile armistice between Russia and Germany failed and German troops swept into Russia, threatening the former tsarist capital Petrograd (known as St Petersburg prior to 1914 and renamed Leningrad in 1924). The Russians were forced, on 3 March, to accept the harsh terms of the Treaty of Brest-Litovsk: in return for the cessation of hostilities, Germany now demanded that Russia surrender Russian Poland, the Baltic States (Estonia, Lithuania, and Latvia) and part of Ukraine. Hitler, please note, it is Germany who is the aggressor, not Russia! In response to the increasing threat from Germany, Russia now declared Moscow, a city strategically less vulnerable than Petrograd, to be its new capital. On the night of 16/17 July, the Romanov dynasty came to an abrupt end when, on Lenin's orders, Tsar Nicholas II and his family were murdered by the (Bolshevik) Red Army.[9]

*   *   *

In August 1918 there was an attempted coup in Moscow and Lenin survived an assassination attempt. His response was to establish a new and ruthless state security agency, the *Cheka*. He now turned his attention to promoting a far-left socialist seizure of power in Germany in the hope that it would result in the formation of a gigantic geopolitical Russian/German bloc which could never be overthrown. Said he, 'The absolute truth, is that without a revolution in Germany, we shall perish'.[15] However, his hopes were quickly dashed when, in November 1918, an attempt by the Spartacists, a left-wing, Marxist, revolutionary movement, to overthrow Berlin's socialist government was ruthlessly suppressed. In the same year, Bolsheviks attempting to overthrow the government of Finland suffered the same fate. Undeterred, the First Congress of Communist Parties, in 1919, continued to emphasize the need for 'a determined struggle for the dictatorship of the proletariat and for the triumph of soviets all over the world'.[10] Workers everywhere were exhorted to 'wipe out boundaries between states, and transform the whole world into one co-operative commonwealth'. In Lenin's view, 'It will not be long [before] we shall see the victory of communism in the entire world ...'.[11]

Had Hitler's remarks, that 'Russian Bolshevism' threatened 'dominion over the world', been applicable to the year 1919, then clearly there was some truth in them, although Lenin would probably have argued that he simply wished to see the Bolshevik *system* established in other countries, albeit by force if necessary, rather than to see the Soviet Union having dominion over them. However, Hitler had made his statement, not in 1919, but five years later, in 1924, by which time the situation in the Soviet Union had changed completely.

Lenin's hopes were again dashed when communist uprisings in Hungary and in Munich were also crushed. And even though, by 1920, Russia's Bolsheviks had largely won the civil war, that August the Red Army was defeated by the Poles on the Vistula river on the outskirts of Warsaw. To Lenin's troubles, there seemed to be no end!

An order by the Tenth Party Congress, on 8 March 1921, for 'the immediate dissolution of all factional groups',[12] meant that Lenin was now a virtual dictator. He, who had formerly been an advocate of democracy, had now put the final nail in its coffin. On 18 March the Soviet Union signed a peace treaty with Poland and, on 16 April 1922, the Soviet Union signed a treaty of friendship and neutrality with Germany – the Treaty of Rapallo – by which the two countries agreed to cooperate, both economically and militarily.

Events had now forced Lenin to see the Soviet Union not as an exporter of communism but as an 'oasis of Soviet power in the middle of the raging imperialist sea'.[13] Now it was he who felt threatened. 'We must remember,' he said, 'that we are at all times but a hair's breadth from any manner of invasion.'[14]

In December 1922, the soviet republics, which included Russia, Ukraine, Transcaucasia, Belorussia, Uzbekistan, Turkmenistan and Tajikistan, became 'a single union of soviet states – the 'Union of Soviet Socialist Republics' (USSR, or Soviet Union).[15]

* * *

Lenin, worn out with the strife and struggle, died on 21 January 1924, which was the year in which Hitler wrote *Mein Kampf*. By that time, the Soviet leader, having been preoccupied with the problems of governing his country, and having seen how communism had failed to take root in other countries – including Germany – had completely abandoned the concept of 'international communism'. Therefore, why did Hitler allege that 'Russian Bolsheviks' intended to 'secure dominion over the world'? This was surely yet another of the Führer's delusions. In fact, it was *he* who sought world domination!

Notes

1. Hitler, op. cit., p. 364.
2. *History of the Communist Party of the Soviet Union: Bolsheviks*, op. cit., p. 20.
3. Ibid, p. 18.
4. Ibid, p. 21.
5. Ibid, p. 130.
6. Ibid, p. 208.
7. Ibid, pp. 208–9.
8. Uldricks, *Russia and Europe: Diplomacy, Revolution and Economic Development in the 1920s*, International History Review, 1, 1979, p. 58.
9. *Russia: Land of the Tsars.
10. *History of the Communist Party of the Soviet Union: Bolsheviks*, op. cit., p. 232.
11. Goodman, *The Soviet Design for a World State*, pp. 30–2.
12. *History of the Communist Party of the Soviet Union: Bolsheviks*, op. cit., p. 254.
13. Ulam, *Expansion and Co-existence: a History of Soviet Foreign Policy, 1917–67*, p. 79.
14. Stalin, *Problems of Leninism*, p. 160.
15. *History of the Communist Party of the Soviet Union: Bolsheviks*, op. cit., p. 261.

Chapter 23

The Jews as Aggressors?

In *Mein Kampf*, Hitler declared,

> The great leaders of Jewry are confident that the day is near at hand when the command given in the Old Testament will be carried out and the Jews will devour the other nations of the Earth.[1]

Strong words indeed, but is there any truth in this statement?

There had been pogroms (manifestations of hatred, often involving beatings, stonings, and massacres, and the burning of businesses and properties) against the Jews of Europe since time immemorial, but particularly during the period of the Crusades in the Eleventh and Twelfth Centuries. Then, mainly at the instigation of the Catholic Church, Jews were expelled from countries such as England, France, Spain, various Germanic states, Portugal, Lithuania and the Ukraine. The murder of Russian Tsar Alexander II in 1881, which was blamed on the Jews, resulted in pogroms throughout Eastern Europe which lasted into the early Twentieth Century. Only in 1965 did the Vatican revise its teaching by exonerating the Jews of the murder of Christ, and accepting the legitimacy of the Jewish religion.

Russia's Jews lived mainly in *shtetls*, segregated, small-town communities, in which they maintained their own way of life, spoke their own language (Yiddish), married within the community, had their own educational system, and practised their own religion. Tsar Nicholas II contributed to their further isolation by issuing anti–Semitic decrees, such as the May Laws of 1882, which restricted their right to settle in the cities and to practise their faith. (Instead, it was his wish that they convert to the Russian Orthodox faith.) Jews were now forced to sell their businesses and their homes, and move into a specially designated quarter of Russia's western province, known as the 'Jewish Pale'.

Lenin, like his predecessor Marx, also had Jewish ancestry, his maternal grandfather being Israel Blak, a Ukrainian Jew who was later baptized into the Russian Orthodox Church.[2] According to his younger sister, Maria Ilyinichna, he was proud of his Jewish ancestry and of the political, scientific and artistic achievements of the Jews, which were out of all proportion to the smallness of their numbers. He also admired the Jews for helping to create a Western European–type culture in Russia.

Russian novelist Maxim Gorky also confirmed that Lenin was fulsome in his praise of the Jews and quoted him as saying, 'We (the Russians) are a predominantly talented people, but we have a lazy mentality. A bright Russian is almost always a Jew or a person with an admixture of Jewish blood.'[3]

Lenin pointed out to his sister Anna that Jewish activists constituted about half of the number of revolutionaries in the southern regions of the Russian Empire. Also, several members of the editorial board of Lenin's Marxist newspaper *Iskra* (a voice for the Russian Social Democratic Labour Party RSDLP) had Jewish backgrounds, including Pavel Axelrod, Julius Martov and Leon Trotsky. However, all had abandoned Judaism in favour of Marxism.

At the Second Party Congress of the RSDLP, held on 29 July 1903 in London, one of the questions to be decided concerned the Jewish *Bund*: its Party members, who were recruited on a purely ethnic basis, were numerous in the western borderlands of the Russian Empire. The *Bund* was aggrieved that it had been allocated only five of the forty-three places at the Congress. However, finding itself unable to persuade the other delegates to increase its representation, the *Bund* responded by demanding autonomy for itself within the Party, but was again thwarted when the Congress once more refused its request.[4] Eight years later, in 1911, the USA cancelled its economic treaty with Russia, on the basis that Jews were denied their basic civil rights throughout the Russian Empire.

In 1914, Lenin again showed his support for the Jews by referring, disapprovingly, to the fact that in the ranks of the Russian imperial armies – which were now fighting the Germans – were to be found so-called 'Black Hundred' gangs (reactionary thugs, who in pre-war days, had organized pogroms of Jews throughout the Russian Empire). However, it was not until September 1916 that Tsar Nicholas II and his Minister of the Interior, Alexander Protopopov, finally gave their endorsement to full civil rights for the Jews. This was welcomed by progressive members of the *Duma*, and described by Prime Minister Alexsandr Kerensky as one of the few positive actions taken by the government.

However, right-wing elements, the army, and even the Tsar's own family, were opposed to the granting of such freedom to the Jews. For example, Alexander Mikhailovich Romanov, husband of the Tsar's sister, Ksenia, in a letter to his brother, Sergei, describes how he told 'N' and 'A' (abbreviations for Nicholas and his wife Alexandra) 'that concessions or new rights for the Jews were unthinkable, that we could not afford to be merciful to a race which the Russian people hate even more now because of their negative attitude towards the war and [their] outright treason …'.[5]

Despite the Tsar's belated support for Jewish civil rights, Russia's Jews gave their full support to the October 1917 Revolution, which is hardly surprising in view of the centuries of persecution which they had endured at the hands of the Romanov dynasty.

Not only that, but following the Bolshevik takeover, those who assumed positions of power were mainly Jews. For example, Leon Trotsky, Head of the Red Army and Chief of Soviet Foreign Affairs; Yakov Sverdlov, the Bolshevik Party's Executive Secretary, Chairman of the Central Executive Committee, and Head of the Soviet

Government; Grigori Zinoviev, Head of the Communist International – or *Comintern* – the agency responsible for spreading revolution abroad; Karl Radek, Press Commissar; Maxim Litvinov, Foreign Affairs Commissar; Lev Kamenev, Chairman of the Central Executive Committee of the All Russian Congress of Soviets; and Moisei Uritsky, Head of the Secret Police, or *Cheka*. Interestingly, these Jewish Bolshevik leaders, who had chosen Marxism instead of Judaism, had also exchanged their Jewish surnames for Russian ones.

The extent of Jewish political dominance is indicated by British journalist and author Robert Wilton who, in his book *Les Derniers Jours des Romanovs*, states that, at the time of the assassination of the imperial family, no less than forty-one of the sixty-one members of the Bolshevik Party's Central Committee were Jews. Furthermore, the Extraordinary Commission of Moscow, *Cheka*, consisted of thirty-six members, twenty-three of whom were Jews; in the Council of the People's Commissars, Jews provided seventeen of the twenty-two members, and of the functionaries of the Bolshevik State in 1918 and 1919, Jews occupied 457 of 556 important positions.

According to Wilton, by 1918 the Central Commission of the Bolshevik Party, which effectively governed the country, consisted of twelve members of whom nine were of Jewish origin, the remaining three being Russian. As for the other Russian socialist parties, including Mensheviks, Communists of the People, Social Revolutionaries (both right-wing and left-wing) and Committee of the Anarchists of Moscow, 'out of sixty-one individuals at the head of these parties, there are six Russians and fifty-five Jews'.[6]

And to the Jews an immediate benefit came when, a few months after taking power, the new Soviet government reflected its leader, Lenin's, benevolent attitude to the Jews by declaring anti-Semitism to be illegal in Russia. Lenin also accused the 'accursed tsarist monarchy' during its final days, of attempting 'to incite ignorant workers and peasants against the Jews', and his sister, Anna, entirely concurred with these sentiments when she declared,

> The tsarist police, in alliance with landlords and capitalists, organized pogroms against the Jews. The landowners and capitalists tried to divert the hatred of the workers and peasants who were tortured by want, against the Jews.

And she proceeded to describe how the Jews had been unjustly persecuted, not only in Russia but elsewhere.

> In other countries too, we often see the capitalists fomenting hatred against the Jews in order to blind the workers, to divert their attention from the real enemy of the working people, [which is] capital ... [i.e., accumulated wealth]. It is not the Jews who are the enemy of the working people. The enemies of the workers are the capitalists of all countries. Among the Jews there are working people and they form the majority. They are our brothers who, like us, are oppressed by capital; they are our comrades in the struggle for socialism.[7]

However, Anna *was* prepared to admit that there were bad Jews, just as there were bad people in all societies.

> Among the Jews there are 'kulaks' (that small minority of the peasantry who are rich – 'bourgeois' – rural capitalists), exploiters, and capitalists, just as there are among the Russians and among people of all nations. The capitalists strive to sow and to foment hatred between workers of different faiths, different nations, and different races. Those who do not work are kept in power by the power and strength of capital.[8]

* * *

Bearing in mind the persecution that they had endured over many centuries, and most recently at the hands of the Romanov dynasty, it is not at all surprising that the Jews gave their support to the Russian Revolution. However, as members of Lenin's Bolshevik administration, they had, by 1924, when Hitler wrote *Mein Kampf*, entirely rejected the concept of 'international communism'. They were, therefore, no threat, either to Germany, or to anyone else, and the fact that Hitler portrayed them as aggressors and enslavers is the opposite of the truth.

Friedrich Heer points out that although Hitler himself never referred to Jörg Lanz von Liebenfels, nevertheless, the German leader's

> talks on 'diabolical' Jewish plutocracies, Russian 'bog/marsh people', the 'satanic' Bolsheviks and his theo–political messages of salvation, illustrate how close his beliefs were to enthusiasts such as Lanz [Liebenfels]…[9]

This is further confirmation of the fact that Hitler's delusions, both about the Jews and about the Bolsheviks, had their origins in the writings of the 'mad monk' – who himself was also clearly deluded.

Notes
1. Hitler, op. cit., p. 351.
2. *The Jewish Role in the Bolshevik Revolution and Russia's Early Soviet Regime.* [This essay appeared in the Jan–Feb 1994 issue of the 'Journal of Historical Review', published by the Institute for Historical Review]; www.ihr.org/jhr/v14/v14n1p-4Weber.html
3. Gor'kii, *Vladimir Lenin*, Russkii sovrenennik, No.1 1924, page 241. (in Service, *Lenin: a Biography*, p. 29).
4. Service, *Lenin: a Biography*, p. 153.
5. *Alexander Palace Time Machine*; www.alexanderpalace
6. *The Jewish Role in the Bolshevik Revolution and Russia's Early Soviet Regime*, op. cit.
7. *Workers' Liberty*,' No. 59, December 1999.
8. Ibid.
9. Heer, op. cit., p. 710.

Chapter 24

Russia Under Stalin

Born in Tiflis, now Tblisi, Georgia, then part of the Empire of the Tsars of Russia, in 1879, Josef Dzhugashvili was the son of a peasant woman and a cobbler father. From 1910 he called himself *Stalin* ('Man of Steel'). Like Hitler, his junior by ten years, Stalin had considered becoming a priest, but was expelled from the Tiflis Theological Seminary, allegedly for disseminating Marxist propaganda.

In 1902 Stalin married Ekaterina Svanidze but she died of typhus in 1907. 'With her died my last warm feelings for people,' he said.[1] In the same year he was arrested and imprisoned by the tsarist police for secretly helping to produce revolutionary publications.

Two years later, Stalin escaped from Siberia, where he was living in exile, and made his way back to Georgia – a distance of over 3,000 miles. Astonishingly, having been recaptured he would perform this feat again no less than five times more. Having, illegally, attended several Party conferences in cities outside Russia, he came to the notice of Lenin, who co-opted him onto the Party's Central Committee and sent him to Russia as one of a group of four men who were organizing the Party's activities there.

In the Bolshevik Revolution of 1917, Stalin did not play a major role. However, when in that same year, Lenin created the Council of People's Commissars – the Bolsheviks' highest government authority – he was appointed Commissar of Nationalities. The following May he became Director of Food Supplies in southern Russia.

In 1922 Stalin became General Secretary of the Communist Party of the Soviet Union's Central Committee. Now, Lenin, whose health had deteriorated, sent him to Georgia which, since the Revolution, had behaved like an autonomous region, in order to achieve its further integration with the Bolshevik state. Stalin, however, instead of looking on his homeland with affection, behaved as a Russian conqueror, and sent the Red Army in to invade and annex Georgia by force.

At the 1923 Party Congress, which he was unable to attend because of ill health, Lenin, who by now had begun to have grave misgivings about Stalin, appealed to Trotsky for his support. Trotsky, however, demurred, choosing not to confront Stalin over the Georgian issue, but instead, presenting his own programme for economic recovery.

* * *

When Lenin died in January 1924 his testament (will) was read out at the Thirteenth Party Congress. It stated that his wish, after his death, was that there should be a collective leadership, comprising Grigori Zinoviev and Lev Kamonev – two senior figures who were former colleagues of his – together with Nikolai Bukharin and Leon Trotsky, although the influence of the latter was now waning. Lenin also desired that Stalin be removed. However, in this, his wishes would be thwarted. Instead, according to Boris Bazhanov (Stalin's Secretariat 1923–26), the following statement was read to the Communist Party Committee.

> Comrades, you know we are sworn to carry out Lenin's will and so we shall, but we are happy to say (that) his fears about our General Secretary (i.e., Stalin) … have turned out to be unfounded. (During) These last months he has worked with the Central Committee excellently … and without friction.'[2]

A vote was then taken and the outcome was that Stalin remained General Secretary.

Stalin established a countrywide network of Party leaders whose appointments he controlled. According to Nadezhda Ioffe (described as 'daughter of Old Bolshevik'),

> as General Secretary, he [Stalin] managed to install his own people … i.e., regional Party secretaries and such like … [who were] already loyal to him [and] who suited him.[3]

He also moved swiftly to eliminate any potential rivals. His rule was to be marked by purges, exiles, *gulags* (corrective labour camps) and great show trials, which were intended to make an example of anyone whom he saw as a potential threat.

* * *

By the mid-1920s many of the peasants had organized themselves into cooperatives, using their new prosperity to purchase tractors, improve the roads, build schools and hospitals, and have electricity installed in their domestic dwellings.

However, at the Fourteenth Party Conference, held in April 1925, it was recorded, with regret, that the Soviet Union was 'as yet the only socialist country, all the other countries remaining capitalist', and that it 'continued to be encircled by a capitalist world'. The question arose, therefore, as to what was to be the relationship between 'the Soviet people' on the one hand, and 'the international bourgeoisie, which hated the Soviet system and was seeking the chance to start armed intervention once again in the Soviet Union …' on the other. And whereas the opinion was that the Red Army

> would be able to beat off a new foreign capitalist intervention, just as they had beaten off the first capitalist intervention of 1918–20 …, this would not mean

that the danger of a new capitalist intervention would be eliminated. It followed from this that the matter of promoting the proletarian revolution in the capitalist countries was a matter of vital concern to the working people of the Soviet Union.[4]

* * *

Tensions still existed between the advocates of 'Communism in one country', i.e., the Soviet Union, on the one hand, and the advocates of 'permanent revolution' throughout the countries of Europe, and eventually throughout the world – as advocated by Leon Trotsky, on the other.

Leon Trotsky

Born in the Ukraine, the son of a Jewish farmer, Trotsky joined the Social Democrats and, in 1898, at the age of nineteen, was arrested as a Marxist and exiled to Siberia. Four years later he escaped to England. In London he met Lenin and collaborated with him on the publication of the journal *Iskra*. In 1903, he broke with Lenin and became leader of the Menshevik wing of the Social Democratic Party.

In the abortive revolution in St Petersburg in 1905, Trotsky became President of the city's soviet. Exiled again to Siberia, he escaped once more, and fled to the West where he joined other Russian émigrés, becoming a revolutionary journalist. He returned to Russia in 1917, joined the Bolshevik Party, and played a major part in the revolution. In the ensuing civil war he served as military commander of the Bolshevik forces.

In his aspirations, however, Trotsky was to be disappointed, for with Stalin's rise to power, the *Comintern* distanced itself from his concept of 'permanent revolution', and instead was content to promote the interests of communism within the Soviet Union only. In November 1927, Trotsky, now portrayed as someone 'ready to spy, sabotage, commit acts of terrorism and diversion, and to work for the defeat of the Soviet Union in order to restore capitalism', was expelled from the Party and exiled to Alma Ata in Kazakhstan.[5] At the Fifteenth Party Congress, held in December 1927, Stalin achieved final victory. All 'deviation' was now condemned, and enemies were purged or exiled.

* * *

From 1928, in place of Lenin's New Economic Policy (NEP), Stalin substituted a series of Five Year Plans with rapid industrialization and collectivization, in which land was seized from the peasants to form collective farms. This resulted in the ejection of some five million *kulaks*.

In April 1929 the Party held its Sixteenth Conference, with the First Five Year Plan as the main item on the agenda. Nineteen and a half billion roubles were to be invested in industrial and electric power development, 10 billion in transport development, 23.2 billion in agriculture.[6] In this way, steel output was increased from four million to eighteen million tons; oil production from eleven million to twenty-eight million tons; aircraft production from 1,000 to over 10,000 per year, and tank production from 170 to almost 5,000. In the same year, Leon Trotsky was expelled from the Soviet Union. He finally found refuge in Mexico.

* * *

Stalin was conscious that, in military terms, Russia had been a continual loser. In the past he said that she had been beaten,

> by the Mongol khans ... by the Turkish beys ... by the Swedish feudal lords ... by the Polish and Lithuanian gentries ... by the British and French capitalists ... [and] by the Japanese barons.

The reason for this was her military, cultural, political, industrial and agricultural backwardness. 'We are fifty years behind the advanced countries. We must make good the distance in ten years. Either we do it, or they crush us.'[7]

In that year, Stalin's fears of external aggression were heightened when Japan, with a view to acquiring colonies, and with them the prestige which was attached to other great colonial powers such as Britain, France and Germany, invaded the Chinese province of Manchuria, and thus acquired a common border with the Soviet Union. The failure of the Allies to intervene against Japanese aggression gave Hitler the confidence to ignore the Versailles Treaty and commence rearmament. Ties between Germany and Japan were strengthened by a five-month visit to Berlin by General Tomoyuki Yamashita, who had been the Japanese Military Attaché to both Germany (1919–22) and Austria (1928–30). When, in February 1933, Germany's Communist Party – the largest in Europe – was destroyed by the Nazi SA in a reign of terror, military cooperation between the Soviet Union and Hitler came to an abrupt end.

Thanks to the First Five Year Plan, Stalin could boast that, whereas in the great world economic crisis of 1930–33, industrial output in the USA and Europe had slumped, in the Soviet Union, it had 'more than doubled ... to 201 per cent of the 1929 output'. Now, in 1933 the Second Five Year Plan was put into operation.[8]

Meanwhile, the philosophy of the *Comintern* had changed. Whereas, even as late as 1933 its members were being sent on 'manoeuvres' to teach revolutionaries how, for example, to use explosives, by 1934 these tactics were abandoned in favour of cooperation with parties such as the Popular Front of communists, socialists, and radicals, created in Paris in July 1935 which were opposed to the 'terroristic dictatorship[s]' as practised by the fascists. [9]

* * *

The signing by Germany of a pact with Poland in 1934 served to exacerbate relationships between the latter country and the Soviet Union, which seems the Poles – who had defeated the Red Army in August 1920 – as a hated enemy.

That September, the Soviet Union adopted a defensive posture by joining the League of Nations. This was 'in the knowledge that the League, in spite of its weakness, might nevertheless serve as a place where aggressors can be exposed', and because the League was an 'instrument of peace, however feeble, that might hinder the outbreak of war'.[10]

The murder of the popular Leningrad Party chief and Secretary of the Central Committee, Sergei Kirov, on 1 December – presumably at the instigation of Stalin – marked the start of a great terror campaign on the part of the Soviet leader. This lasted for several years. There were purges of the opposition, with for example, as many as 1,500 to 2,000 'enemies of the people' being shot in a single day in the summer of 1937. Unrest by the peasants was suppressed and they were herded into collective farms. Nationalists, religious leaders, critical intellectuals and internal Party opponents were arrested and imprisoned.

In May 1935 the Soviet Union signed a treaty of mutual assistance with both France and Czechoslovakia 'against possible attack by aggressors'. In 1936, when the new so-called Stalin Constitution came into being, Stalin reiterated the sentiments of his predecessor Lenin, when he declared that 'the export of revolution is nonsense'.[11] That March the Soviet Union signed a similar treaty with the Mongolian People's Republic. In August 1937 the Soviet Union signed a non-aggression pact with the Republic of China. The Third Five Year Plan, which commenced in 1938, saw the completion of the collectivization of agriculture, and the further industrialization of the Soviet Union – a fact that would have serious implications for any would-be aggressor.

The exclusion of the Soviet Union from the Munich Agreement of 29/30 September 1938 enhanced that country's feeling of isolation. Stalin now realized that he must face the fact that 'The Soviet Union will stand alone. Alone and unaided, she will have to wage war against Hitler … To save our country from this war, I would be prepared to treat with the devil'.[12]

Meanwhile, in his purges, Stalin is estimated to have murdered in excess of forty million of his own citizens: amongst them were some 35,000 of his most senior army officers. When the distinguished Russian neuropathologist Professor Vladimir Bechterew diagnosed Stalin as suffering from paranoia, the professor died soon afterwards – allegedly poisoned by his patient.

On 10 March 1939 Stalin addressed the Eighteenth Party Congress. The Soviet Union would 'continue the policy of peace'; the Party would be 'open, cautious' and we 'would not allow our country to be drawn into conflicts by warmongers who are accustomed to have others pull the chestnuts out of the fire for them'.[13]

In July 1939 hostilities broke out between the Soviet Union and Japan along the Soviet-Manchurian border with Mongolia. However, the Japanese were pre-empted by Stalin's General Georgi Zhukhov who, in a surprise attack, secured a total victory in which over 20,000 soldiers of the Japanese Imperial Army were killed. This would prompt Japan, on 27 September 1940, to join the tripartite Axis pact with Germany and Italy.

That August, Britain and France made a half-hearted attempt to come to an accord with the Soviet Union, but the talks petered out in an atmosphere of mutual mistrust. This left the door open for Germany to sign a non-aggression pact with the Soviet Union in which the lands lost by the latter country to Poland would be restored. It was also agreed that, from henceforth, the Baltic States and Finland would come under the Soviet sphere of influence. Also, Germany would grant the Soviet Union credit of 200 million Reichsmarks at an interest rate of 5 per cent, to be used to finance orders by the Soviets of German machine tools and industrial plant, together with a limited quantity of optical instruments and armour plate. In return, the Soviets would supply the Germans with raw materials.[14]

This agreement gave the Soviets a much-needed breathing space, which they used to expand their army numerically, by a factor of 2.5, and to produce, in the two years from June 1939, 7,000 tanks and 81,000 artillery pieces.[15]

*   *   *

Karl Marx had urged the workers to free themselves from their chains. Lenin had created a more egalitarian society, at a cost, but he had failed to realize his dream of turning Russia into a democratic society. However, he did acknowledge the role Russia's Jews had played in helping to overthrow the autocratic tsar.

Stalin came to power in 1924, the year that Hitler wrote *Mein Kampf*. And in *Mein Kampf*, in reference to Bolshevism, Hitler declared that

> To all external appearances, this movement strives to ameliorate the conditions under which the workers live; but in reality its aim is to enslave and thereby annihilate the non-Jewish races.[16]

Whatever the truth of the first part of this statement may be, the second part is a complete fabrication, for Stalin was quick to realize Russia's military weakness, and he also acknowledged her failure to spread communism worldwide. His industrialization of his country would, however, stand Russia in good stead should war with Germany – which he neither envisaged nor desired – finally ensue. However, the fact was that, by the mid-1930s, it was Stalin who felt threatened, both by capitalist countries on his western borders, and by militaristic Japan in the east. Therefore, for Hitler to maintain that the Soviet Union was any kind of a threat to Germany, was a complete travesty of the truth. Nevertheless, this is precisely what he did. Said he, in June 1941,

> We had no conception of the gigantic preparations of this enemy against Germany and Europe, of how tremendously great this danger really was, and how very narrowly we escaped this time the annihilation not only of Germany, but of all Europe.[17]

Notes

1. *Stalin.
2. Ibid.
3. Ibid.
4. *History of the Communist Party of the Soviet Union: Bolsheviks*, op. cit., pp. 274–5.
5. Ibid, p. 330.
6. Ibid, p. 296.
7. Stalin, op. cit., Speech to the First All-Union Conference of Managers, 4 February 1931, p. 356.
8. *History of the Communist Party of the Soviet Union: Bolsheviks*, op. cit., p. 300.
9. McKenzie, in *Comintern and World Revolution*, pp. 143–5.
10. *History of the Communist Party of the Soviet Union: Bolsheviks*, op. cit., p. 335.
11. Overy, *The Road to War*, p.199.
12. Haslam, *The Soviet Union and the Struggle for Collective Security*, pp.196–97.
13. Stalin, op. cit., Report to the 18th Congress of the CPSU, 10 March 1939, p.606.
14. Toland, op. cit., p.541.
15. Zhukov, *The Memoirs of Marshal Zhukov*, pp.197–201.
16. Hitler, op. cit., pp.181–2.
17. Prange, op. cit., 3 October 1941, p.271.

Chapter 25

World War

As the war progressed Hitler's leadership of it, as Commander-in-Chief of Germany's armed forces, provides a further valuable insight into his character. It would present him with two golden opportunities: firstly at Dunkirk where he could, had he been so minded, have crushed the Allied forces and thus nullified any further resistance on his Western Front. This he conspicuously and incomprehensibly failed to do. Secondly, the opportunity for winning the war in the east would come later in Operation BARBAROSSA, the invasion of the Soviet Union.

Poland
At 4.00am on 17 September 1939, seventeen days after Germany had invaded Poland from the west, the Red Army invaded that country from the east. Ten days later, on 27 September, Ribbentrop arrived once again in Moscow for the signing of the Soviet-German Boundary and Friendship Treaty. Western Poland, including the Polish capital, Warsaw, would now come under the German sphere of influence whereas eastern Poland, including the strategically important oilfields of Borislav-Drohbysz, and the Baltic States would come under Soviet control.

Norway and Denmark
On 9 April 1940 Hitler launched a simultaneous attack on Denmark and Norway. This, he said, was to have 'the character of a peaceful occupation, designed to protect, by force of arms, the neutrality of the northern countries; however, any resistance would be broken by all means available'.[1]

As Nordic peoples the Norwegians were, in Hitler's view, akin to the Aryans and, therefore, he was not particularly antagonistic towards them. In the event, the Norwegians were able to put up only a limited resistance to Hitler, and the Danes even less. On the down side, however, the German navy sustained heavy losses when, off the Norwegian coast and at Narvik, there was damage and destruction to nineteen vessels including two battle cruisers, two heavy cruisers, and one pocket battleship, caused by the Royal Navy.

Holland, Belgium and Luxembourg
Hitler decided that, when he invaded Holland, Belgium and Luxembourg on 10 May 1940, there would be no bombing by the Luftwaffe of the cities of those

countries. Despite this, the Luftwaffe did drop ninety-eight tons of high explosive bombs, which were intended to destroy Dutch resistance, onto the centre of the city of Rotterdam.

Dunkirk

When, by May 1940, the forces of Generals Fedor von Bock and Gerd von Rundstedt had broken through the Belgian and Dutch frontiers, by-passing the French Maginot Line, the expectation was that the Allied forces, consisting of the British Expeditionary Force, three French armies, and the remnants of the Belgian Army, a Czech division and Polish troops, now trapped between the Germans and the sea, would be destroyed. However, this was not to be the case.

To the astonishment of German commanders on the ground, at 12.45pm on 24 May 1940, their Fourth Army was ordered to halt. It should be noted that Hitler had previously postponed the date for the invasion of France on numerous occasions. The outcome was that, by the time Hitler finally gave the order to advance, no fewer than 338,226 British and Allied troops had managed to make their escape to England by sea between 26 May and 4 June 1940.

Hitler's remarks to Frau Gerdy Troost, wife of German architect Professor Paul Ludwig Troost, indicate that he would have taken no pleasure in seeing the British army destroyed. 'The blood of every single Englishman is too valuable to be shed,' he said. 'Our two peoples belong together, racially and traditionally; this is and always has been my aim, even if our generals can't grasp it,' he added.[2] However, in view of his subsequent behaviour, and in particular his bombing of Britain's cities, these remarks should be viewed with some scepticism.

There is no doubt that Hitler was in a position to deliver the knockout blow to Allied forces at Dunkirk. Why did he, therefore, not choose to do so? He had only to give the order to his generals. Instead, his failure to act decisively left them bemused and exasperated. Was he relying on Hermann Göring's Luftwaffe to complete the task, and thereby save the lives of German soldiers? Hardly, for his soldiers' welfare had never been one of Hitler's concerns. In the event, the Luftwaffe was thwarted, both by the soft sands of the Dunkirk beaches, which absorbed the explosions of the aerial bombardment, and by the mauling it received from the Royal Air Force. Or was he hoping against hope that, even at this late stage, Britain would throw in the towel as it were? Or did the explanation have more to do with what was going on inside the mind of Hitler himself, rather than with any external factors or influences?

*   *   *

As the Germans advanced, Hitler, instead of paying visits to the various battlefields, which he did only rarely, and to the concentration camps, which he did not do at all, preferred to live in an escapist world of glamorous women and motion pictures, spending as much time as possible at his idyllic retreat, the Berghof, where he dreamed up and made drawings of the architectural buildings which he hoped would one day grace his new German Reich and, in particular, 'Germania' – the new Berlin – which he aspired to make the capital city of the whole world.

* * *

Although, in the pre-war years, Stalin had been careful to avoid direct conflict with Germany, now that the war had begun and German forces were engaged against Britain and France in the west, the wily Soviet leader was not averse to exploiting the difficult situation in which Hitler found himself. To this end, in early August 1940, the Soviet Union annexed the Baltic states of Lithuania, Latvia and Estonia. And on 28 June 1940, five days after the French had capitulated, Soviet troops occupied the Romanian regions of Bessarabia, acquired by Romania from Russia at the end of the First World War, and Bucovina. Fortunately for Hitler, however, this did not include that part of the country which contained the rich resources of oil upon which his military machine depended. Supplies from elsewhere had been curtailed by the British naval blockade of Germany.

Astonishingly however, even with the war in progress, Stalin was still entirely ignorant of Hitler's real intentions. This is demonstrated in an exchange of views between himself and Sir Stafford Cripps, British Ambassador to the Soviet Union. According to Cripps,

> The British Government was convinced that Germany was striving for hegemony in Europe. This was dangerous to the Soviet Union as well as to England. Therefore, both countries ought to agree on a common policy of self-protection against Germany, and on the re-establishment of the European balance of power …

Stalin's response was as follows. He did not see any danger of the hegemony of any one country in Europe, and still less the danger that Europe might be engulfed by Germany. Stalin observed the policy of Germany and knew several leading German statesmen well. He had not discovered any desire on their part to engulf European countries. Stalin was not of the opinion that German military successes menaced the Soviet Union and her friendly relations with Germany.[3]

With the fall of France in June 1940, Hitler travelled to Compiègne, where, in the same railway carriage in which French Marshal Ferdinand Foch had accepted Germany's surrender on 11 November 1918, he presented the French with Germany's terms for armistice. This having been signed, he visited Paris and, in particular, the Emperor Napoleon Bonaparte's tomb at Les Invalides. However, he failed to learn from the emperor's mistakes, as will soon be seen.

The Problem of Britain
By the end of July 1940 Hitler had come to the conclusion that, given the strength of the British navy, an invasion of that country was impracticable. To his generals, he said,

England mainly puts her hopes in Russia. If Russia is crushed, England's last hopes will have gone. Germany will be the master of Europe and the Balkans. Decision: Russia will have to be finished off. (proposed) Date: Spring 1941.[4]

To this end, between July and mid–September, more than half of Germany's divisions in the west were transferred to the east for a proposed attack on the Soviet Union. From material, which included 8mm cine film, smuggled out of Moscow by the German Military Attaché there, Lieutenant General Ernst Koestring, Hitler was aware of the growing strength of the Red Army and of the new tanks which Russia was producing. '[W]e have to hurry up and beat them to it,' he said.[5]

When Hitler decided to launch an intensive air campaign against Britain, aimed at destroying that country's air power prior to the launch of an amphibious attack, Herbert Döhring (a member of Hitler's household staff) stated that

They [the Nazis] didn't have military intentions, but political ones. They hoped that politicians like [British Liberal politician and former Prime Minister] Lloyd George would somehow rise up together with the English people. That was the aim of this bombardment.[6]

In other words, British leader, Winston Churchill, was seen as an impediment to peace.

On 13 August 1940, the so–called Eagle Day (*Adler Tag*), the Luftwaffe launched an all–out attack against Britain and, on the night of 24/25 August, German bombs fell on central London for the first time. On the night of the 25th/26th the British retaliated by bombing Berlin. Following this, on 4 September, Hitler declared,

If the British Air Force drops two, three, or four thousand kilos of bombs, then we will drop 150,000 or 180,000; 230,000; 300,000; 400,000 kilograms in one night. When they say they will mount large scale attacks on our cities, then we will eradicate theirs.[7]

On 7 September 1940, Hitler duly ordered a massive bombing raid on London, which would be the first of seventy consecutive night raids on the British capital, together with the daylight raids. However, by 15 September, the Germans had lost so many bombers in action that they realized the daylight attacks could not be sustained.

On 28 October 1940 Italy invaded Greece, by which time Hitler had already sent troops into Romania. For the two Axis leaders there was now resentment on both sides, for each had acted without the full consent and backing of the other. Hitler, whose forces were now infiltrating ever more eastwards, now gave Romania a guarantee of her new frontiers against foreign attack, that country being immensely valuable to him on account of its Ploesti oilfields. On 3 November British troops and units of the RAF landed in Greece to help repel the invading Italian army.

On 12 November 1940 Germany's Foreign Minister Ribbentrop and Soviet Foreign Minister Vyacheslav Molotov, met in Berlin. On 26 November, Molotov, who had now returned to Moscow, informed the German Ambassador of the terms under which the Soviet Union would agree to join the Axis Pact. They were as follows: German troops to be withdrawn from Finland; a mutual assistance pact to be signed between the Soviet Union and Bulgaria; the granting to the Soviets of control over the Arabian and Persian oil fields and over the Dardanelles; and the renunciation by Japan of her rights to concessions for coal and oil in the Soviet province of Northern Sakhalin.[8] In the same month, Molotov returned to Berlin to meet with Hitler. However, much to the Führer's embarrassment, the meeting coincided with a British bombing raid on the city, which forced the pair to retreat into an air-raid shelter.

Far from improving relationships between the two countries, the visit was a dismal failure, the Russians being only too well aware of the build up of German forces along their border. As for Hitler, the Soviet proposals were totally unacceptable. He was now convinced that

> sooner or later, Stalin will abandon us and go over to the enemy [the enemy being Britain and France].[9] The Third Reich, defender and protector of Europe, could not have sacrificed these friendly countries on the altar of communism. Such behaviour would have been dishonourable ... War with Russia had become inevitable whatever we did ... I therefore decided, as soon as Molotov departed, that I would settle accounts with Russia as soon as fair weather permitted.[10]

Greece and Yugoslavia

When Mussolini's Italian troops were defeated in Albania and Greece, Hitler realized that, before he launched Operation BARBAROSSA against the Soviet Union, it was essential for Greece to be occupied and subdued. Between Germany and Greece, however, lay four countries: Hungary, Romania, Bulgaria and Yugoslavia. Of these, the first two were already under German occupation; the third, Bulgaria, had in March 1941 joined the Axis Tripartite Pact. Therefore, only Yugoslavia, a country hostile to either German or Russian occupation of the Balkans, remained as an obstacle to Hitler's ambitions.

Hitler calculated that, were he to invade Greece, Yugoslavia would be sure to intervene against him. So, having made his decision, he agreed to appease the Hungarians once more so that, in return for their collaboration, Hungary would be permitted to regain territory lost to its neighbours in 1920 under the Treaty of Trianon.

Hitler now invited Prince Paul, Regent of Yugoslavia, to the Berghof for discussions. However, although the Prince's Crown Council agreed to sign the Axis Pact, such was the opposition to this within his country that, on 27 March 1941, pro-Allied army officers staged a coup, overthrew the government, and replaced Paul with his nephew Peter. The Soviet Union instantly recognized King Peter and his new government, and signed a pact with Yugoslavia on 5 April. Faced with this setback Hitler declared, 'Now I intend to make a clean sweep of the Balkans …',[11] and he issued a directive whereby Yugoslavia and Greece were to be attacked simultaneously.

First, the Yugoslav forces were overwhelmed in a devastating *Blitzkrieg*-type attack and, on 17 April 1941, the Royal Yugoslav Army surrendered to the Germans. On 23 April, the Greek Army followed suit. However, in order to achieve this goal, Hitler had been forced to employ no less than twenty-nine German divisions.

Japan

In the spring of 1941 Hitler invited the new Japanese Ambassador, General Hiroshi Ōshima, to a secret briefing in which he outlined his plan for a global war to be fought by Germany and Japan, with a view to conquering the world – Operation ORIENT. And this world included the Soviet Union. The proposal was for one German force to sweep across North Africa, Egypt, Iraq and Iran; for another to cross the Soviet Union into the oil-rich Caucasus. And having joined together, the combined forces would move to attack India, the 'Jewel in the Crown' of the British Empire. Meanwhile, Japan would conquer Europe's colonies in the East, before rendezvousing with the Germans in India.

Notes

1. Toland, op. cit., p. 599.
2. Ibid, p. 611.
3. *Documents on German Foreign Policy*, Files of the German Foreign Office, pp. 207–8.
4. **Hitler's Britain.*
5. Ibid.
6. Ibid.
7. Ibid.
8. *Nazi-Soviet Relations* Dispatch of Schulenburg. 26 Nov 1940, NSR. pp. 258–59.
9. Toland, op. cit., p. 646.
10. Ibid, p. 646.
11. Ibid., p. 653.

Chapter 26

The Planned Invasion of the Soviet Union

Up until this point, Hitler's armed forces had carried all before them, but now, for the German military, came the greatest test of all.

It is chilling to note that in his book *Mein Kampf*, written seventeen years previously, when he was aged thirty-five, there are powerful indications that Hitler would, were he in a position to do so, wage war on the Soviet Union. And nothing in his writings or utterances made since that time, leads to any other conclusion than that this was his great and overriding ambition.

As already demonstrated, whereas the Soviet Union, with its aim of spreading communism worldwide, may have posed a threat to Germany, and to other European countries prior to the writing by Hitler of *Mein Kampf* in 1924, then, and subsequently, it posed no threat whatsoever. On the contrary, Lenin was preoccupied with the task of internal government, and Stalin positively sought peace with the outside world. However, the deluded Hitler believed otherwise.

In *Mein Kampf*, however, Hitler reveals his own aggressive and expansionist tendencies, as he states, in respect of 'the inexorable cosmopolitan Jew, who is fighting for his own dominion over the nation'

> the sword is the only means whereby a nation [Germany] can thrust that clutch from his throat. Only when national sentiment is organized and concentrated into an effective force can it defy that international menace which tends towards an enslavement of the nation. But this road is, and will always be marked with bloodshed.[1]

And in combating the 'international menace', Hitler would conveniently, and in accordance with his policy of *Lebensraum*, appropriate Russian territory for the use of the Germans.

> We, as National Socialists, must stick firmly to the aim that we have set for our foreign policy, namely that the German people must be assured [of] the territorial area which is necessary for it to exist on this earth.[2]

In future, this territory would not be obtained 'as a favour from other people, but we will have to win it by the power of a triumphant sword'.[3]

And in a final, ominous, warning, he declares, 'Today, Germany is the next battlefield for Russian Bolshevism!'[4] And so, with Liebenfels' favourite descriptions of the Bolsheviks as 'Satanic', the Jews as 'hybrid beasts,' and the 'Bolshy-Jewish bloodhounds [which] remind us of the horrible faces of antediluvian dragon-monsters,' no doubt echoing in his mind, the deluded Hitler embarked on the last of a series of military campaigns which would cost, all told, the lives of approximately sixty million people. The race war, as advocated by the mad monk in his *Ostara* journals, was now to become a reality.

* * *

In March 1941, Hitler issued the so-called Commissar Order by which, following the invasion of the Soviet Union, the entire Soviet leadership, both military and civilian, was to be eliminated. However, so that Hitler should not personally be implicated in the decision, the order was not put in writing.

On 20 March 1941, Yōsuke Matsuoka, the Japanese Foreign Minister arrived in Berlin, where he urged the Führer to make peace with Stalin, with the object of creating a German-Soviet-Japanese alliance. This proposal was anathema to Hitler, who in turn urged the Japanese to attack the Russians in the east. The Japanese responded by massing their troops in Manchuria. However, on 13 April, and greatly to Hitler's fury, Japan signed a neutrality pact with the Soviet Union. This action would be of immense help to Stalin in the months to come, by allowing him to transfer many of his eastern divisions to his Western Front.

* * *

In deciding to invade the Soviet Union, Hitler failed to learn from the experience of French Emperor Napoleon Bonaparte, who had invaded Russia in 1812, seventy-seven years before the Führer was born, and with catastrophic results. Instead, the German leader preferred to focus, optimistically, on the Great War Battle of Tannenberg (26–30 August 1914) in which the Germans routed the Russian army. This battle he recreates with relish in *Mein Kampf*, where he describes the 'interminable columns of Russian war prisoners' which 'poured into Germany', a stream which he thought would never end for 'as soon as one [Russian] army was defeated and routed, another would take its place. The supply of soldiers which the gigantic [Russian] Empire placed at the disposal of the Tsar seemed inexhaustible …'.[5]

Hitler, however, revealed that he was aware that, were he to invade the Soviet Union, he would be breaking the rules of military strategy, when he told Martin Bormann, Head of the Party Chancellery,

I had always maintained that we ought, at all costs, to avoid waging war on two fronts [Since February 1941, German forces had been engaged – with the

Italians – against the British in North Africa], and you may rest assured that I pondered long and anxiously over Napoleon, and his experiences in Russia.[6]

However, because of his aggression towards, and paranoia towards an enemy which, in his deluded state of mind, he had created for himself, Hitler was resolved to ignore both the experience of the great French general, and the tenets of military warfare.

Notes
1. Hitler, op. cit., p. 364.
2. Ibid, p. 359.
3. Ibid, p. 360.
4. Ibid, p. 364.
5. Ibid, p. 116
6. Toland, op. cit., p. 650

Chapter 27

Operation BARBAROSSA

Operation BARBAROSSA, which was delayed on account of Hitler having to divert military resources to Greece and Yugoslavia, commenced on 22 June 1941. Up until the previous month, the unsuspecting Soviets had supplied Germany with approximately 1.5 million tons of grain, 100,000 tons of cotton, 2 million tons of petroleum products, 1.5 million tons of timber, 140,000 tons of manganese and 25,000 tons of chromium.[1] This was hardly the action of a country which was expecting to be invaded imminently by the recipient of these commodities which, of course, the Soviet Union was not.

This was to be a multi-pronged attack, involving not only German forces, but also those of Finland, Italy, Romania and Hungary. The three main formations concerned were Army Group North (AG North), under Field Marshal Wilhelm von Leeb, which would advance towards Leningrad – which the Finns would also attack from the north, cutting off Soviet forces in the Baltic States in the process; Army Group Centre (AG Centre), under Field Marshal Feodor von Bock, which would drive directly towards Moscow; Army Group South (AG South), under Field Marshal Gerd von Rundstedt, which would drive towards the Ukraine, overrun that region's industrial centres, capture the town of Rostov and the Crimea, then, finally, the valuable oilfields of the Caucasus. Further south still, German and Romanian troops would advance towards Odessa and the Black Sea.

On that very day, 22 June 1941, German Ambassador to the Soviet Union, Count Friedrich von der Schulenburg, went to the Kremlin to accuse the Soviet Union of being 'about to fall on Germany's back'. He told Soviet Foreign Affairs Commissar Molotov that the Führer had therefore ordered the Wehrmacht 'to oppose this threat with all the means at its disposal'. To this, Molotov retorted 'It is war! Your aircraft have just bombarded some ten [Russian] "villages". Do you believe that we deserve that?'[2] But German Propaganda Minister Goebbels was unmoved. Said he

Now that the Führer has unmasked the treachery of the Bolshevik rulers, National Socialism, and hence the German people, are reverting to the principles which impelled them – the struggle against plutocracy and Bolshevism.[3]

Such was the unpreparedness of the Soviet Union for an attack by Germany, that by the time Stalin had finally consented to Soviet commander Marshal Zhukov putting his frontier forces on the alert, it was too late for them to take effective action. As for the Red Air Force, the majority of its aircraft were destroyed on the ground before they even had the chance to take off.

As the German forces advanced they were followed by four SS *Einsatzgruppen* (Special Groups, a euphemism for murder squads), each consisting of 3,000 men whose aim was to eliminate Bolshevik leaders, Jews, gypsies, and the mentally and physically sick. Hitler now transferred his headquarters to the *Wolfsschanze* (Wolf's Lair) near Rastenberg in East Prussia.

The Jews of Russia, instead of acting in a way consistent with that in which Hitler had liked to portray them, i.e., as people who were antagonistic to the Germans and anxious to spread Bolshevism throughout the world, welcomed the invaders as liberators. Their reward was to be rounded up and despatched to concentration camps and killing centres. In the words of Obergruppenführer von dem Bach–Zelewski, Senior SS and Police Commander for Central Russia, 'Never before has a people gone as unsuspectingly to its disaster'.[4]

The initial objective of BARBAROSSA was to destroy the Red Army, and, at first, all went to plan. In huge pincer movements, German forces cut off their Soviet counterparts: at Minsk on 9 July 1941, 290,000 were captured; at Smolensk on 12 July, 300,000 were trapped; at Umlan on 4 August 100,000 prisoners were taken. The Germans' greatest success, however, was at Kiev on 19 October, when 665,000 Soviet troops surrendered.

By 14 July 1941, AG North had reached Leningrad and was in occupation of its suburbs. The city, invested as it was to the north by the Finns, was now only able to hold out by being supplied across Lake Ladoga. As for AG Centre, it encountered serious Soviet resistance at the Battle of Smolensk from 10 July to 10 September, but continued with the drive towards Moscow.

On 2 October 1941, Hitler said,

Only when the entire German people becomes a single community of sacrifice can we hope and expect that providence will stand by us in the future. Almighty God never helped a lazy man. Nor does He help a coward.[5]

A fatal flaw in Nazi strategy now became apparent. Whereas Hitler had envisaged that, after the initial onslaught, AG Centre would divert to support AG North rather than press on to Moscow, Field Marshal Walther von Brauchitsch and General Franz Halder, Chief of the General Staff, believed that the attack on Moscow – the centre of Russian communications and armament production – should be the primary objective. Nonetheless, contrary to the advice of his generals, Hitler ordered that armoured units of AG Centre were to be diverted, some to be sent north to AG North to facilitate the capture of Leningrad, and others to the south to AG South to assist with the drive into the Ukraine. 'My generals understand nothing of the war economy,' he said.[6]

Finally, on 5 September 1941, Hitler, at the urging of Brauchitsch, changed his mind once again and ordered that the focus be, once more, switched to Moscow which, on 2 October, was attacked with seventy-seven divisions in Operation TYPHOON. This was despite warnings from Field Marshal Fedor von Bock that it was too late in the season to risk an attack.

Further catastrophes befell the Soviets, when at Bryansk and Vyazma another 650,000 prisoners were taken. By October, when the Germans were barely fifty miles from Moscow, around three million Soviet troops had been either killed, captured, or wounded.

Halder, in his response to Hitler's statement that the Russians were 'finished', told his Führer that the army's own intelligence showed that this was far from the case. The former subsequently commented that

> Hitler's decisions had ceased to have anything in common with the principles of strategy and operations as they have been recognized for generations past. *They were the product of a violent nature following its momentary impulses, which recognize no limits to possibility, and which made its wish-dreams the father of its acts* ...[7] You didn't have to have the gift of a prophet, to see what would happen when Stalin unleashed those million and a half troops against Stalingrad and the Don flank. I pointed this out to Hitler very clearly.

The outcome was that Halder was dismissed.[8]

Heavy rains caused the German Mark IV tanks to flounder in the mud. Not only that but the Luftwaffe, which normally would have supported their attacks by Blitzkrieg, could not fly, owing to poor visibility. Boch was right. The attack had come too late. Even worse, the Germans now found themselves facing a new and able Russian Commander, General Georgi Zhukov.

When, in November 1941, Colonel General Heinz Guderian, Commander of the Second Panzer Army, informed Bock that he could 'see no way of carrying them [i.e., Bock's orders] out' because of the poor condition of his men, Bock ignored him and ordered another assault on Moscow (the domes of its buildings were clearly visible to the Germans) to commence on 15 November. Now came snow, ice, and temperatures of minus 40 degrees Celsius, for which the German troops were ill-prepared due to an earlier edict by Hitler which prohibited the making ready of winter clothing for the men. On 5 December, Guderian was forced to halt his attack on Moscow. AG Centre's losses alone had by now amounted to 55,000 dead and 100,000 wounded or suffering from frostbite.

On 6 December 1941, after a huge Russian counter-attack on a 200-mile front, Hitler was finally forced to admit to Colonel General Alfred Jodl, Chief of OKW's Operations (*Oberkommando der Wehrmacht*, high command of the armed forces) that 'Victory could no longer be achieved'.[9] Meanwhile, on 7 December, Japan, anxious to prevent America from intervening in her plan to conquer Europe's Far Eastern colonies, attacked the American Fleet at Pearl Harbor. Japanese forces went on to capture Singapore, Hong Kong, Malaya and Dutch Indonesia.

On 11 December 1941, Hitler, together with Italy, declared war on America – an act of crass stupidity, given the fact that there was in the USA, a substantial anti-war lobby, a fact of which its President, Franklin D. Roosevelt was well aware.

By 13 December 1941 it was clear that Hitler's attempt to surround Moscow had failed. His response? To dismiss Brauchitsch and assume personal command of the army himself. Now, instead of sanctioning a retreat he gave the order 'Stand fast: not one step back!' and with an air of supreme arrogance, declared,

> This little affair of operational command is something anybody can do. The commander-in-chief's job is to train the army in the National Socialist Idea, and I know of no general who could do that as I want it done. For that reason, I have taken over control of the army myself.[10]

Between December and January 1942, Hitler dismissed not only the commanders of the army groups which had embarked on Operation BARBAROSSA, but thirty-five other generals as well.[11] In the words of Ulrich de Maizière of Hitler's General Staff,

> One of Hitler's greatest weaknesses as a commander was that, in that mood, any feelings for logistics deserted him. Thus the operational aims he set, and his decisions, became more and more unreal … further and further from reality.[12]

Here, once again, the mental health of the Führer is being questioned.

On 28 May 1942, AG South captured Kharkov and, on 24 July, Rostov on the Don river. In the far south, the Germans reached the Crimea, where the newly formed Eleventh Army, under General Fritz Erich von Manstein, isolated the fortress of Sevastopol.

Stalingrad

In numerous documentary films, Hitler is to be seen, splendidly attired in military uniform, poring over maps with his military commanders. This former corporal in the German Army of the Great War, with little or no training in military strategy and tactics, would now be instrumental in orchestrating the complete destruction of *his own* fighting forces on the Eastern Front.

The events at Stalingrad during the winter of 1942–43 would provide a graphic demonstration not only of Hitler's incompetence as a commander but also of his utter lack of concern for the well-being of his armed forces. At first, for the Germans, all went well: when Soviet Marshal Semyon Timoshenko's forces attacked on 12 May 1942 at Kharkov, they were routed, with 600 tanks lost and 250,000 troops taken prisoner.

Fall Blau (or Case Blue) was an operation designed by Hitler to drive through the Caucasus to the Caspian Sea, capturing the oilfields of Grozny and Maikop on the way. On 28 June 1942, AG South, commanded by Field Marshal Feodor von Bock, duly launched the attack but failed to encircle and destroy the Soviets in the customary classic pincer movement, which hitherto had been so successful.

On 13 July 1942, Hitler dismissed Bock, and divided his forces into Army Group A (AG A) under Field Marshal Wilhelm von List, and Army Group B (AG B) under Field Marshal Maximilian von Weichs. List's AG A in Operation EDELWEISS was to continue the drive to the Caucasus; Weichs' AG B in Operation SIEGFRIED was to drive towards Stalingrad, an industrial city situated on a great bend in the river Volga. In this operation Italian, Hungarian and Romanian forces would also be engaged on the German side.

Hitler also ordered the Eleventh Army to withdraw from the south and, instead, travel north to join the attack on Leningrad: this had the effect of extending the German southern front from 500 to 3,000 miles. In another bizarre move, Hitler transferred General Hermann Hoth's Fourth Panzer Army from General Friedrich Paulus' Sixth Army (Paulus was Deputy Chief of the Army General Staff under General Franz Halder, and his Sixth Army was the main element of AG B) to the south, to be placed under the command of AG A. This weakened Paulus' offensive capability and thereby retarded his advance on Stalingrad. List's AG A captured Rostov on 23 July 1942, but by the time it reached the Caucasus it found the mountain passes had been blocked by the Soviets.

At the end of August 1942, Paulus, whose supply line stretched 1,200 miles back to Berlin, commenced his attack on Stalingrad, much of which was reduced to rubble by German artillery fire and aerial bombing. However, the Soviets capitalized on this by using the ruins as defensive fortifications. By early October the Germans, in hand-to-hand fighting, managed to occupy roughly 70 per cent of the city and the Russian Sixty-second Army was pinned down, with its back to the Volga river.

The Russian winter found the German soldiers much less adequately clothed than their Russian counterparts; neither was their equipment designed to deal with the sub-zero temperatures which pertained. In the words of Kurt Sametreiter (of 1st SS-Panzer Division *Leibstandarte SS Adolf Hitler* – created from the SS bodyguard, or *Leibstandarte* to Adolf Hitler), the temperature fell to minus 46 degrees Celsius. 'I saw how my fellow soldiers' (frozen) ears fell off,' he said, 'so we got some rope and tied our ears to our heads, and that's how we coped.' Not possessing overcoats of their own, the only way for the German soldiers to obtain them was from dead or captured Russians.[13]

By early November 1942, 90 per cent of Stalingrad was in the hands of the Germans. Nevertheless, in a holding operation of unsurpassed tenacity, heroism and improvization, the Red Army, under General Vasily Chuikov, whose overall commander, General Georgi Zhukov, had organized and directed the successful counter offensive before Moscow, was reinforced from across the river and managed to hold on. Now it was Zhukov's turn to take the offensive. On 19 November he launched Operation URAN, a counter-attack made simultaneously on three fronts. Prior to this, General Kurt Zeitzler, Halder's successor as Chief of Army General Staff, had flown back to Hitler's headquarters to request permission to withdraw his forces before the Russian counter-offensive began, but the Führer had declined his request. Zeitzler now urged Hitler to give permission for the Sixth Army to withdraw from Stalingrad to the Don bend, in order that the German front line, which had been fractured by the Soviets, could be restored. Hitler responded, with characteristic anger and stubbornness, 'I won't leave the Volga! I won't go back from the Volga!'[14]

On the evening of 22 November 1942, General Paulus signalled by wireless message that his Sixth Army of 250,000 men, which consisted of twenty German and two Romanian divisions, was now surrounded by the enemy. Hitler's response was that the Sixth Army would be supplied by Göring's Luftwaffe, until it could be relieved. Paulus declared that he would need a minimum of 750 tons of supplies per day to be flown in. In the thick fog and freezing conditions, this proved to be well beyond the capability of the Luftwaffe.

On 25 November 1942, Hitler hastily ordered Field Marshal von Manstein back from the Leningrad Front and gave him command of Army Group Don, newly improvised from part of the AG A, with the task of relieving the Sixth Army from the south west. Manstein believed that the only chance of success would be for the Sixth Army to break out of Stalingrad, while he made his own assault against the intervening Russian armies. However, once again, Hitler refused to countenance a withdrawal from Stalingrad.

Manstein commenced his attack on Stalingrad on 12 December 1942 in Operation WINTER TEMPEST, and advanced to within thirty miles of the southern perimeter of the city, from where Paulus' besieged army could see the signal flares of their would-be rescuers. Had the Sixth Army chosen this moment to break out from Stalingrad, they would almost certainly have met with success, but Paulus stubbornly obeyed Hitler's orders not to retreat. By now the Volga river had frozen over, thus facilitating the relief of the city by the Soviets.

Finally, on 21 December 1942, Hitler gave Paulus permission to break out, but only provided that he also retained possession of Stalingrad! Said Chief of Staff Zeitzler,

I begged Hitler to authorise the breakout. I pointed out that this was absolutely our last chance to save the 200,000 men of Paulus' army. However, Hitler would not give way. In vain I described to him conditions inside the so-called fortress [of Stalingrad]: the despair of the starving soldiers, their loss of confidence in the Supreme Command, the wounded expiring for lack of proper attention, while thousands froze to death. *He remained as impervious to arguments of this sort as to those others which I had advanced.*[15]

On 8 January 1943, General Konstantin Rokossovski, Commander of Soviet Forces on the Don Front, offered General Paulus terms for surrender. When Hitler, yet again, vetoed Paulus' request that he be permitted to comply with Rokossovski's demand, the Soviets, on 10 January, began what would be their final assault on the city. Meanwhile, in their great misery and desperation, many Germans soldiers began to commit suicide.

On 24 January 1943, when the Soviets again offered Paulus the chance to surrender, he sent a wireless message to Hitler,

Troops [are] without ammunition or food. Effective command no longer possible ... 18,000 wounded without any supplies or dressings or drugs ... Further defence senseless. Collapse inevitable. Army requests immediate permission to surrender in order to save lives of Romanian troops.

To which the Führer replied with utter callousness,

Surrender is forbidden. VI Army will hold their positions to the last man and the last round, and by their heroic endurance, will make an unforgettable contribution towards the establishment of a defensive front and the salvation of the western world.[16]

'One must cut off one's own lines of retreat; then one fights more easily and with greater determination,' said Hitler. In other words, there was to be no way out for Paulus, however dire his situation.

On 30 January 1943, in a supremely ironic gesture, Hitler promoted Paulus to the rank of field marshal. The following day, Paulus' army surrendered, by which time, of his 285,000 soldiers, only 91,000 remained alive, together with 20,000 Romanians. Awaiting them now were the prisoner-of-war camps of Siberia, places of such harshness that only 5,000 would ever see their homeland again.[17] For the Germans, the only consolation was that tying down seven Soviet armies at Stalingrad had successfully allowed their armies in the Caucasus to be evacuated.

Throughout the battle, Hitler had displayed a mixture of arrogance, aloofness and indifference as to whether a single soldier of his was lost, or a whole army. His adjutant, Reinhard Spitzy, attempted to explain this by stating that

Hitler always wanted to gamble. He risked everything. Before the war Göring said, 'We should stop risking everything.' To which Hitler replied, 'We've always risked everything and I always will risk everything.'[18]

German lawyer and legal historian Otto Gritschneder went further.

What he (Hitler) called BRAVELY was really the 'all or nothing' PSYCHOSIS OF A MADMAN. There are people who take the greatest risks, so as to feel the joy and thrill of adventure. He certainly wasn't a realist.[19]

Said Count Johann Adolf Kielmansegg of Hitler's General Staff, 'For me, it [the experience of Stalingrad] destroyed [not only] any respect [I had] for Hitler as a commander, but also as a man, as a leader'. Vincenz Griesemer, who fought at Stalingrad, said, 'For us, Hitler was, by this stage, our grave-digger'.[20]

* * *

Following the German defeat at Stalingrad on 2 February 1943, Hitler promoted Martin Bormann to the post of Secretary to the Führer, in charge of all the affairs of state. Bormann, the son of a postal worker, was a mediocre student who had failed to gain his high school diploma. In the First World War he fought as an artilleryman. Having been released in 1927, following his imprisonment for the murder, when he was serving in the *Freikorps*, of a former school teacher, he joined the German National Socialist Workers' Party, and, finally, the staff at Nazi Party Headquarters in Munich. In 1933 Hitler appointed him Head of the Office of Deputy Führer Rudolf Hess.

Not surprisingly, Bormann was viewed with contempt by senior members of the armed services. They saw him as an uneducated person, and as someone who deliberately restricted their access to the Führer.

* * *

The defeat of Nazi forces at Stalingrad would prove to be the turning point of the war. Yet Hitler seemed strangely unmoved, preferring to blame his generals but not himself for yet another debacle. To them, and to his party officials and close acquaintances, it must have seemed that Hitler was working to a different agenda, one to which they were not privy, and which they were unable to comprehend.

* * *

Hitler once more displayed his intransigence when, in February 1943, following a Soviet counter-attack, Rundstedt realized that his position in the town of Rostov was untenable and that he must withdraw. When Hitler duly, and predictably, ordered him to remain where he was, Rundstedt replied, 'It is MADNESS to attempt to hold. First the troops cannot do it, and second, if they do not retreat, they will be destroyed. I repeat that this order must be rescinded, or that you find someone else [to command]'.[21] 'Madness' was a word which was now being used more and more frequently in relation to the Führer. To this, Hitler replied, 'I am acceding to your request. Please give up your command.' Rundstedt was replaced by Field Marshal von Reichenau and Rostov fell to the Red Army on 14 February 1943.

* * *

Hermann Rauschning described how Hitler's acolytes did not help the situation when they, metaphorically, 'threw sand in Hitler's eyes'. He believed that,

> The German people, once the most objective and scientific of peoples, now went to unbelievable extremes of lying servility. Hitler was never told the uncomfortable truth. By favourably coloured reports, he was pushed ever further along the road to ruin.[22]

Hitler subsequently made it clear where, in his opinion, the blame lay for the defeat, both at Stalingrad and elsewhere. Not of course, with himself, but with his fellow countrymen, of whom he made a scapegoat. Said he:

> If many people are shattered by this trial of will, then I shall shed no tears for them. They deserve this fate. They have forged their own destiny. They do not deserve any better.[23]

By the end of 1944 more than two thirds of German towns and cities had been bombed, but Hitler did not take the trouble to visit them.

Newsreels and press reports designed for homeland consumption revealed nothing of Germany's defeat at Stalingrad and the huge losses sustained by her forces; nor of the untold atrocities committed by the Nazis, and in particular by the Waffen SS, which by now was so short of manpower that, among others, Balkan Muslims and Ukrainian Slavs were recruited into its ranks. These atrocities included the SS massacre at the Russian military hospital at Kharkov in March 1943, and the destruction of the village of Oradour-sur-Glane in south-west France on 10 June 1944, when its menfolk were shot to death in a barn, and its women and children locked in a church which was then set on fire – to name but two atrocities.

* * *

In 1944, dissatisfied with the existing German legal system, Hitler set up the People's Court, designed to facilitate the swift incarceration of his opponents. Those who did not confess their crimes – either real or fabricated by the prosecution – were beaten ('intensive interrogation' being a phrase used by the Gestapo for torture). Even those acquitted were sent to concentration camps. When students of Munich University's White Rose Society denounced Hitler as a mass murderer, they were sentenced to death.

General Kurt von Schleicher, former Reichs Chancellor, who was seen as an obstacle to the Nazis, was shot to death, along with his wife. And when civil servants working in Secretary of State Roland Freisler's Reichs Ministry of Justice prepared a document describing this as a 'political murder', Freisler, according to German lawyer Otto Gritschneider, ordered the document to be destroyed saying, 'That was no political murder, that was suicide.'[24]

It was felt by some in Germany that if Hitler could be assassinated then the Home Guard* could take power and bring the war to a close. To this end, on 20 July 1944, German Army Colonel Klaus von Stauffenberg placed a bomb under a table

---

* This was the *Volkssturm*, created on 18 October 1944 whereby males between the ages of 16 and 60 were conscripted for the defence of the homeland.

in a room where Hitler was holding a conference. Although the bomb exploded, Hitler sustained only minor injuries. Stauffenberg and his fellow conspirators were arrested, the Gestapo having discovered their identities, and they were tried at the Supreme Court in Berlin the following month with Freisler, whose vicious shrieking and snarling surpassed even that of Hitler himself, presiding over the proceedings.

General Beck was given the opportunity to commit suicide. Stauffenberg and General Friedrich Olbricht, together with their two adjutants, were sentenced to death for high treason, and executed by firing squad. Other prisoners to be executed included Field Marshal Erwin von Witzleben and Generals Erich Hoepner, Helmuth Stieff and Paul von Hase. As for Colonel Mertz von Quirnheim and Lieutenant Werner von Haeften, they suffered a slow and agonizing death by being hanged with piano wire from meat hooks. It is believed that approximately 5,000 men and women suspected of being involved in this so-called July Plot were executed by the Nazis.

Notes

1. Toland, op. cit., p. 667.
2. Ibid, pp. 671–72.
3. Ibid, p. 673.
4. Ibid, p. 676.
5. Ibid, p. 685.
6. *Hitler: a Profile: The Commander*.
7. Halder, *Hitler als Feldherr*, p. 50.
8. Shirer, op. cit., p. 917.
9. Toland, op. cit., p. 690.
10. Ibid, p. 697.
11. Campbell, *The World War II Fact Book*, p. 102.
12. *Hitler: a Profile: The Commander*.
13. *The SS: Himmler's Madness*.
14. Zeitzler, *The Fatal Decisions*, Essay on Stalingrad in Freidin, 1956, New York.
15. Shirer, op. cit., p. 927.
16. Ibid, p. 930.
17. Ibid, p. 932.
18. *Hitler: a Profile: The Blackmailer*.
19. Ibid.
20. *Hitler: a Profile: The Commander*.
21. Toland, op. cit., p. 689.
22. Rauschning, op. cit., p. 204
23. *Hitler's War: Air War over Germany*.
24. *Hitler's Henchmen: Freisler: the Executioner*.

Chapter 28

The 'Final Solution'

Hitler never met Liebenfels, nor did he ever acknowledge that *Ostara* (and probably other of Liebenfels' works) were the source of his core beliefs. However, whereas, for the deluded Liebenfels, the journal was merely an outlet for his insane ramblings, Hitler, in 'The Final Solution', would make the mad monk's sickening notions a reality.

The full implications of The Final Solution – the Holocaust – would be felt not only in Germany but throughout all the countries occupied by the Nazis. Its seeds, however, had been sown long before Adolf Hitler arrived on the scene. During the Christmas period of the year 1920, the Nazi Party's message was carried to its readers on the front page of its newspaper *Der Volkischer Beobachter*. It read as follows: 'Germans! Buy your Christmas presents at German stores, but not from Jews or in Jewish stores.'[1]

However, when the Nazis came to power in 1933, Eugene Levine, German Communist Youth, 1930 to 1933, said that because a substantial number of the Storm Troopers had Jewish girlfriends, many German Jews thought, 'It's not going to be so bad … They can't hate us all.'[2] In fact, life for the Jews became worse.

On 1 April 1933 the Nazi Party organized a boycott of all Jewish shops for a period of one day. On 10 May, outside Berlin's Opera House, there was a great bonfire of books, perceived to contain un-German or pro-Jewish sentiments.

It was decided that Jews, gypsies, Slavs and those with hereditary disabilities – either physical or mental – would play no part in the production of an Aryan master race. Therefore, from 1933 onward, nurses and doctors were required to report them to the health authority where a *eugenics committee* would decide who was, and who was not, worthy to procreate. Those designated as unworthy were labelled 'a-socials' and compulsorily sterilized. The message was reinforced by propaganda films demanding that women should question whether the genes of their forebears were worthy to be passed on.

One of Dr Josef Goebbels' propaganda films showed two scorpions fighting with each other, as the 'professor' who is commentating on the film declares, 'All animals live in a permanent struggle, whereby the weak is destroyed.'[3]

On 27 July 1934 Hitler offered Hjalmar Schacht, President of the Reichs Bank, the additional post of Economics Minister. Schacht, one of the few of Hitler's acolytes with a conscience and with courage enough to stand up to the Führer, first enquired, 'Before I accept, I want to know how you wish me to handle the Jewish question', for it was Schacht's view that, as far as international trade was concerned, and particularly that with America, 'Jews should not be molested in commerce, since any hampering of Jewish-operated trade brings unemployment for German employees'.[4] To this, Hitler replied, 'In matters which concern the economy, Jews can participate as they did in the past'.[5]

Pressure continued to mount on Germany's Jews, and on 15 September 1935, the Nuremberg Blood Laws for the 'protection of German blood and German honour' came into effect. Now, Germans with Jewish ancestry who were either 'full', 'half', or 'quarter–bred' were categorized as being non-Aryans. It became a criminal offence for pure-bred Germans to marry, or even have sexual intercourse with Jews, who were declared to be non-German citizens. Jews also faced prohibitions on residence and employment. According to Johannes Zahn, German economist and banker from 1931, 'The general opinion was that the Jews had gone too far in Germany', and he pointed out that of the 4,800 lawyers in Berlin, 3,600 were Jews and, apart from German orchestral conductor Gustav Furtwangler, 'there was hardly a theatre director who wasn't a Jew'.[6]

Jews were forced to wear Stars of David on armbands or on their jackets as a means of identification, and Jewish children were ejected from the state education system. In Munich one of the largest synagogues in Germany was demolished to make way for a car park. Posters appeared in the streets saying:

BEWARE OF JEWS AND PICKPOCKETS
JEWS ARE NOT WELCOME HERE
JEWS ARE NOT WELCOME IN OUR GERMAN FORESTS[7]

Propaganda Minister, Goebbels, pleased his Führer by announcing, subsequently, that as a result of the activities of the Nazi Party,

We have German films, a German press, German literature, German art, and German broadcasting. The objection that was often raised against us in the past, that it was not feasible to remove Jews from the arts and from cultural life because there were too many of them, and that we'd be unable to fill all the vacant positions – all this has brilliantly been proved wrong.[8]

Economics Minister Schacht, however, realized the danger of anti-Semitism to foreign trade, and pointed out at the 1935 Nuremberg Party Rally that, instead of 'a display of turbulence in the racial wars [being waged against the Jews]' action must be 'conducted within a legal and controlled framework and co-ordinated with the country's economic necessities'. Although Hitler's Nazi henchmen were infuriated by these remarks, Hitler himself did not intervene. Now, the emboldened Schacht, instead of keeping a low profile, made a point of attending Lutheran religious services presided over by Pastor Martin Niemöller, a Great War submarine commander, at his local church in the wealthy Berlin suburb of Dahlem.

Niemöller was subsequently arrested by the Nazis; he would spend a total of eight years in various concentration camps.

During the Berlin Olympic Games in the summer of 1936, when German athletes won thirty-three gold medals, which was more than any other country, all traces of anti-Jewish activity were concealed for a period of three weeks, and the ubiquitous banners proclaiming that 'THE JEWS ARE OUR MISFORTUNE' were temporarily removed. Meanwhile, visitors to the Games, who had travelled from all parts of the world, would have had no idea that a mere sixty kilometres away slave labourers were demolishing the Oranienburg Concentration Camp and replacing it with a new one called Sachsenhausen. On 1 August 1937 the Buchenwald Concentration Camp was opened; by the time war broke out there would be a total of six such establishments, holding approximately 50,000 detainees.

When Hitler annexed Austria on 11 March 1938, anti-Jewish pogroms were initiated and the same anti-Semitic laws applied there as were in force in Germany. The result was that the Jews, having been robbed by the SS of their homes, businesses, capital, and possessions, embarked on a mass exodus from that country.

As for Reichs Chief of Police Heinrich Himmler, he chose the picturesque Austrian village of Mathausen as the site for a new concentration camp. Gypsies, as well as Jews were targeted, declared to be 'inveterate criminals', and subjected to forced labour and mass sterilization.[9] In fact, a special section for gypsies was created within Buchenwald Concentration Camp where, during the holocaust, between a quarter and a half million were exterminated.

Reinhard Heydrich of the Reichs Security Head Office had a network of informers within the Catholic Church in Vienna. Even nuns were not immune from Nazi persecution. Helen Kafka Restituta, for example, had for twenty years been a nurse, working in the operating theatre of a hospital in the town of Modling near the capital. According to her friend Gertrude Jancsy, she had hung crucifixes on her wall and had refused to remove them, having been ordered to do so by the Nazis. 'I will happily put a cross up, but I will certainly not take one down,' she said.

When Sister Restituta disseminated the words of a soldier's song criticizing the Nazis, she was denounced by a doctor colleague and, on Ash Wednesday 1942, was accused of 'aiding and abetting the enemy in the betrayal of the Fatherland, and for plotting high treason'. The Gestapo forced her to leave the Order, and despite the pleas of her colleagues, she was condemned to death and executed. She was beatified by the Pope in 1998.[10]

In July 1938, at an international conference held at Evian-les-Bains in France, the problem of Jews who were unable to emigrate from Germany because of restrictive quotas imposed by other countries was discussed, but no solution was forthcoming.

In November 1938 Schacht requested a meeting with Hitler at which he proposed that all Jewish holdings in Germany and Austria be paid into a trust fund, which would issue twenty-five-year bonds which Jews throughout the world would be invited to purchase. Part of the dividends from these bonds would then be paid to German and Austrian Jews to assist them to emigrate. To this, Hitler agreed.

Sadly, Schacht's scheme for Jewish emigration failed to gain the support of western countries, particularly America, where it was felt that this was an attempt by the Germans to extort ransom money for each Jewish life.

In that same month of November, Hitler received a telegram informing him that Ernst Eduard vom Rath, Third Secretary to the German Ambassador in Paris, had been assassinated by a seventeen-year-old Polish Jew named Herschel Grunspan, who was angry about the way his family had been treated by the Nazis. This was Goebbels' opportunity to persuade Hitler to take even more extreme action against the Jews. Reinhard Heydrich now issued a series of statements to the police and SS units across the Reich.

> Demonstrations against Jews are expected and must not be prevented. Jewish property may be destroyed but not looted ... As many Jews as possible, for now only healthy males, are to be arrested. All concentration camps are to be alerted to accommodate them.

At that time the Jewish population of Germany numbered about half a million.

The result was that, on 9/10 November 1938, some 7,500 Jewish homes, 275 synagogues, and hundreds of businesses were destroyed by the Nazis in 150 towns and villages throughout the Reich. Even Jewish hospitals, such as the one for sick children in Laupike, were attacked. Some 26,000 Jews were arrested, of whom ninety were murdered. Only a few managed to escape abroad. This became known as *Kristallnacht* (literally, night of broken glass) – the name deriving from the fact that glass from the shattered windows of Jewish shops littered the streets of Berlin and other towns and villages throughout the Reich. The event was timed to coincide with the anniversary of Hitler's first attempt to seize power in Munich, fifteen years previously.

Having perpetrated these horrors on the Jewish population, Goebbels now added insult to injury by extorting a billion Reichsmarks from the Jews in order to pay for a clean up of the operation. He also announced ominously, that a resolution of the Jewish question would require a 'final solution'.[11]

Schacht was open in his contempt for the way Germany was treating its Jews. At the annual Reichsbank Christmas party of December 1938, he made a speech saying, 'The burning of Jewish synagogues, the destruction and looting of Jewish businesses, the ill-treatment of Jewish citizens, was so disgraceful that every decent German must blush with shame ...'.[12]

At about this time, Hitler received a letter from a father who sought permission to terminate the life of his mentally disabled child. Having already ordered the compulsory sterilization of the disabled, the Führer now approved a secret policy for the selection and murder of disabled infants within a few days of their birth. Within months the remit spread to include disabled children also. They were given lethal injections of morphine in special children's units. However, in every case the cause of death was recorded as 'measles', or even 'general weakness'.[13]

With the German invasion of Czechoslovakia on 15 March 1939, Heydrich was dispatched to the region of Bohemia–Moravia to effect the 'Germanization' of the region, and to co-opt the Czechs into supporting the German war effort. Dissidents were sent to Mathausen Concentration Camp whereas Jews were incarcerated in the ghetto at Terezin (in German, Theresienstadt) before being moved on to death camps further east. Meanwhile, former Czech President Edvard Beneš fled to England where he became head of the Czech government in exile.

Homosexual men were clearly of no value when it came to promulgating the Master Race and, over the next decade, 50,000 or so of them would be sent to their deaths in the concentration camps. The same strictures did not apply, however, to lesbian women, the theory being that they could always be forcibly impregnated and so produce children for the Führer.

Following the invasion of Poland by Germany on 1 September 1939, the Nazis began rounding up all Polish Jews, a total of about three million, and moving them into ghettos, which were created in all the major towns and cities in order to facilitate their deportation. It was decided, however, that rather than let all the Jews in the ghettos perish from starvation and disease, some should be used as slave labourers in the making of textiles, construction of roads, or even the building of palaces for their Nazi masters. Nevertheless, in consequence of Nazi policies, almost one in five Poles would die during the Second World War.

The Danes were regarded by the Nazis as fellow Nordics. They were therefore treated more leniently, a fact which enabled Denmark, after the German invasion of 8 April 1940, to evacuate virtually its entire population of some 8,000 Jews to the safety of neutral Sweden. However, in Lithuania, by August 1941, no less than 38,324 Jews had been murdered by the Nazis.

In June 1940 an official in the German Foreign Office, Hans Rademacher, proposed that the Jews throughout the Reich be resettled on the French island of Madagascar. However, in wartime, this proved not to be a feasible project. Madagascar might, at first, seem a strange choice, unless the long arm of Lanz von Liebenfels, who advocated throwing the 'untouchables' out 'into the forest of the monkeys' had somehow influenced Hitler's – and therefore Rademacher's – decision.

SS Brigadeführer Arthur Nebe was Commander of *Einsatzgruppe* B (the *Einsatzgruppen* were special extermination units which followed Germany's fighting troops into the occupied territories – in this case, the Soviet Union). He complained to Himmler that the execution of Jews by shooting was having an adverse effect on the morale of his men. Himmler agreed, having seen at first-hand the execution of 100 Jews and partisans when he had visited the Front Line and Russian city of Minsk. Experiments were therefore made to discover which gas, when pumped into a sealed room full of victims, was most efficacious to use. And by a process of trial and error, the one most effective for the purpose was found to be hydrogen cyanide – Zyklon B.

Himmler now announced that not only Jewish men but also women and children were to be executed and, to this end, in September 1941, he issued a secret order decreeing that all Jews from Germany, Austria and the occupied Czech lands should be transported to camps in the east. By December 1941 in Vienna, Hitler's home capital, virtually none of that city's original community of 180,000 Jews remained: all had been transported to death camps.

Chief of the Reichs Chancellery Hans Lammers makes reference to a Führer Order which was 'transmitted by Göring to Heydrich …' entitled 'Final Solution of the Jewish Problem'.[14] No copy of this order has ever been found and it was probably never committed to paper. This led Heydrich to convene a meeting of the SS and SD at the Berlin suburb of Wannsee on 20 January 1942 to work out details of how all Jews in occupied Europe were to be deported and killed. The outcome was, as he explained, that Jews capable of work were to be brought to 'the East' – i.e., to concentration camps in Poland – where they were to be 'employed in road building, in which task undoubtedly a great part will fall through natural diminution' (i.e., they would be worked to death). And then, said he, ominously,

> The remnant, that finally is able to survive all this – since this is undoubtedly the part with the strongest resistance – must be treated accordingly, since these people representing a natural selection, are to be regarded as the germ cell of a new, Jewish development.[15]

From Berlin alone 55,000 Jews were deported and, by the end of 1942, experiments with gas had enabled the Nazis to set up no less than seven extermination centres in Poland at Auschwitz, Birkenau, Belzec, Sobibor, Chelmno, Majdanek and Treblinka. It was now logistically possible to abduct and exterminate Jews from all the territories which Germany occupied.

The search for a method of creating a perfect Aryan race would find its ghastly apotheosis in the work of one man, Dr Josef Mengele, who, as camp doctor at Auschwitz, performed medical experiments on the concentration camp's inmates.

* * *

Of the estimated sixteen million people murdered by Hitler's Nazi regime between 1933 and 1945 – in the so-called 'holocaust' – around six million were Jews. This represented approximately 67 per cent of the Jewish population of Europe. They met their deaths by shooting, hanging, torture and gassing, with many being burned alive in the incinerators of the concentration camps on occasions when the gas ran out. Many died as a result of ghoulish medical experiments performed by qualified doctors of the Third Reich, who subjected their unfortunate victims to hypothermia, hyperthermia, and deliberate wounding and infection, the idea being to study how best they could treat their own wounded from the battlefield. Hitler, however, did not trouble himself to visit a concentration camp. How the Jews and others met their end was, to him, a matter of supreme indifference.

Notes

1. *Der Volkischer Beobachter*, 25 December 1920.
2. **The Nazis: A Warning from History, Part 1.*
3. Ibid.
4. Weitz, *Joachim von Ribbentrop: Hitler's Diplomat*, pp.185–6.
5. Schacht, *76 Jahre meines Lebens*, p.404.
6. **The Nazis: A Warning from History, Part 2*
7. **Hitler: a Profile: The Criminal.*
8. **The Nazis: A Warning from History, Part 2*
9. **The Third Reich in Colour.*
10. **The SS: Himmler's Madness.*
11. **Kristallnacht: 9 November 1938.*
12. Schacht, op. cit.
13. **The Nazis: A Warning from History, Part 3.*
14. *A Trial of the Major War Criminals: Nuremberg Documents and Testimony*. TMWC, xi, p.141
15. Shirer, op. cit., pp.965–6.

Chapter 29

Hitler and his 'Inner Voices'

As has already been demonstrated, Hitler suffered from delusions (i.e., 'erroneous beliefs that usually involve a misrepresentation of perceptions or experiences'). But are there any other clues which might shed further light on the workings of the Führer's mind – a mind which has remained largely a mystery for over half a century? The answer is yes, and these clues are to be found in the hitherto long neglected memoirs of two of his contemporaries, Otto Wagener and Hermann Rauschning, which have survived for posterity. They not only reveal, in depth, the precise nature of Hitler's delusions but also that he experienced hallucinations (perceptions that occur in the absence of an external stimulus) of a particular type.

Otto Wagener (1888–1971)
In the introduction to Wagener's book, *Hitler – Memoirs of a Confidant* (published in 1978), American historian Henry Ashby Turner Jr describes the author as 'a prominent official in the Nazi Party, with close ties to Adolf Hitler from the Autumn of 1929, until the Summer of 1933'.

Prior to the outbreak of the Second World War, says Turner,

Wagener served as Chief of Staff of the Storm Troop Auxiliary, the SA; headed the Economic Policy Section of the Party's National Executive [*Reichsleitung*]; worked on special assignment for Hitler in Berlin; headed the Party's Economic Policy Office during the early months of the Third Reich; and briefly served as Commissar for the Economy. [However] Wagener fell into disfavour with Hitler at the end of June 1933. This cost him his posts in the Party and the government … He retained only his nominal rank as SA Group Leader, and a meaningless seat in the rubber-stamped Nazi legislature, the Reichstag, which rarely even convened.[1]

During the Second World War, Wagener … served in the army. He entered as a captain, and had attained the rank of major general by the end of the war, when he surrendered the remaining German forces to the British on the island of Rhodes. After seven years in British and Italian internment he returned to Germany in 1952 and settled in Bavaria, where he dabbled in nationalistic politics until his death in 1971 at the age of 83.[2]

It was in 1946, during his time of internment in a British camp for German officer prisoners of war at Bridgend in Wales, that Wagener wrote his memoirs which provide the most vital piece of information ever about the workings of the Führer's mind. This is to be found in Chapter 25, entitled 'Hitler's Thought Processes'. Here Wagener relates a discussion that he had with Hitler at the Elephant Hotel in Weimar during one of their 'political trips,' where Hitler told him

> I'm now and then aware, that it is not I who is speaking, but that something speaks through me. On such occasions, I frequently feel as if there were a mistake in human logic or as if it had limits of which it is not aware. Now and then ideas, concepts, views occur to me that I have read nowhere, heard nowhere, and never before thought, nor can I justify them by logic, and they do not even seem to me capable of being logically justified.[3]

> I owe to [Albert] Einstein* the scientific proof that there are things which, recognized by man's senses, nevertheless cannot be understood and justified, though they are true and could form the basis for a new way of thinking, perhaps even of a new conception of the world. In future, I will know how to console myself when some perception comes to my mind to which I am lacking a logical bridge. I shall nevertheless have the courage to build on it.[4]

Hitler is here showing that, whereas he is bemused by what the voices are saying to him, nevertheless he hopes to adopt the ideas which they are putting forward.

When asked by Wagener, 'Do you always know whether such a perception comes from beyond or through the agency of the human senses within this world?' Hitler replied,

> In general, at such moments I have a sensation like an inner vibration, as if I were being touched by an invisible charge. Whenever I have seized the impulse, what I said or did as a result of that feeling always turned out to be correct. Whenever I have let it go, almost invariably it turned out later that it would have been right to follow the inner voice.[5]

Says Turner,

> Wagener's accounts of public events, his descriptions of organizations, especially those of the Nazi Party, and his identifications of individuals and their positions, provide many opportunities to check the accuracy of his memory. [And he concluded that] In the instances where such checks could be made, Wagener's memory proved highly reliable.[6]

---

* Hitler had recently attended a lecture by the mathematical physicist on his Theory of Relativity.

Wagener was not the only person to have first-hand evidence that Hitler's actions were being orchestrated by an 'inner voice', for Hermann Rauschning arrived, independently, at precisely the same conclusion. In the parlance of modern-day psychiatrists, what Wagener is describing in Hitler are delusions, in which 'alien thoughts have been put into his mind ("thought insertion")', so that henceforth his 'body or actions are being acted on or manipulated by some outside force ("delusions of control")'. Psychiatrists characterize such delusions as 'bizarre' – i.e., in that they express a loss of control over mind or body'.[7]

Hermann Rauschning (1887–1961)

The Free City of Danzig had been established in 1920 under the terms of the Treaty of Versailles. When, in 1933, the Nazis won control of that city's government, Rauschning, the son of a Prussian army officer, became President of its Senate on 20 June. Rauschning subsequently became disillusioned with the Nazis and, in 1936, fled to Switzerland. In 1939, Danzig was annexed by Germany.

Rauschning's book *Hitler Speaks* is described as 'A Series of Political Conversations with Adolf Hitler on his Real Aims'. Published in December 1939, it, too, contains vital information about the Führer's way of thinking, which is to be found in Chapter 14, entitled 'A New Social Order, A New Economy'. Here, Hitler, in conversation with Rauschning, explains his decision-making process.

> Unless I have the inner, incorruptible conviction, [that] *this is the solution,* I do nothing. Not even if the whole Party tries to drive me to action. I will not act; I will wait, no matter what happens. But if the voice speaks, then I know the time has come to act.[8]

These few words of Hitler's have never been accorded the importance which they deserve, for, as will now be seen, they provide the crucial key to understanding the Führer's psyche. Continued Rauschning,

> He [Hitler] seemed to take it for granted that the ideas [which he expounded] were his own. He had no notion of their actual origin, and considered that he had worked them out himself, and that they were inspirations, the product of his solitude in the mountains.[9]

In Chapter 18 of *Hitler Speaks*, entitled 'Hitler Himself', Rauschning describes how

> undeniable powers enter into Hitler, genuinely daemonic powers, which make men his instruments. The common united with the uncommon – that is what makes Hitler's personality so desperate a puzzle to those who come into contact with him.[10]

And crucially, in the same chapter, he describes how Hitler

> loves solitary walks. He hears voices. I have met him when in this mood. He recognizes nobody then: he wants to be alone. There are times when he flees from human society.[11]

German historian, Theodor Schieder, says this of Rauschning's book. It is 'a document of unquestionable value, since it contains views derived from immediate experience'.[12]

And in respect of both these key witnesses – Wagener and Rauschning – Turner declares that

> One cannot regard the utterances Wagener attributed to Hitler and others as verbatim quotations. On the other hand, Wagener's recollections, like those of Rauschning, come from a person who repeatedly experienced Hitler at first-hand.[13]

What conclusions may be drawn from the testimony of Wagener and Rauschning, and how may this be interpreted in the light of modern-day psychiatric experience?

Modern-day psychiatrists describe the hearing of voices by an individual, in the absence of any physical source for these voices, as 'auditory hallucinations' – these being 'perceived as distinct from the person's own thoughts'.[14] The presence in an individual of both bizarre delusions and of auditory hallucinations, provided that these symptoms were ongoing, as they undoubtedly were in the case of Hitler, is sufficient evidence to satisfy the criteria for a diagnosis of schizophrenia to be made.[15] Furthermore, of the various subtypes of schizophrenia which are currently recognized, it is clear from his symptoms that Hitler suffered from the 'Paranoid Type' of schizophrenia in which 'delusions are typically persecutory or grandiose'.[16]

Notes

1. Wagener, *Hitler – Memoirs of a Confidant*, p. ix.
2. Ibid, p. xiii.
3. Ibid, p. 150.
4. Ibid, p. 151.
5. Ibid.
6. Ibid, p. xvii.
7. American Psychiatric Association, *Diagnostic and Statistical Manual of Mental Disorders*, p. 299.
8. Rauschning, op. cit., p. 181.
9. Ibid, p. 220.
10. Ibid.
11. Ibid, p. 255.
12. Wagener, op. cit., p. xv.
13. Ibid, p. xvi.
14. American Psychiatric Association, op. cit., p. 300.
15. Ibid, p. 298.
16. Ibid, p. 313.

Chapter 30

Hitler's Schizophrenia: the Most Dangerous Type of All

People who hear voices which only they can hear, instructing them to perform a particular act or behave in a particular way, are, in modern parlance, experiencing 'Command Hallucinations' which, as already stated, are a symptom of schizophrenia.

Recently, author Louise G. Braham et al, of the University of Birmingham's Department of Clinical Psychology in the United Kingdom, have reviewed a decade of studies pertaining to the association between command hallucinations and dangerous behaviour.[1] Firstly, the authors issue a warning, that the 'action instructed' by the commanding voice

> may be dangerous and can result in offending behaviour. The key feature that distinguishes them from ordinary hallucinations is that, phenomenologically, the voice is experienced as commanding rather than commentating, and there is a significant probability that the hearer will comply with the command.[2]

And they point to studies which show that this 'significant probability' is between 32.9 per cent and 88.5 per cent.[3]

What are the factors which determine whether or not the hearer of the voice will act on the command?

> As well as beliefs about the voice, severity of [the] command, and the environment in which the voice was heard, [the] presence of a delusion congruent with the command hallucination is also considered to influence compliance.[4]

In other words, to give a theoretical and somewhat extreme example, if the voice says, 'Cut off your finger', the recipient is more likely to do so if he or she has a pre-existing delusion that the aforesaid finger is an offending article.

Another study showed that, in the context of command hallucinations,

> psychotic symptoms are likely to lead to violence/anti-social behaviour if they cause a person to perceive others as out to harm them ...[5]

Here, it should be remembered that Hitler was convinced that both the Bolsheviks and the Jews were out to harm not only himself and his country, but the whole world. And yet another study states that

> Perhaps most disturbing is the capacity of these hallucinatory commands to exact unquestioning obedience, often on a frequent basis.[6]

Other signs of schizophrenia in Hitler

What other features of Hitler's behaviour correlate with him having schizophrenia? Unity Mitford, in a letter to her sister Diana, written from Munich on 19 September 1935, inadvertently described one of them. She had met Hitler at the city's *Osteria Bavaria* restaurant the previous day, and declared, 'He couldn't seem to keep still. He moved backwards & forwards the whole time, with his hands on his knees, you know how he does.'[7] In other letters to her sisters, Unity also made several references to Hitler's 'giggling', or to his 'uncontrollable giggling'.

The rhythmical 'rocking' movements described by Unity are typical of the 'abnormalities of psychomotor activity' (i.e., activity relating to mental processes) which are sometimes an associated feature of schizophrenia. The same may be said of Hitler's 'uncontrollable giggling', this being known, in psychiatric terminology, as 'inappropriate affect (eg, smiling, laughing, or [putting on] a silly facial expression in the absence of an appropriate stimulus').

Other 'motor activities' commonly seen in those suffering from schizophrenia are 'grimacing, posturing, odd mannerisms, ritualistic or stereotyped behaviour' (viz, Hitler delivering a speech at a Nuremberg Rally).

'Affective flattening' (i.e., a decrease in the level of emotion displayed by an individual) is also common in schizophrenia, with

> the person's face appearing immobile and unresponsive, with poor eye contact and reduced body language. Although a person with affective flattening may smile and warm up occasionally, his or her range of emotional expressiveness is clearly diminished most of the time.[8]

(Viz, Hitler, in his last few weeks and months, as he shuffles along in a zombie-like state – although by this stage, his Parkinson's disease had also become a factor in the equation).[9]

The origin of Hitler's schizophrenia

August Kubizek, Hitler's acquaintance from his youthful period spent in Vienna, was of the opinion 'that the biological effect of the intermarriage in the [Hitler] family ... [had] produced [what he described as Hitler's] 'arrested complexes' and his 'particular type of character'[10] – i.e., of his schizophrenia (though Kubicek himself did not use this term). Two questions now arise: was Kubicek correct in stating that Hitler was inbred and, if so, was this inbreeding the cause of his schizophrenia?

No records exist of Hitler's family tree in the archives (*Oberösterreichisches Landesarchiv*) of the Austrian town of Linz. However, as Kubizek points out, when Hitler's father, Alois, and his mother, Klara, made the decision to marry, because of the closeness of the family relationship between the couple, they were first required as Roman Catholics to apply for a special Ecclesiastical Dispensation from the Pope before the marriage could take place. And just how close this relationship was is indicated in the attachment that accompanied their application, dated 27 October 1884, from which it may be deduced that Hitler's paternal grandfather, Johann Georg Hiedler, and Hitler's maternal grandfather, Johann von Nepomuk Hiedler, were brothers.[11]

However, US psychiatrist E. Fuller Torrey and senior medical researcher Judy Miller point out that

> Studies in Canada, Norway, Saudi Arabia, and the Sudan have shown that inbreeding associated with consanguineous marriages does *not* increase the prevalence of schizophrenia. Similarly, inbreeding rates are highest in Japan, Brazil, India, and Israel but none of these countries has abnormally high rates of schizophrenia.[12]

Kubicek was therefore correct in his first assumption – that Hitler was inbred, but he was incorrect about the second – i.e., that this inbreeding was responsible for his abnormal mental state.

Nevertheless, there is a familial pattern to the illness, it being the case that 'the first-degree biological relatives [i.e., parents, offspring, siblings] of individuals with schizophrenia have a risk for schizophrenia that is about 10 times greater than of the general population'.[13] It is therefore pertinent to enquire whether Hitler's schizophrenia was a disorder which he had inherited from his forebears? If this is the case, then one would expect to find other schizophrenics in his family and, sure enough, there is at least one.

Aloisia Veit

Paradoxically, it was because of the Gestapo – Hitler's secret police – that definitive proof of the presence of schizophrenia in the Führer's family came to light.

As a result of a rumour which was circulating 'alleging that relations of Hitler who were half-wits or deranged, were resident in [the Austrian city of] Graz', the Gestapo sent one of their agents to that place. Here, the agent encountered a couple, Maria and Conrad Pracher, who lived in the St Peter's district of the city.

The Prachers informed the agent that just prior to his death, in 1904, one Josef Veit asked the Prachers whether they would look after his and his wife Aloisia's two daughters, Josefa and Viktoria Veit, the Prachers being their great-aunt and uncle. The agent also learnt that the Prachers had had a son who had committed suicide at the age of twenty-one, and another daughter, also called Aloisia, born in 1891 who will be discussed shortly.

Maria Pracher told the agent that Josefa Veit was 'a half-wit and worked in a bakery in Graz'. Maria also said that Josefa's sister Viktoria Veit was married, lived in Graz, and was 'mentally retarded'.

Most importantly, said the Prachers, Josef Veit had entrusted them with a collection of letters and documents which demonstrated that the Veit family and Hitler were related, in that Hitler's paternal grandmother, Maria Anna Schicklgruber, and Josef Veit's maternal grandmother, Josefa Böhm (née Schicklgruber), were sisters. Therefore, Adolf Hitler and Josef Veit's children, who included Aloisia, were distant cousins.[14]

The younger Aloisia Veit was born on 18 July 1891 in Polz, Austria. On 23 January 1932 at the age of forty-one, she was admitted to a psychiatric clinic in Vienna. Prior to that she had worked, for six years, as a chambermaid in the city's *Hotel Holler*. The doctor's grounds for referring her were 'strange behaviour for one week'.

Three days later, Aloisia's mental condition was regarded as so serious that she was admitted, first to Vienna's General Hospital, and then to Vienna's *Steinhof*, Austria's State Asylum. Whilst there it was recorded that she saw an apparition of the face of Jesus Christ (in psychiatric terms, a visual hallucination) whereupon, she 'got down on her knees and prayed'.

At the *Steinhof* the doctor noted that Aloisia was 'a scatty patient with lively facial expressions and aural hallucinations'. On 18 February 1932, she was diagnosed as 'a schizophrenic who is deranged, helpless, and scatty and suffering from depression, hallucinations and delusions'.

A week later, Aloisia was confined to a cot for reasons of safety after she had become violent and 'aggressive towards fellow patients and nurses'. At the end of 1933 she began to refuse food, and from May 1935 she was fed through a tube. On 3 June 1933 Aloisia was certified as 'incapable of managing her own affairs'.[15]

In 1936, Maria Pfeiffer from Vienna became Aloisia's attorney. In October of that year, Maria informed the hospital staff that at least one of Aloisia's siblings were suffering from schizophrenia. Said she,

Aloisia had a sister in Graz who was mentally ill [a reference either to Josepha or to Viktoria], and that the parents [Josef and the older Aloisia] had seemingly, also suffered from mental illness.

Meanwhile, it was recorded that between March 1936 and September 1940, Aloisia's weight fluctuated between 29.5 kilograms and 42.5 kilograms.

On 28 November 1940, Aloisia was transported to a 'euthanasia-holding institution' on the Danube river, prior to being transferred on 6 December to an 'unknown institution'.[16] In other words, despite the fact that she was Hitler's cousin, she was murdered, in accordance with his policy of euthanasia.

Both Hitler and Aloisia had schizophrenia, a disorder which, in its aetiology, is known to have a strong genetic component. The action of not one, but of a cluster of genes is believed to be responsible for this illness. The conclusion must be, therefore, that both of them inherited their disorder from their common ancestors, namely Johannes Schicklgruber, a farmer from the hamlet of Strones, situated to the north of Vienna, and his wife, Theresia (née Pfeisinger), who were the parents of Josepha (Aloisia's forebear) and Maria Anna (Hitler's forebear).

Finally, Hitler's father, Alois senior, was a violent and controlling person. This does not mean that he had schizophrenia, but the possibility cannot be ruled out.

Notes

1. Braham, Trower and Birchwood. *Acting on Command Hallucinations and Dangerous Behaviour: a Critique of the Major Findings in the Last Decade*. University of Birmingham, UK: Department of Clinical Psychology, p. 513.
2. Ibid, p. 514.
3. *Clinical Psychology Review*, 24 (2004), pp. 513–28, in Braham et al, op. cit., p. 515.
4. Junginger, 1990, in Braham et al, op.cit., p. 519.
5. Link, Steuve & Phelan, 1998, in Braham et al, op.cit, p. 520.
6. Rogers et al. p.1306, in Braham et al, op.cit, p. 524.
7. Mosley, *The Mitfords: Letters Between Six Sisters*, p. 64.
8. American Psychiatric Association, *Diagnostic and Statistical Manual of Mental Disorders*, p. 304.
9. McKenna, *Schizophrenia and Related Syndromes*, pp. 19, 21 & 22.
10. Kubizek, *Young Hitler*, p. 30.
11. Linz. 1884. *Archives of the Episcopate*: No. 6.911/II/2, in Kubizek, op. cit., p. 29.
12. Foster, *What really causes Schizophrenia?*, p. 15.
13. American Psychiatric Association, *Diagnostic and Statistical Manual of Mental Disorders*, p. 309.
14. Hinz-Wessels, *Aloisia Veit – Ein Euthanasie Opfer aus Hitler's Familie*, in *Das Vergessen der Vernichtung ist Teil der Vernichtung selbst*, by Petra Fuchs et al., pp. 280–1.
15. Ibid, pp. 274 & 276.
16. Ibid, p. 278.

Chapter 31

Finale

In 1944, after an acquaintance of fifteen years, Eva Braun was still 'ostensibly' Hitler's mistress. But even as late as June of that year, when her sister Gretl married SS General Otto Hermann Fegelein, he still declined to marry her.

Bernd Freytag von Loringhoven, of Hitler's General Staff, described Hitler's appearance in July 1944.

> I saw a wreck standing in front of me ... a stooped man, already dragging one leg, who could only offer his shaky left hand because his right hand was more or less unusable owing to a contusion from the attempt on his life. I saw no shining eyes able to hold one spellbound. His eyes were dull. And a worn out figure stood in front of me.[1]

In fact, Hitler at this time was suffering from Parkinson's disease, and this is why his left arm and hand were shaking.

In early December 1944 Hitler, against the advice of his generals, made Himmler Commander-in-Chief of the Army Group Upper Rhine. When Himmler duly failed to stem the tide of Germany's collapse, he was reassigned, in January 1945, to command Army Group Vistula which, by mid-January 1945, was also overrun by the Red Army. Himmler now retired to the SS military hospital at Hohenlychen, from where he claimed to be suffering from influenza.

As the final months of the Second World War played themselves out, Hitler, from 16 January 1945, took up permanent residence in Berlin at the so-called *Führerbunker*, situated some fifteen metres beneath the gardens of Berlin's Reichs Chancellery building. 'I expect every German to do his duty to the utmost,' said the Führer and, 'to take upon himself every sacrifice which must be required of him.'[2]

On 30 January 1945, Hitler made his last broadcast to the German people.

> However grave the crisis may be at the moment, through our unalterable will, our readiness for sacrifice and our own abilities, we will overcome the crisis. We will endure. It is not Central Asia that will win, but Europe, led by this nation, which for 1,500 years has defended and will continue to defend Europe against the East – our greater German Reich – the German nation.[3]

Hitler's words applied not only to adults, for he was anxious that those members of the Hitler Youth 'who can fight, do fight, and that we sacrifice ourselves together'.[4] Referring to the fact that the defence of Berlin was being carried out mainly by children, Baldur von Schirach, who had been instrumental in their military training declared, 'I didn't know ... that young people were deployed there. I had no influence any more. But on looking back, I can't understand how people [Hitler and the Nazis] could send children into battle. I feel you can't justify it, not biologically'.[5]

These sentiments were echoed by Walter Goergen, formerly of the Hitler Youth. Referring to boys of just sixteen or seventeen who had fought for Germany at the end of the war against hopeless odds, he said, 'They didn't realize that the war had been lost long before. Those lads sacrificed themselves for Germany for nothing'. Hans Jürgen Habenicht, also formerly of the Hitler Youth, said, 'I am furious that we were used in a hopeless situation, just to prolong Hitler's life by a couple of days'.[6] Said Ingeborg Seldte, 'That's what I reproach Hitler for most. He led the youth astray. He betrayed them and he took their lives.'[7]

However, Hitler remained unchallenged both as Chancellor of Germany and Supreme Commander of her armed forces.

On 7 March 1945 Eva Braun, who had become intensely frustrated at her long separations from Hitler, came to Berlin to be with him, even though this was against his wishes.

* * *

With the advance of the Soviets, Hitler issued, on 19 March 1945, the so-called *Nero Decree*: the implementation of a scorched earth policy, designed to deprive the Allies of any facilities which might be useful to them. At the same time, all traces of the concentration camps were to be removed. The following day, Himmler was dismissed by his disillusioned Führer.

On 20 April 1945, Hitler, who had been joined by Bormann and Goebbels for the final few days of the battle, celebrated, if that is the correct word, his fifty-sixth birthday. Camera footage shows him shaking hands with his soldiers with his right hand while the left hand is held behind his back, shaking rhythmically and uncontrollably from the elbow down at the fast rate of about five times per second.

Himmler would now play his last card for, on that very day, he crept away from the *Führerbunker* to a prearranged meeting in a mansion north of Berlin with Norbert Masur, a Jew who was spokesman for the Jewish World Congress. To save Germany from total defeat, Himmler proposed a new alliance between Nazi Germany and the western Allies against the Soviet Union. Part of the bargain would be the release by the Nazis of some 15,000 women prisoners, including some 2,000 Jews, from Ravensbrück Concentration Camp. Himmler also used Hungarian Jews as bargaining counters and, as a result of this meeting, the lives of approximately 350,000 inmates of the camps were saved. Others were not so fortunate and, as the camps were evacuated by the SS, many Jews died as a result of forced marches.

However, when Himmler began making peace overtures in the direction of British Prime Minister Winston Churchill, they were rejected out of hand. As for Hitler, when he learnt that Himmler had offered Great Britain and the United States but not the Soviet Union unconditional capitulation, he stripped the latter of all his offices of state.

On 23 April 1945, Albert Speer, having said his goodbyes to Hitler, unexpectedly flew back to the besieged city of Berlin's Reichs Chancellery. It has been suggested that Speer was anxious NOT to be named by the Führer as his successor as he felt that this might adversely prejudice the part that he hoped to play in reconstructing a new, post-Hitler Germany.

On the night of 28 April 1945, Hitler married Eva Braun in the *Führerbunker*. Only two days previously, his wartime ally, Mussolini, along with his mistress, Clara Petacci, had been executed by Italian partisans. After the executions the angry mob in Milan had hanged both bodies up by their feet.

Lieutenant General Hans Baur, Hitler's personal pilot, who was interrogated by the Soviets, said that on the morning of 30 April 1945 Hitler sent for him. The Führer 'talked about being betrayed by his generals [and said] that his soldiers refused to fight for him'. He then gave Baur an order, 'You must see to it that my body is burned so that it cannot be carried to Moscow and displayed like Mussolini's'.[8] Hitler's valet, Heinz Linge, who was also interrogated by the Soviets, was also told by Hitler that, after he [Hitler] had shot himself, both his body and also that of his wife, Eva, were to be burned.

There were no eyewitnesses, said Linge, as to what happened after Hitler and his wife Eva entered their sitting room at about 3.30pm that afternoon. However, Hitler had in his possession two pistols, Eva had one, and each had a small box of cyanide capsules. When they were discovered moments later, it appeared that Eva had bitten on a cyanide capsule and died swiftly whereas Hitler had put a cyanide capsule between his teeth and shot himself at the precise moment when he bit into it. Hitler had previously ordered that Blondi, his German shepherd dog, be used as a guinea pig for testing the cyanide capsules which he and Eva intended to use on themselves.

Rochus Misch, the *Führerbunker*'s switchboard operator, is adamant that the bodies, having been cremated on Hitler's orders, were buried in a bomb crater near the exit to the bunker. 'The bodies of Hitler and Eva Braun were placed here. They were wrapped in blankets and petrol was poured over them ... that's how Hitler was burned.'[9]

German radio announced, 'Soldiers of the German army. Our Führer, Adolf Hitler, is dead. The German people bow in grief and reverence.'[10] According to Ulrich de Maizière, General Staff Officer in Hitler's headquarters in 1945, however, Hitler had said shortly before his death that 'after the end of him [i.e., Hitler] and of National Socialism, the German people could not survive. It would be destined to collapse'.[11]

The fact that Hitler committed suicide would have come as no surprise to American psychoanalyst Dr Walter C. Langer – in fact, Langer had previously predicted that this was a course of action which the Führer might one day embark upon. Also, it is now recognized that approximately 10 per cent of individuals with schizophrenia commit suicide.[12]

On 1 May 1945 Admiral Karl Dönitz, Commander-in-Chief of the German navy, made a radio broadcast to the German people, telling them that the Führer, Adolf Hitler, had perished and that he [Dönitz] had been appointed his successor.[13] And from the Naval Academy at Mervik-Flensburg, where Field Marshal Wilhelm Keitel, Chief of the High Command of the Armed Forces (OKW), and Colonel General Alfred Jodl, Chief of OKW's Operations Office, were also in attendance, Dönitz made the decision to surrender in the West, but to carry on fighting in the East in order to save as many Germans as possible from capture by the Russians.

Himmler, now dressed as a soldier and disguised with an eye patch, intermingled with retreating troops. It was to no avail. He was captured by the Allies and confessed to his identity. But, on 23 May 1945, he took poison. He was buried by the British in an unmarked grave near Luneburg.

On 2 May 1945 Soviet troops reached the Reichs Chancellery and entered the *Führerbunker*, where only twenty or so personnel remained alive. Here they found the charred bodies of Josef and Magda Goebbels. The Propaganda Minister had shot himself and his wife, after which their bodies had been burned by his adjutant. As for their six children, they were all found dead, having been poisoned by their mother.

On 4 May 1945 Field Marshal Sir Bernard Law Montgomery, the victor of El Alamein and Commander-in-Chief 21st Army Group, accepted the partial surrender of the Wehrmacht, the German Armed Forces, at Luneberg Heath in northern Germany. On 7 May Jodl agreed to unconditional surrender on all fronts.

Notes

1. *Hitler: a Profile: The Commander.*
2. Ibid.
3. *The Nazis: A Warning from History, Part 5.*
4. *Hitler's Henchmen: Schirach, the Corrupter of Youth.*
5. Ibid.
6. Ibid.
7. *Hitler: a Profile: The Commander.*
8. *Hitler's Death: The Final Report.*
9. Ibid.
10. *Hitler's Henchmen: Bormann.*
11. *The Nazis: A Warning from History, Part 5.*
12. American Psychiatric Association, 2000, *Diagnostic and Statistical Manual of Mental Disorders*, p.304.
13. *Hitler's Henchmen: Karl Dönitz.*

Chapter 32

Aftermath

Twenty-two former principal Nazi figures stood trial before the International Military Tribunal, convened at the Palace of Justice in the German town of Nuremberg, from November 1945 to October 1946 – where the Nazis had previously promulgated their racial laws – having been indicted for crimes against peace, war crimes, and crimes against humanity.

Hermann Göring

At Nuremberg, Göring told his doctor,

> I'm determined to go down in German history as a great man. If I can't convince the court, I shall at least convince the German people that everything I did was done for the greater German Reich. In fifty or sixty years there will be statues of Hermann Göring all over Germany.

Unlike his fellow accused who admitted their guilt, or blamed Hitler for their crimes, Göring, having been confronted with incriminating cinematographic evidence, told the Tribunal that he would accept guilt neither for himself, nor for his country.[1] He was due to be executed on 15 October 1946 but, hours before his execution, he committed suicide by taking cyanide.

Rudolf Hess

In his address to the court Hess said,

> It was my privilege to spend many years of my life working for the greatest son whom my people have produced in their thousand year history. Even if I could ... , I would not want to erase that time from my life. I am happy in the knowledge that I did my duty towards my people, my duty as a German, as a National Socialist and as a loyal follower of the Führer. I regret nothing.[2]

Hess was found guilty at Nuremberg and sentenced to life imprisonment.

By 1966, Hess was the only prisoner remaining in Berlin's Spandau Prison. He remained unrepentant. 'If I had my time again I would act as I have acted, I regret nothing,' he said.[3] Only in 1969 did he permit himself to receive visits from his family, including his son Wolf Hess. On 17 August 1987, while still a prisoner in Spandau, he hanged himself. He was aged ninety-three.

Albert Speer

At Nuremberg, Speer was the only defendant to accept collective responsibility for Hitler's deeds. However, to the end of his life, he claimed to have had no knowledge of the crimes of the Nazi regime (which was demonstrably untrue, viz, his visits in the capacity of Armaments Minister to the slave-labour camp of Dora-Nordhausen). Sentenced to twenty years' imprisonment, he was released in 1966 and died in 1981.

Martin Bormann

Bormann, who in the final phase of hostilities had managed to escape from the Reichs Chancellery, was sentenced in his absence to death by hanging. In 1972 construction workers in Berlin unearthed two bodies. By comparison of teeth and dental records, and by DNA testing one of these bodies was positively identified as being that of Bormann, who is believed to have committed suicide. DNA testing did not exist in 1972 but, in 1998, DNA from the skull of the remains was compared with that of Martin Bormann junior and a match confirmed. (There was no corroborative confirmation, because no samples were sent to an independent laboratory.)

Alfred Rosenburg

Rosenburg was found guilty of crimes against humanity and hanged in October 1946.

Joachim von Ribbentrop

In a statement made to the Nuremberg Tribunal, Ribbentrop said,

> For years Hitler tried to counteract the danger from the East by concluding an alliance with Britain. The Naval Agreement of 1935 and the waiving of German claims to Alsace-Lorraine, were, among other things, an earnest [indication] of the intentions of German foreign policy; they showed that Germany was ready to make sacrifices. But Britain could not be won over. She regarded Germany's growing strength, not as a reasonable correction [of the Treaty of Versailles] and as a safeguard against the East, but only as a threat to the 'balance of power'. I worked for an understanding between Germany, France and Britain for twenty years of my life, and later wrestled with Britain to achieve an alliance. Up to the last hour I made efforts to avoid the war. Britain, fully resolved to prevent the further growth of Germany's strength, concluded her alliance with Poland. This made a peaceful German-Polish settlement impossible.[4]
>
> [As for the current charges] I declare myself not guilty as charged.[5]

Ribbentrop however, had prevailed on Mussolini to permit the deportation of Italian Jews to concentration camps and, on this count alone, he was found guilty of crimes against humanity and sentenced to death by hanging.

Baldur von Shirach

With the Red Army on the outskirts of Vienna where he was *Gauleiter*, Schirach left his command post and fled into the mountains of the Austrian Tyrol, but was captured nevertheless. At Nuremberg he said, 'I declare myself not guilty as charged'. When confronted with graphic pictures of the concentration camps, however, he put the blame on Hitler. 'I'm guilty of having trained young people for a man who was a murderer a million times over. I believed in this man. That's all that can be said in my defence.'[6] Schirach was found guilty and would serve a term of twenty years' imprisonment in Spandau Prison.

Karl Dönitz

Grand Admiral Dönitz was captured by the British when the German fleet surrendered. In his trial at Nuremberg, he said, 'I think the conduct of this war was justified – and I acted according to my conscience. I would do exactly the same again.' He served a ten-year sentence in Spandau Prison and was released in October 1956.

Josef Mengele

With the approach of the Russian Army, Mengele, on 18 January 1945, fled from Auschwitz, exchanged his SS uniform for that of an ordinary German soldier and joined a retreating German army unit as a doctor. Despite being captured by the Allies, his true identity remained a secret because, for some reason, his blood group had not been tattooed onto his skin, as was normal procedure for the SS.

Mengele made his way to his home-town of Gunzburg in southern Germany where he worked on a farm. He then fled to Italy and from there to Buenos Aires, choosing Argentina because there was a secret organization called Odessa which helped former SS members to evade capture. Here he set up in medical practice. In the early 1950s he found employment in the Argentine branch of his family's farm-implement retailing business. When the German government tried to extradite former Nazis from Argentina, Mengele escaped to Paraguay. A 3.4 million dollar reward was offered for his capture.

When in June 1985, in Brazil, a body, said to have been buried in 1979, was exhumed from a cemetery, subsequent DNA analysis revealed that this was the remains of Mengele.[7] Eye witnesses at the time stated that he had drowned, having suffered a stroke while swimming in the sea.

Hjalmar Schacht

Schacht was one of only three to be acquitted at Nuremberg, the other two being former Chancellor Franz von Papen, and Hans Fritzsche – an official in the

Propaganda Ministry. However, with the coming of the new Federal Republic of Germany in 1949, Schacht was arrested once more and it was not until 13 September 1950 that he was finally cleared on the charge of being a Nazi.

Subsequently the energetic Schacht not only went on to found two banks of his own but became financial consultant adviser to various governments, including those of Egypt, Syria, and Indonesia. A resident of Munich, he died on 4 June 1970 at the age of ninety-three.

Josef Stalin

Russian historian Dmitri Volkogonov, head of a special Russian parliamentary commission and Stalin's official biographer, has concluded from newly available Soviet KGB documents, that under Stalin's twenty-nine-year leadership '21.5 million (Soviet) people [including Jews] were repressed. Of these, 1/3 were shot, and the rest sentenced to imprisonment, where many also died'.[8] In fact, it was only by Stalin's death from a stroke on 5 March 1953 that another purge of the Jews was avoided. He was buried in Moscow's Red Square in the same tomb as Lenin.

Following Stalin's death Marshal Lavrenti Beria attempted to seize power in a failed coup. Nikita Khruschev then became First Secretary of the Soviet All Union Party. At the Twentieth Party Congress in 1956, Khruschev astonished the world by his frankness in condemning much of what Stalin had done. Soon he would introduce greater freedoms, relax press censorship, and free prisoners from the gulags.

Shortly after the Twenty-second Party Congress of October 1961, Stalin's body was removed and reburied near the Kremlin wall, close to those of the former leaders of the Bolshevik Revolution.

Czechoslovakia

Following Germany's defeat in May 1945, Edvard Beneš and his government returned from exile to the Czech capital, Prague. Now, in excess of two million Sudeten Germans were expelled from Czechoslovakia, thereby increasing the population of Germany and thus achieving the opposite of what Hitler had intended by his policy of *Lebensraum*. Against this, however, must be offset the total German dead of the Second World War – estimated to be in the region of four million.

Communism Worldwide

Communism was finally dismantled in Eastern Europe in 1989 and in the Soviet Union at the end of 1991. Elsewhere, it had failed to take root except in a handful of countries, such as North Korea and Cuba. As for China 'which was never slavishly Soviet in its ideology and practices', that country has 'quietly abandoned its beliefs in everything except the dictatorship of the Party, particularly after the death of Deng Xiao Ping in 1997. The same is broadly true of the communist regime in Vietnam.'[9]

The Holocaust in Perspective

'The Holocaust', as it came to be known, resulted in the murder of an estimated sixteen million people by Hitler and his regime between 1933 and 1945. They included around six million Jews (of whom three million were from Poland) and ten million Ukrainians, Russians, Romanies, socialists, homosexuals, and those labelled mental or physical 'defectives'.

With regard to the Jews, not only working people, shopkeepers and businessmen, but also doctors, chemists, musicians, composers, teachers, artists, philosophers and such people were eliminated, i.e., those who had most to contribute when it came to enriching the culture and civilization of the society in which they lived, and, of course, children.

The loss to the world was incalculable and the degree of human suffering unquantifiable. As for mankind in general, the holocaust produced not one single benefit, but instead would taint those who planned and perpetrated it for all times.

To the credit of the majority of the German people, they have not tried to hide the fact that the holocaust actually took place. In fact, since the war, numerous Germans have come forward to describe exactly what they saw, both inside and outside the labour camps and the extermination camps, in the proximity of which, the stench of death was all pervading. Also, German school children are taken specially to see the camps as part of their educational curriculum.

Hitler's Legacy

In his will Hitler left his art collection to the art gallery of the town of Linz, objects of 'sentimental value' to his 'faithful co-workers', including his secretary, and anything else of value to the Nazi Party.

For him, as for his henchmen, there would be no monument or memorial. His beloved Berghof was bombed to destruction by the Allies while his Reichs Chancellery bunker is now the site of a children's playground.

The Hitler Family

Paula. During the Second World War, Hitler's sister Paula worked as a secretary in a military hospital. In the spring of 1945, following the destruction of Dresden by Allied bombing, Hitler arranged for her to be taken from there to Berchtesgaden where she lived at Hitler's request under the assumed name of Paula 'Wolff'. In 1945 she was arrested by US intelligence officers and interviewed. After her release she returned to Vienna for a while until, in 1952, she returned to Berchtesgaden. She died in 1960.

Alois. In 1945, Hitler's half-brother Alois, fearful of recriminations on account of his close relationship to Hitler, fled with his wife Hedwig from Berlin to Hamburg, where he went into hiding. He changed his name to 'Hiller' and adopted a child – a girl. He was subsequently cleared of being a Nazi and, having lived a privileged existence in the Third Reich, was obliged to take up menial employment. He died in 1956 and is buried in Hamburg Cemetery.

Angela. Hitler's half-sister Angela Raubal also lived *incognito* in Munich until her death in 1949.

William. In the spring of 1944 thirty-three-year-old William Patrick Hitler joined the US Navy. When William first tried to enlist in the US Navy, his relationship to the Nazi dictator caused such concern in official circles that his application to become a sailor eventually landed on President Roosevelt's desk for a decision. He retired from the Navy in 1946 and set up in private practice as a haematologist.

William married a German lady, Phyllis Jean-Jacques, and they had four sons, of whom Howard (a tax inspector, and the only one to marry) was killed in a road-traffic accident in 1989 at the age of thirty-two. Of the remaining three children, two are gardeners, and one is a psychiatrist.

There was a degree of ambivalence in William's attitude to Hitler, his uncle, in that he too sported a characteristic Hitler-style moustache, gave his first-born son, Alexander, the second name of Adolf, and, in his latter years, adopted for himself and for his sons the surname 'Stuart-Houston' in which, no doubt, he was inspired by Houston Stewart Chamberlain, a person whom Hitler had admired greatly. William's mother, baptized Bridget (but Brigid, on her tombstone), died in 1969. William died in 1987 and is buried in the same tomb.

William's three remaining sons appear to have made a positive decision not to have children of their own. They also steadfastly refused to contest Hitler's will, describing any royalties to which they might have been entitled from the sale of Hitler's book, *Mein Kampf*, as 'blood money'.

Heinz. On 10 January 1942 Alois's son Heinz (by his second marriage to Hedwig), an army officer, was declared missing in action on the Eastern Front. Having been captured, he endured months of interrogation and torture, and died in a military prison in Moscow in the same year.

Jörg Lanz von Liebenfels
Liebenfels outlived his 'clone', Hitler, by nine years. He died on 22 April 1954, aged seventy-nine.

Notes
1. *Hermann Göring: Ambition without Conscience*.
2. *Hitler's Henchmen: Hess, The Deputy*.
3. Ibid.
4. *Joachim von Ribbentrop*. www.spartacus.schoolnet.co.uk/GERribbentrop.htm
5. *Hitler's Henchmen: Ribbentrop, the Puppet*.
6. *Hitler's Henchmen: Schirach, the Corrupter of Youth*.
7. *Josef Mengele: Medical Madman of Auschwitz*.
8. *The Jewish Role in the Bolshevik Revolution and Russia's Early Soviet Regime*. [This essay appeared in the Jan-Feb 1994 issue of the 'Journal of Historical Review', published by the Institute for Historical Review]; www.ihr.org/jhr/v14/v14n1p-4Weber.html
9. *Chambers Dictionary of World History*.

Epilogue

Hitler's racism, warmongering, lying, bloody-mindedness and lack of compassion have been seen by some simply as the product of an evil mind. Others, however, who are more inquisitive and discerning, have realized that there must be more to it than simply this; for the use of such emotive words as 'evil', 'wicked', 'devilish', 'monstrous', etc, fail to address the long-standing question as to what, exactly, were the thought processes of the Führer.

Clues to the answer to this conundrum, as has been shown, are to be found both in the writings of Hitler himself and in particular of two people who were acquainted with him – Otto Wagener and Hermann Rauschning. These clues reveal that the Führer heard voices, which, together with his delusions, confirm a diagnosis of schizophrenia.

Hitler refers to 'the voice' – as if it came from a single source, as, for example, when he told Hermann Rauschning (as already mentioned),

Not even if the whole Party tries to drive me to action. I will not act; I will wait, no matter what happens. But if the voice speaks, then I know the time has come to act.

It is almost certain that Hitler heard 'the voice' even before he became Führer of Germany in 1934. He was then aged forty-five, and the onset of schizophrenia, typically, occurs between the late-teens and the mid-thirties. He had scarcely any insight into his condition and therefore did not realize that he was mentally ill. He was, however, often bemused by what the voice was telling him. Nevertheless, he felt obliged to obey the commands of the voice, even though he often found the commands to be illogical, and this is what makes his particular type of schizophrenia such a dangerous one.

Had the Allies, in 1945, managed to capture Hitler alive, he would undoubtedly have been tried at Nuremberg and convicted and hanged, along with his henchmen. Today, however, his counsel would surely have pleaded that his client was insane. He would then have been sent to a mental institution, just like his cousin, Aloisia Veit, to be treated humanely (unlike Aloisia, who was murdered as part of the Nazi's euthanasia programme).

The fact that Hitler was at the mercy of delusions and command hallucinations makes it possible now, and for the first time, to understand why, having achieved power, he embarked on a course which led his great country, Germany, to utter destruction, and caused untold mayhem and suffering throughout the world. Now, for the first time, the reason for his irrational hatred of Jews, Bolsheviks, and others, and for his asinine military decisions – notably at Dunkirk and at Stalingrad, which helped to win the war for the Allies – is explained.

Can we imagine, for a moment, a Hitler without the schizophrenic gene? Someone who was kind, courteous, and compassionate, like the person we catch a brief glimpse of in Eva Braun's films, taken on the terrace at the Berghof: where a little girl shows him her new shoes and they both admire them; where he smiles with genuine pleasure as he talks to a little boy, or embraces and kisses his favourite dog on the head? Alas and alack, we can only imagine!

Appendix

'Ostara': Index

The author (if other than Liebenfels) is indicated in brackets.

Ostara: First Series. (1905–1916)
Titles:

1. The German/Austrians and Election Reform. 1905.
2. Economic Trade and Law Reform. March 1906.
3. Revolution or Evolution: A Free conservative Easter Prayer: The Supremacy of the European Race. April 1906.
4. Hungary's Economic Bankruptcy and how to bring it under control. May 1906.
5. 'Be Hard, Lord' – An Old German story, retold in modern German. (Hagen). June 1906.
6. The Empire's Treasure returns to the Empire! Guiding Humanitarian Principles for our Future. July 1906.
7. The Resurrection of Man. (Harpf) August 1906.
8. The Austro-German regions of the Alps as Meat and Milk producers – A study of the Local Economy. (Bernuth) August 1906.
9. The People's Thoughts – The Aristocratic Principle of our Time. (Harpf) September 1906.
10–13. Anthropology – Primitive Peoples and Race in the Historical Literature. October 1906.
11–12. Women's Affairs – A Cultural Study. (Harpf). January 1907.
14. Israel's Triumph. (Freydank) March 1907.
15. Women's Earning Capacity and Prostitution. (Liszt) April 1907.
16. Judas' Monopoly of Money in the Ascendancy and Zenith. (Wahrmund) June 1907.
17. The Technician's Headline. July 1907.
18. Race and Welfare Work – a call for a Boycott of Indiscriminate Charity. December 1907.
19–20. The Time of Eternal Peace: an Apology of War as a Cultural and Racial Purifier. (Harpf) January 1908.
21. Race and Women, and her Preference for an Inferior Breed of Man. March 1908.
22/23. The Statute of Emmanuel and Racial Cultivation. April 1908.

55.	The Social, Political and Sexual Life of Women in Our Time. 1912.
56.	The Racial Upbringing and Liberation of the Blonds from the Reign of Terror of Dishonourable Education. 1912.
57.	The Order of Races in the Economy and the Liberation of the Blonds from the Reign of Terror of Dishonourable Education as an Exploiter. 1912.
58.	The Immoral and Criminal Woman's Lifestyle of Our Times. 1912.
59.	The Aryan Christendom as a Racial Cult Religion of the Blonds – an Introduction to the Literature of the New Testament. 1912.
60.	Racially Conscious and Unconscious Life and Lovemaking – a Breviary for the Ripe Blond Youth. 1912.
61.	Racial Mixing and Racial De-mixing, 1912.
62.	The Blonds and Darks as Commander-in-Chief and Commander. 1913.
63.	The Blonds and Darks as Soldiers, 1913.
64.	Many or Few Children. 1913.
65.	Race and Illness: a Summary of General and Theoretical Racial Pathology. 1913.
66.	Naked and Racial Culture in a Struggle against Hypocrisy and a Dishonourable Culture. 1913.
67.	The Relationship of the Darks and Blonds to Illness: a Summary of Specialist and Practical Racial Pathology. 1913.
68.	The Resurrection of the Blonds to Wealth and Power – an Introduction to Racial Sociology. 1913.
69.	The Holy Grail as the Mystery of Aryan Christendom: a Racial Cult Religion.
70.	The Blonds as Creators of Technical Culture. 1913.
71.	Race and Nobility. 1913.
72.	Race and External Politics. 1913.
73.	The Blonds as Creators of Music. 1913.
74.	Racial Metaphysics or the Immortality of Higher Peoples. 1914.
75.	The Blonds as Bearer and Victim of Technical Culture. 1914.
76.	Prostitution in Women, and Men's Rights – A Judgement. 1914.
77.	Races and Architecture in Antiquity and the Middle Ages. 1914.
78.	Racial Mystique – an Introduction to the Aryo-Christian Esoteric Doctrine, 1915.
79.	Racial Physics of War. 1915.
80.	An Introduction to Practical Racial Metaphysics. 1915.
81.	Racial Metaphysics of War, 1914–1918. 1915.
82.	A Prayer Book for Enlightened and Spiritual Aryo-Christian I. 1915.
83.	Race and Poetry. 1916.
84.	Race and Philosophy. 1916.
85.	Race and Architecture in the New Age. 1916.
86.	Race and Painting. 1916.
87.	Race and Internal Politics. 1916.
88.	A Prayer Book for Enlightened and Spiritual Aryo-Christian II. 1916.
89.	Racial Metaphysics of the Holy.

90.   Abbot Bernhard of Clairvaux, praise prize of the new Knights Templar.
91.   The Saint as Cultural and racially historical Hieroglyphs.
92.   Race and Sculpture.
93.   Racial metaphysics of the Saints.
94.   The Language of the Ario-heroic Flood.
95.   Leviticus or Moses as a Racial Hygienist.
96.   Information about the Names of Places
97.   Numeri (Bible – Book of Numbers) or Moses as a Renewer of the Race.
98.   Ario-heroic Personal Names.
99.   Deuteronomy or Moses as a Racial Law Giver.
100. Ario-heroic Family Names.

Ostara: Second Series. (1922)
1.   Ostara and the Blond Empire.

Ostara: Third Series. (1927–1931)
1.   Ostara and the Blond Empire. 1927.
2.   World War as a Racial Struggle of the Darks against the Blonds. 1927.
3.   World Revolution as the Blonds' Grave. 1927.
4.   World Peace as an Achievement and Victory for the Blonds. 1928.
5.   Theozoology or Natural History of the Gods 1: the Old Testament and the Old God. 1928.
6/7. Theozoology or Natural History of the Gods 2: the Sodom Stone and Sodom Water. 1928.
8/9. Theozoology or Natural History of the Gods 3: Sodomfire and Sodomair. 1928.
10.   Anthropology – Primitive Peoples and Race in the Historical Literature. 1931.
11.   Economic Resurrection by the Blonds – an Introduction to Private Business in the Racial Economy. 1929.
12.   The Dictator of the Blonds Patrician – an introduction to Political Economy of the Racial Economy. 1929.
13/14. The Zoological and Talmudish (i.e., Jewish traditional law) origin of Bolshevism. 1930.
15.   Theozoology or Natural History of the Gods 4. The New Testament and New God. 1929.
16/17. Theozoology 5 – the Divine and Spiritual Father of Immortality in Substance and Spirit. 1929.
18.   Theozoology or Natural History of the Gods 6: the Son of God and the Immortality of Origin and Race. 1930.
19.   Theozoology 7: The Immortal Church of the Gods. 1930.
101. The work of J. Wolfl and L. Liebenfels – an Introduction to their Theories. 1927.

From Daim, pp.311–314 (Kindly translated by Nicholas Dragffy and Martin Clay)

Bibliography

Books, Papers, Articles

Aarons, Mark, and Loftus, John, *The Secret War Against the Jews* (St Martin's Press, New York, 1994)

Allen, Gary, *The Rockefeller File* (76 Press, Seal Beach CA, 1976)

American Psychiatric Association, *Diagnostic and Statistical Manual of Mental Disorders (DSM-IV-TR)* (American Psychiatric Association, Washington DC, 2000)

Barker, Alan, *Invisible Eagle: The History of Nazi Occultism* (Virgin Books, London, 2000)

Barnett, Correlli, *Hitler's Generals* (Weidenfeld and Nicolson, London, 1989)

Binion, Dr Rudolph, 'Hitler's Concept of Lebensraum' in *History of Childhood Quarterly* (No. 1, 1973)

Bloch, Dr Eduard, 'My Patient Hitler' in *Colliers Magazine* (Vol. I, 15 March 1941, pp. 11, 35–9 & 22 March 1941, pp. 69–73)

Bloch, Michael, *The Secret File of the Duke of Windsor* (Bantam Press, London, 1988)

——, *The Duchess of Windsor* (Phoenix, London, 1997)

Braham, Trower and Birchwood, *Acting on Command Hallucinations and DAngerous Behaviour: a Critique of the Major Findings in the Last Decade* (University of Birmingham, Birmingham)

Bryan, J., & Murphy, Charles J. B., *The Windsor Story* (William Morrow and Co., New York, 1979)

Bullock, Alan, *Hitler: A Study in Tyranny* (Book Club Associates and Hamlyn, London, 1973)

——, *Hitler and Stalin: Parallel Lives* (Book Club Associates and HarperCollins, London, 1991)

Campbell, Christy, *The World War II Databook* (Macdonald and Co., London, 1985)

Commission of the C.C. of the CPSU (B) (eds), *History of the Communist Party of the Soviet Union: Bolsheviks* (Foreign Languages Publishing House, Moscow, 1943)

Daim, Dr Wilfried, *Der Mann, der Hitler die Ideen gab*. (Böhlau, Cologne, Vienna & Graz, 1985)

Dalley, Jan, *Diana Mosley: A Life* (Faber and Faber, London, 1999)

Degrelle, Leon, 'The Enigma of Hitler' in *The Journal for Historical Review* (May/June 1994)

Devrient, Paul, *Mein Schuler Adolf Hitler* (Universitas, Munich, 2003)

Domarus, Max, *Hitler, Speeches and Proclamations 1932–1945* (in four volumes) (I. B. Tauris & Co., London, 1992)

Douglas-Hamilton, James, *The Truth About Rudolf Hess* (Mainstream Publishing, London and Edinburgh, 1993)

~ Flood, Charles Bracelen, *Hitler: The Path to Power* (Houghton Miffilm, Boston MA, 1989)

~ Fest, Joachim, *Hitler* (Penguin Books Ltd, London, 1974)

Foster, Harold D., *What Really Causes Schizophrenia* (Trafford, Victoria BC, 2003)

Fuchs, Petra, *Das Vergessen der Vernichtung ist Teil der Vernichtung selbst* (Wallstein, Göttingen, 2007)

Gardner, David, *The Last of the Hitlers* (BMM, Worcester, 2001)

Gilbert, Martin, *Winston Churchill – The Wilderness Years* (Macmillan, London, 1981)

Goodenough, Judith, Wallis, Robert A. and Maguire, Betty, *Human Biology* (Saunders College Publishing, Harcourt Brace College Publishers, New York and London, 1998)

~ Goodricke-Clarke, Nicholas, *The Occult Roots of Nazism* (New York University Press, New York, 1992)

Goring, Emmy, *An der Seite meines Manne: und Begebenheiten und Bekenntuisse* (Schutz, Göttingen, 1967)

Gregory, Richard L., *The Oxford Companion to The Mind* (Oxford University Press, Oxford, 1987)

Greiner, Josef, *Das Ende des Hitler-Mythos* (Amalthea-Verlag, Zürich, Leipzig, Vienna, 1947)

Griffiths, Richard, *Patriotism Perverted: Captain Ramsay, the Right Club and British Anti-Semitism 1939–40* (Constable, London, 1998)

Halder, Franz, *Hitler als Feldherr* (Munchener Dom-Verlag, Munich, 1949)

~ Hamann, Brigitte, *Hitler's Vienna: A Dictator's Apprenticeship* (Oxford University Press, Oxford, 1999)

' Hamilton, General Sir Ian, *The Hamilton Papers* (Liddell Hart Centre for Military Archives, King's College, London, nd)

Hanisch, Reinhold, 'I Was Hitler's Buddy' in *The New Republic*, 5 April 1939, pp. 239–42; 12 April, pp. 270–2; 19 April, pp. 297–300 (New York, 1939)

Heer, Friedrich, *Der Glaube des Adolf Hitler: Anatomie einer politschen Religiosität* (Esslingen, Munich, 1968)

~ Heiden, Konrad, *Hitler: A Biography* (Constable, London, 1936)

~ Higham, Charles, *Trading With The Enemy* (Dell Publishing, New York, 1984)

——, *Wallis: Secret Lives of the Duchess of Windsor* (Sidgwick & Jackson, London, 1988)

~ Hitler, Adolf, *Mein Kampf* (Hurst and Blackett, London, 1942)

~ Hougan, James, *Spooks* (Bantam Books, New York, 1978)

Jenkins, Roy, *Churchill: A Biography* (Macmillan, London, 2001)

Jenks, William A., *Vienna and the Young Hitler* (Columbia University Press, New York, 1960)

Keegan, John (ed), *Encyclopaedia of World War II* (Book Club Associates and Bison Books, CT and London, 1977)

Kershaw, Ian, *Hitler 1889–1936: Hubris* (Allen Lane, London, 1998)

King, Greg, *The Duchess of Windsor* (Aurum Press, London, 1999)

Kogan, Eugen, *The Theory and Practice of Hell* (Berkeley Books, New York, 1980)

Kubizek, August, *Young Hitler* (George Mann Books, Maidstone, 1973)

Lambert, David (and the Diagram Group), *Body Language* (HarperCollins, Glasgow, 1996)

Langer, Walter, *The Mind of Adolf Hitler* (Secker and Warburg, London, 1973)

Lenman, Bruce P.(ed), *Chambers Dictionary of World History* (Chambers Harrap Publishers, Edinburgh, 2000)

Liebenfels, Jörg Lanz von, *Bibliomystikon oder Die Geheimbibel der Eingweihten, Vols 1–10* (Berlin Privatdruckverlag, Pforzheim, 1930–8)

——, *Theozoology* (Europa Germanic Translations, Sandusky, Ohio, 2003)

List, Guido von & Flowers, Stephen E. (introduction by; also editor & translator), *The Secret of the Runes* (Destiny Books, Vermont, 1988)

Lloyd George, David, *War Memoirs of David Lloyd George, Vols I & II* (Odhams Press, London, 1938)

Lovell, Mary S., *The Mitford Girls* (Little, Brown and Co., New York, 2001)

Lumsden, Robin, *SS Regalia: A Collector's Guide to Third Reich Militaria* (Ian Allan Publishing, London, 1995)

Machtan, Lothar, *The Hidden Hitler* (Perseus Press, Oxford, 2001)

Matthews, John, *The Grail* (Thames and Hudson, London, 1981)

McKenna, P. J., *Schizophrenia and Related Syndromes* (Psychology Press, London and New York, 1997)

McLeod, Kirsty, *Battle Royal* (Constable, London, 1999)

McGovern, Una (ed), *Chambers Biographical Dictionary* (Chambers Harrap Publishers, Edinburgh, 2002)

Mintz, Morton and Cohen, Jerry S., *Power, Inc. Public and Private Rulers and How to Make them Accountable* (Bantam Books, New York, 1977)

Morrison, James M., *DSM-IV Made Easy: The Clinician's Guide to Diagnosis* (Guilford Press, New York, 1995)

Mosley, Charlotte (ed), *The Mitfords: Letters between Six Sisters* (Harper Perennial, London, 2008)

Mosley, Sir Oswald, *My Life* (Nelson, London, 1968)

Muhlen, Norbert, *Schacht: Hitler's Magician* (Alliance Book Corporation, New York, 1939)

Nedava, Joseph, *Trotsky and the Jews* (The Jewish Publication Society of America, Philadelphia PA, 1972)

Olden, Rudolf, *Hitler the Pawn* (Victor Gollancz, London, 1936)

Osborne, R. Travis, Noble, Clyde, and Weyl, Nathaniel (eds), *Human Variation: The Biopsychology of Age, Race and Sex* (Academic Press, New York, 1978)

Overy, Richard, *The Road to War* (Macmillan, London, 1989)

Pia, Jack, *SS Regalia* (Ballantine Books, New York, 1974)

Pick, Heller, *Simon Wiesenthal: A Life in Search of Justice* (Phoenix, London, 1997)

Prange, Gordon, *Hitler's Words* (American Council on Public Affairs, Washington DC, 1944)

Ramsay, Archibald M., *The Nameless War* (Britons Publishing Society, London, 1955)

Rauschning, Hermann, *Hitler Speaks* (Thornton Butterworth, London, 1939)

Schacht, Hjalmar, *76 Jahres meines Lebens* (Kindler und Schiermeyer Verlag, Bad Worishöfen, 1955)

Schwarz, Dr Paul, *This Man Ribbentrop* (Julian Messmer, New York, 1943)

Seldes, George, *Facts and Fascism* (In Fact Inc., New York, 1943)

Service, Robert, *Lenin: A Biography* (Macmillan, London, 2000)

Shirer, William L., *The Rise and Fall of the Third Reich* (Secker and Warburg, London, 1972)

Speer, Albert, *Inside the Third Reich* (Sphere Books, London, 1971)

Sutton, Antony C., *Wall Street and the Bolshevik Revolution* (Arlington House, New Rochelle NY, 1974)

Toland, John, *Adolf Hitler* (Doubleday with Book Club Associates, London, 1977)

Trevor-Roper, H. R. (ed), *Hitler's Secret Conversations, 1941–1944* Weidenfeld and Nicolson, London, 1953)

Unger, Michael (ed), *The Memoirs of Bridget Hitler* (Gerald Duckworth, London, 1979)

Vorres, Ian, *The Last Grand-Duchess* (Hutchinson, London, 1964)

Wagener, Otto (ed by Turner, Henry Ashby, Jr) *Hitler – Memoirs of a Confidant* (Yale University Press, New Haven and London, 1985)

Walther, Herbert (ed), *Der Führer* (Bison Books, London, 1978)

Weidemann, Fritz, *Der Mann, der Feldherr werden wollte* (Blick und Blick, Lieben Velbert/Kettwig, 1964)

Weitz, John, *Hitler's Banker* (Little, Brown and Co., New York, 1977)

——, *Joachim von Ribbentrop: Hitler's Diplomat* (Weidenfeld and Nicolson, London, 1992)

Wheen, Francis, *Karl Marx* (HarperCollins, London, 1999)

Williams, Susan, *The People's King* (Allen Lane, London, 2003)

Windsor, The Duke of, *A King's Story: The Memoirs of HRH The Duke of Windsor KG* (Putnam, New York, 1947)

Wolman, Benjamin (ed), *The Psychoanalytic Interpretation of History* (Harper Torchbooks, New York, 1971)

Ziegler, Philip, *King Edward VIII, the Official Biography* (Collins, London, 1990)

Journals, Newspapers, Magazines
'Colliers Magazine', 1905–1957 (P. F. Collier & Sons, New York)
Krause, Karl 'Die Fackel' (satirical journal of which 922 issues were published between 1899 and 1912)
'Ostara' – various editions

Official Records
National Archives, Kew, Richmond, Surrey: Security Service material from the series KV.

Film Documentaries
Betrayal: Oswald Mosley, the English Führer. © 2003, AP Traitor Productions Ltd. History Channel
Churchill, Pt 1. Renegade and Turncoat. © 1992, BBC. UK History
Eva Braun. © ZDF 2001. History Channel
Hermann Göring: Ambition without Conscience. © 2002, A&E Television Networks
Hitler: A Profile: The Betrayer. © 1995, ZDF
Hitler: A Profile: The Blackmailer. © 2001, Channel 5 Broadcasting Ltd
Hitler: A Profile: The Commander. © 1995, ZDF
Hitler: A Profile: The Criminal. © 1995, ZDF
Hitler: A Profile: The Dictator. © 1995, ZDF, Discovery Channel
Hitler: A Profile: The Seducer. © 1995, ZDF
Hitler's Britain. © 2002, Lion Television Ltd, Sea Lion Productions, Inc History Channel
Hitler's Death: The Final Report. © 1995, BBC
Hitler' Henchmen: Bormann: The Shadow Man. © 2001, ZDF
Hitler's Henchmen: Freisler: The Executioner. © 1998, Discovery Communications Inc.
Hitler's Henchmen: Hess, The Deputy. © 1996, ZDF Enterprises. Discovery Channel
Hitler's Henchmen: Karl Dönitz. © 1984, Granada, UK
Hitler's Henchmen: Ribbentrop, The Puppet. © 1998, Discovery Communications Inc, Discovery Channel
Hitler's Henchmen: Schirach, the Corrupter of Youth. © 1998, Discovery Communications Inc
Hitler's Henchmen: Speer, the Architect. © 2001, Atlantic Alliance Inc, The History Channel
Hitler's Mistress Eva Braun. © 1991, Castle Communications plc
Hitler's War: Air War over Germany. © 2002, ZDF. History Channel
Hitler's Women. © 2001, Spiegel TV. History Channel
Josef Mengele: Medical Madman of Auschwitz. © 1996, A&E Television Networks
Kristallnacht: November 9, 1938. © 2003, BBC
Nazis: The Occult Conspiracy. © 1998, Discovery Communications Inc, Discovery Channel

Pius XII: The Pope, the Jews and the Nazis. © 1994, BBC 'Reputations'
Russia: Land of the Tsars. © 2003, A&E Television Networks, History Channel
Secret History: The Nazi Expedition. © 2004, MFIV Ifage Productions
Sex and the Swastika: The Making of Adolf Hitler. © 2002, BBC 'Timewatch'
Simon Wiesenthal. © 1997, BBC/A&E Networks co-productions, History Channel
Stalin. © 1990, Thames Television plc, History Channel
The Brits who fought for Hitler © 2002, Channel 5 Broadcasting Ltd, History Channel
The Hitler Family: In the Shadow of the Dictator. © 2005, Channel 4, ZDF, History Channel
The Last Nazi Secret. © 2002, Channel 4 Television Corporation
The Nazis: A Warning from History. Part 1: Helped into Power
The Nazis: A Warning from History. Part 2: The Wrong War
The Nazis: A Warning from History. Part 3: The Wild East
The Nazis: A Warning from History. Part 4: The Road to Treblinka
The Nazis: A Warning from History. Part 5: Fighting to the End © 1997, BBC
The SS: Himmler's Madness. © 2002, ZDF, History Channel
The Third Reich in Colour. © 1999, Spiegel TV, History Channel
World at War: Hitler's Germany: The Only Hope, 1933–1936. © 1975, Thames Television Ltd

Websites

www.intelinet.org/swastika14.htm The Swastika and the Nazis
www.antiqillum.com/glor/glor_005/nazimyth.htm information from *Ostara*
www.huskyl.stmarys.ca/-mills/course203/16_Fascism_2.html St Mary's University – Wallace G. Mills' course on Fascism Pt II
www.ihr.org/jhr/v14/v14n1p-Weber.html Institute for Historical Review
www.spartacus.schoolnet.co.uk/GERribbentrop.htm Educational website

Index